Spinners and weavers of Auffay

Spinners and weavers of Auffay

Rural industry and the sexual division of labor in a French village, 1750 – 1850

Gay L. Gullickson
The University of Maryland

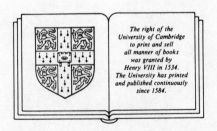

The right of the
University of Cambridge
to print and sell
all manner of books
was granted by
Henry VIII in 1534.
The University has printed
and published continuously
since 1584.

Cambridge University Press
Cambridge
London   New York   New Rochelle
Melbourne   Sydney

Published by the Press Syndicate of the University of Cambridge
The Pitt Building, Trumpington Street, Cambridge CB2 1RP
32 East 57th Street, New York, NY 10022, USA
10 Stamford Road, Oakleigh, Melbourne 3166, Australia

© Cambridge University Press 1986

First published 1986

Printed in the United States of America

Library of Congress Cataloging-in-Publication Data
Gullickson, Gay L.
    Spinners and weavers of Auffay.
        Bibliography: p.
    1. Weavers – France – Auffay – History. 2. Auffay
(France) – Occupations – History. 3. Sexual division
of labor – France – Auffay – History. I. Title.
HD8039.T42F834 1986   331.4'877'02822094425   86-6808

British Library Cataloguing in Publication Data
Gullickson, Gay L.
    Spinners and weavers of Auffay: rural
industry and the sexual division of labor
    in a French village, 1750–1850.
    1. Textile industry – France – Auffay –
Employees 2. Sexual division of labor –
        France – Auffay – History
                I. Title
    305.9'677'094425   HD9862.8.A9/
    m ℛ   ISBN 0 521 32280 4

For my parents
Gene and Margaret Gullickson

Contents

Preface

This study began ten years ago when, having survived my Ph.D. exams, I began to search for a dissertation topic. My desire to study changes in women's economic and family roles in connection with some aspect of industrialization gradually developed into a study of cottage industry and agriculture in Normandy, as one research question led to another and I moved from general research in the Bibliotheque Nationale in Paris to more focused study in the Archives Départemental de la Seine-Maritime in Rouen.

Many people helped me along the way, and I am grateful to them all. Joan Wallach Scott, who directed my dissertation, encouraged my interest in the history of women, helped me find my way through the French archives, provided thoughtful and just criticism, discussed ideas, and constantly challenged me to become a better historian. George V. Taylor kindled my interest in French history in his graduate seminars. Franklin Mendels graciously endured my criticisms of proto-industrial theory and supported my work by encouraging me to submit paper proposals for international conferences on proto-industrialization. James Lehning introduced me to the computer, shared his ideas about proto-industrialization, and commented wisely on the manuscript in its final stages. Joseph Carens supported my desire to study history and discussed ideas with me as I worked them through. The staff and archivists of the Archives Départemental de la Seine-Maritime brought me one dusty tome after another, searched out misfiled documents, and even found me a room in which to type, an incredible luxury in an archive. Richard Herr, Rachel Fuchs, and Elaine Kruse read parts of the manuscript and improved its clarity. Susannah Gourevitch helped me find my voice as a writer. My colleagues at the University of Maryland, College Park, provided me with a forum for discussions of my research and inspired me through the example of their own work. Peggy and Van Quinn cheerfully offered me their guest room and endured my frantic work schedule on my flying trips to use the University of North Carolina computer. Darlene King transformed my typescript and handwritten notes into a perfectly typed manuscript, and cheered me on by telling me she thought it was interesting.

The Georges Lurcy Foundation supported my initial research in France. A National Endowment for the Humanities summer fellowship to attend a seminar on "Agriculture and Rural Society" directed by Richard

ix

Herr at the University of California, Berkeley, gave me a chance to discuss ideas in a congenial and challenging academic setting. An Andrew Mellon postdoctoral fellowship at the University of Pittsburgh gave me the time to turn the dissertation into a manuscript and funded further research in France in 1981–82. Grants from the General Research Board of the University of Maryland, College Park, enabled me to polish and improve the manuscript. Portions of Chapters 3, 5, 6, and 7 have appeared in *French Historical Studies,* Vol. XII; the *Journal of Economic History,* Vol. XLIII; and *Peasant Studies,* Vol. IX.

Finally, I would like to thank my parents, to whom this book is dedicated, for encouraging me from childhood to pursue the things that interested me, for providing me with a good education, and for giving me their unfailing love and moral support.

I am, of course, responsible for any errors of fact or interpretation that remain in the book.

G.L.G.

I

~·~

Introduction

In the eighteenth century, travel and the transportation of crops and goods by road or water were laborious and time-consuming throughout Europe. As a result, regions produced grain crops, the staple of the peasant diet, even when the terrain and climate were poorly suited to their cultivation; cities were small; rural artisans produced shoes, barrels, plows, bricks, and furniture for local consumption; and peasant families who were basically identified with farming produced a variety of manufactured goods during the dead season in agriculture. For most peasants, the family's survival depended on the participation of everyone but the youngest children in this alternation of farming and manufacturing.

Some peasant families produced the raw materials from which they made goods to sell in local markets. Linen weavers and cord or rope makers often wove flax or braided hemp from their own plants, and weavers sometimes wove the wool from their own sheep. Other families received raw materials from merchants who put work out into the homes of peasants or cottage workers. Raw fibers or spun thread or yarn might come either from nearby areas or from some distance. All over Europe, weavers who produced high-quality woolens worked with wool from Spain's merino sheep. Silk weavers throughout France depended on the silk produced in the Rhone Valley, where mulberry trees and hence silk worms could be raised. Cotton spinners and weavers worked with cotton from the Orient and the New World.

Sometimes entire families participated in the production process, with children and women preparing raw materials for final production by men. In the textile industry, for instance, women and children cleaned and combed raw fibers and spun yarn for men to weave. Other times, men and women produced unrelated products. Women often spun thread, wove ribbons, made hats, or knit stockings while their husbands worked in the fields, forged iron, milled flour, or cut wood.

In the late eighteenth century, demographic growth and the opening of new colonial markets for manufactured goods encouraged urban merchants to increase production. As long as urban populations remained small and technology remained simple, production could be increased only by expanding the rural putting-out system, despite the difficulty and expense of transporting raw materials and finished products between urban markets and rural producers.

In 1972, Franklin Mendels identified this expansion of the putting-out system as a distinct stage in the economic development of Europe.[1] Large-scale cottage industries, or "proto-industries" as Mendels called them, were organized in the same manner as their small-scale forerunners. Work was put-out into the countryside by merchants who reclaimed the completed articles for finishing and sale. Unlike small-scale cottage industries, however, proto-industries dominated local labor markets, employing large numbers of rural residents rather than just a handful of families, and the goods produced in the system were sold in national and international markets rather than locally.

Under proto-industrialization, cottage workers were unlikely to know the putting-out merchants who remained in urban areas. Work assignments and money were distributed by traveling porters or local merchants who themselves were now employees of the urban putting-out merchants rather than independent agents. The manufacturing system became less and less personal, and the income and economic well-being of large numbers of people became more and more tied to the vagaries and fluctuations of national and international markets, long before most workers lived in cities and worked in factories.

Proto-industrialization began and ended at different times in different places, appearing in some places, at least briefly, as early as the fifteenth century.[2] The phenomenon is primarily identified with the expansion of the textile industry in the eighteenth and nineteenth centuries, however, and is based on Mendels's study of the linen industry in Flanders, Rudolf Braun's study of the cotton industry in the canton of Zurich, and David Levine's study of the knitting industry in Leicestershire, England.[3] The similarities in the experiences of these three regions produced a picture of proto-industrialization that quickly assumed the status of a model to which it was expected other regions (as they were studied) would inevitably conform. Proto-industrialization, it was argued, was most likely to occur in subsistence or pastoral farming regions with large populations and fragmented land holdings, which were being driven out of urban grain markets by richer-soiled, more prosperous regions. As the work available in cottage industry expanded, entire families were drawn into the production of goods for the putting-out merchants. More of the children in these families married and they married at younger ages than their peasant counterparts because their unions were based not on the inheritance of land or workshops and pain-stakingly acquired dowries but on current income and optimistic assumptions about future earnings. Cottage industry families also bore more children than peasant families as a result of their early marriages and the availability of work for children. This demographic behavior resulted in further population growth and set the stage for family and regional crises whenever work in cottage industry contracted. Such crises became particularly acute when proto-industries began to lose ground to urban factory production in the nineteenth century. As work in cottage industry declined, cottage workers attempted to reduce expenses and maximize household income by forming extended family households. The overabundance of hand workers combined with competition from low-priced, machine-produced goods drove wages lower and lower, however, until most families, having already lost their ties to the land, were forced to seek jobs as agricultural laborers to migrate to urban areas where they entered the factory labor force.

This picture or model of proto-industrialization forms the context for this work on the pays de Caux and the village of Auffay in the old French province of Normandy, the scene of a rapidly expanding cottage textile industry in the eighteenth century. Differences between the Caux and Flanders, Zurich, and Shepshed raise serious problems for the model built on the latter regions, however. The Caux was not a subsistence or pastoral farming region. On the contrary, it was one of the most fertile cereal-producing regions in France. Nor was it a region with fragmented land holdings. Instead, most of the land was contained in large farms and worked by day laborers and domestic servants. In addition, demographic behavior changed very little in the village of Auffay, where a substantial percentage of the population worked for the putting-out merchants throughout the proto-industrial period; this lack of change appears to have been typical of the region. Except for a brief period in the early nineteenth century, when the mechanization of spinning produced high piece rates and constant work for weavers, marriage ages remained stable and high, and couples responded to slumps in demand by limiting child-bearing, migrating to Rouen, and delaying marriage even when the woman was pregnant, not by increasing the number of workers in the household.

The contrast that the Caux provides to earlier studies is important because it allows us to draw a more accurate and complex picture of the economic and demographic consequences of proto-industrialization. It points to the complementarity of urban and rural needs as a determining factor in the location of proto-industries and shifts the focus from subsistence and pastoral farming to the seasonal nature of traditional agriculture, and from the general fragmentation of land to landpoorness, regardless of its causes, as essential features of proto-industrial regions. The contrast also illustrates that the sexual composition of the agricultural and cottage labor forces was a key factor in determining both the compatibility of agriculture and cottage industry and the social, economic, and demographic consequences of proto-industrialization.

This book is the story of the eighteenth-century urban – rural complementarities that made proto-industrialization possible in the Caux, the breakdown in the sexual division of labor in textiles that allowed it to continue in the nineteenth, and the rural community's adaptation to the social and economic changes that followed in the wake of the Rouen putting-out merchants. It is also the story of a largely female cottage labor force, since the majority of the textile workers in the Caux were women.

In the last decade, the research of such historians as Olwen Hufton, Joan Scott, and Louise Tilly has illustrated the importance of women's earnings to a majority of peasant, artisan, and proletarian families in eighteenth- and nineteenth-century Europe and the prevalence of sexual divisions of labor in the preindustrial and industrializing eras.[4] Nevertheless, the existing studies of proto-industrial communities have made only passing references to women's work and have not analyzed the sexual division of labor in either cottage industry or agriculture. As a result, they have obscured one of the fundamental features of the proto-industrial labor market and have left us with only half a picture of proto-industrial families and communities. In the Caux, in particular, a focus on male occupations exclusively would underestimate the size of the textile industry, would fail to see the entry of women into the time-honored male domains of nonharvest agriculture and hand weaving, and would overlook the importance of women's earnings to their families and to the region as a whole.

This study integrates research on women with research on proto-industrialization. It examines the experiences of both women and men during the proto-industrial period in the Caux. It also bridges the gap between such highly quantitative studies of proto-industrial regions as those of Mendels and Levine and nonquantitative studies like that of Braun. The book begins with an examination of history, customs, social divisions, and everyday life in the pays de Caux in the eighteenth century, based on government reports, notarial and judicial records, local memoirs, municipal council minutes, and the village *cahiers de doléances* from 1789. These materials provide the human context for the quantitative analysis that follows. That analysis is based on eighteenth-century tax records, manuscript censuses for the years 1796, 1841, 1846, and 1851, and the reconstitution of the families of the 727 couples who married in Auffay between 1751 and 1850.

Family reconstitution is an analytical method developed in the 1950s by the French demographers Michael Fleury and Louis Henry.[5] It consists essentially of constructing family trees for the residents of a particular area (or occupational group within an area) from birth (or baptismal), marriage, and death (or burial) records. In the eighteenth century, these records were kept for Auffay by the local priests. During the French Revolution, the state officially took over the recording of vital statistics, although the church continued to keep its own records.[6] Both the priests and the state kept remarkably complete records, although the amount of information in them varies from era to era and recorder to recorder. In particular, the recording of women's ages and occupations varies, apparently according to what the record keeper thought was important.

The reconstitution of families reveals changes in occupational patterns and demographic behavior that cannot be determined in any other way. It makes it possible to study the extent to which men and women pursued one or multiple occupations during their lifetime and whether children followed the occupations of their parents, married into families with the same occupations as their own, and so forth. Reconstitution also yields information about such things as the number of children women bore, the average interval between marriage and the birth of the first child, the length of subsequent birth intervals, the number of couples who experienced the death of an infant or child, and how many children in a family married. The occupational information contained in the parish and civil registers and in the reconstituted family study, combined with that in the eighteenth-century tax roles and the nineteenth-century enumerated censuses, forms the basis for the discussion in Chapters 4 through 6 of the effects of proto-industrialization on male and female occupations, wages, occupational endogamy, family occupations, and the sexual division of labor. Similarly, the demographic information contained in these records provides the basis for the discussion in Chapters 7 through 9 of the effects of proto-industrialization on demographic behavior.

Throughout the study, I have combined quantitative and nonquantitative data in an attempt to uncover both what people did and how they thought and felt. In particular, I have tried to explore how families and individuals did and did not adapt to developments that at times must have appeared a godsend (the creation of jobs); at other times, a disaster (the demise of hand spinning); and, at still other times, disorienting and distressing (the breakdown of the sexual division of labor). I have tried to understand, or at least to speculate about, what events like the arrival of the putting-out merchants, harvest failures, and the deaths of children and spouses meant to these eighteenth- and nineteenth-century families. In a broad way, I have sought to understand both how the economic system worked and what it was like to live in a proto-industrial community.

2

The pays and the village

The pays de Caux

The Seine River, winding slowly toward the English Channel from Paris, passes through the old province of Normandy, dividing it into two distinct sections. The smaller section lying to the north of the river was called both Haute-Normandie and Normandie Orientale, the combination describing its location in the upper, eastern portion of the province. The larger and lower part of the province, known as Basse-Normandie, lay to the south of the Seine and stretched much farther west, ending in the Cotentin Peninsula. When France was reorganized into departments during the Revolution, Upper Normandy became the Département de la Seine-Inférieure, a name that was later changed to the Département de la Seine-Maritime.

Rouen, the capital of the province and later of the Seine-Inférieure/Seine-Maritime, lay halfway between the eastern boundary of the province and the English Channel, on the northern bank of a large loop in the Seine. Connected to both the domestic markets of Paris and the export markets of England, Spain, and Portugal by short water routes, Rouen was an important commercial center well before the beginning of the eighteenth century. It was the fourth largest provincial city in France with a population that rose slowly from about 55,000 in 1700 to 100,000 in 1850.[1]

North of Rouen lies the pays de Caux, a large triangular-shaped plateau covered with grain fields and woods and punctuated occasionally by small rivers that flow into the Seine or into the sea near Dieppe and Fécamp. The region was named for the Gallic tribe – the Caletes (hard) – which inhabited the plateau before the arrival of the Normans in the ninth century. The exact amount of territory held by the Caletes is unclear, but it appears that their control extended eastward across the plateau from the English Channel to the Bethune River and southward from the coast to the Seine River Valley.[2]

7

The Caletes's area corresponds closely to the pays de Caux, even to the point of the lack of clarity about the region's boundaries. The triangular-shaped *pays* is bordered on two sides by water but is not generally regarded as extending all the way to these natural barriers. The Seine River Valley and the maritime villages along the English Channel are not on the plateau and are not, strictly speaking, part of the *pays*. The eastern boundary is roughly a line drawn from Rouen to Dieppe, although exactly where the line should be is unclear. (This border area is sometimes known as the Petite Caux.) By the time one reaches the Bethune River, one clearly has left the Caux, but precisely when one left it is not evident.

For eighteenth- and nineteenth-century peasants, the question of the Caux's boundaries was not a problem. Their sense of the *pays* was based on its cultural, geographical, and economic characteristics. To them, it was the large plain extending around Yvetot, a large textile-producing town, for a radius of about 30 miles. It was the part of the plateau where people spoke *cauchoise* and raised cereal and industrial crops and some cattle. It lay within the reach of the Rouen textile merchants, lived under the *coutume de Caux* in the eighteenth century, and was oriented toward Rouen and Dieppe. To the northeast lay the pays de Bray, a hilly depression in the plain suited to the raising of dairy herds and not to cereal agriculture. To the southeast, under the pays de Bray, lay the Vexin Normand, a fertile grain-producing region that served as part of the Paris breadbasket.[3]

For the social historian, as for the peasant, an exact determination of the boundaries of the pays de Caux is unnecessary. What is important is not where the pays ends, but what life was like within it, and, for this study, how people reacted to the economic changes that swept across the plateau in the eighteenth and nineteenth centuries, eliminating some jobs, creating others, and confronting the villagers with threats to their familiar social and cultural order, threats to which they responded in a variety of ways.

Topographically, the Caux is a large chalk plateau covered with fine-textured, thick, well-aerated clay that is easy to work and loose enough to support the cultivation of cereal crops. In various places, a subsoil of thicker clay retains moisture and supports pasture land and cattle rearing.[4] The region was and is, as Jules Sion observed in 1909, "among the best land in France," altogether a "*bons pays,* a region where nature recompenses man for his work."[5]

If the soil made the *cauchois* peasant's life easy, the weather did not.

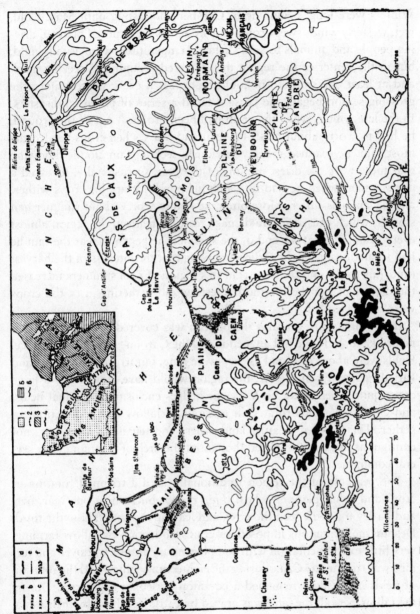

Figure 2.1. Topography and regions of Normandy (*Source:* René Musset, *La Normandie*)

Winters were long, beginning in October and lasting until May. Cold, wet, westerly winds swept continuously across the exposed plateau, driving people and animals to seek shelter. Temperatures were usually mild, but in the center of the region they hovered around the freezing mark and at least one snowstorm could be expected every winter. Once the growing season began, the peasant faced a series of potential disasters. In the late winter, when the grain had begun to push out of the ground, he had to worry about frost. In April and May, when crops needed the most rain, he scanned the sky anxiously seeking rain clouds, knowing that these were the driest months of the year. Occasionally, he faced a dry summer, when he had to watch his pond dry up, his crops wither, and his animals suffer. More often, he had to worry about summer hail storms, which caused severe damage to some fields in the region almost every year. Then, at the end of the summer, he began to fear the rain he had so anxiously sought earlier, knowing that the lateness of the harvest (mid-July to the end of August) in this region of cool summers increased the danger of rain before the harvesting and gathering-in of the crops were completed.[6]

In the eighteenth century, the plateau was covered by open, irregular fields like those found in Languedoc and the Garonne in southern France. Fields were about as broad as they were long, but irregular in shape and varied in size. From the air, the region would have looked like a large crazy quilt. There were no fences or hedges enclosing individual fields, and clusters of fields rotated in and out of fallow and production together. The fields of wealthy landowners and tenant farmers were not contiguous but were scattered thoughout the area of a commune or several communes.[7]

The peasants of the region traditionally used a triennial rotation of crops and fields, planting wheat (*blé*), rye, or buckwheat one year, oats and barley for cattle feed the next, and leaving the land fallow the third. Despite the limitations imposed on grain production by fallow farming, very little experimentation with complementary crops like clover and turnips was tried in the Caux during the eighteenth century, and the rotation of fields into fallow remained a common agricultural practice. During the fallow period, the land was grazed by cattle, fertilized by their dung, and fortified for another round of crop bearing. For poor peasants and agricultural day laborers (*journaliers*) who had little or no land of their own, the practice of fallow farming provided some advantage over other systems because it involved the practice of grazing the cows and sheep of each commune together on the fallow, regardless of who owned the land,

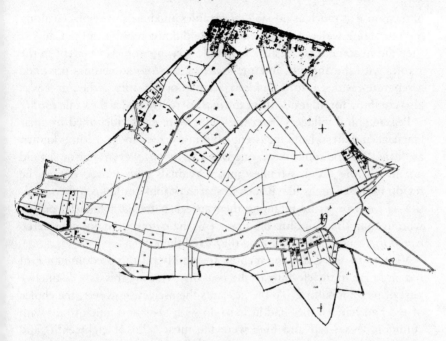

Figure 2.2. Irregular open fields in the pays de Caux, 1804–14 (*Source:* Service du Cadastre, Hôtel des Impôts, Dieppe)

thus allowing them to keep some farm animals in spite of their meager land holdings.[8]

The center of peasant life in the Caux was the *masure,* an enclosed farmyard varying in size and surrounded by a raised dike of earth called a *fossé* (which actually means a ditch or moat).[9] The *fossés* were planted with trees, which provided firewood for the family and protected the inhabitants, animals, and buildings in the interior from the winds that swept across the plain. The tree-planted *fossés* made *masures* visible from considerable distances but gave the family within a sense of security and privacy, even when several *masures* were strung together in a hamlet, as was the common practice. The farmhouse, sheds, and barns of the *masure* lined its perimeter, leaving the interior space open for grazing young animals and chickens, for planting a garden, and for the pond that provided water for both the animals and the peasant family. When possible, houses were positioned on the opposite side of the *masure* from the road, with all windows facing south to receive maximum light. To reduce the danger of fire, the oven or bakehouse (*four*) was placed across the *masure* from the farmhouse; to remove the smell of animals from the residents of the house as much as possible, the stables and barns were placed along the remaining walls. Animals and people did not cohabit in the Caux as they did in some regions, although male servants sometimes slept in the stables with the animals. In large *masures*, the *four* sometimes provided a separate residence for an elderly relative or servants, although it was also common for all residents of the *masure* to live under the same roof.[10]

Peasants and villagers from the Caux were easily identified by their language and dress. Until the twentieth century, they spoke a patois known as "*caux.*" If one spoke *caux*, one was a *cauchois(e)* even if he or she did not live in the Caux. Families and individuals who moved out of the region to urban areas like Rouen in search of jobs could keep their identity as *cauchois(e)* by retaining their speech patterns. Similarly, people who lived in the Caux but did not speak the patois were not considered *cauchois(e)*, no matter how long they lived there.[11]

Visitors to the Caux commented frequently on the predominance of red and blue in the clothing of the peasants, viewing this as a distinctive part of peasant culture. To the peasants themselves, however, the choice of red and blue clothes had little to do with taste and much to do with common sense; red and blue were the most solid of eighteenth- and nineteenth-century dyes and were less likely than other colors to fade in the rain and hot sun of the *pays*. Consequently, skirts, jackets, pants, women's scarves, and men's neckerchiefs were either solid blue or red or were striped or checked with white.[12]

A peasant woman usually wore a linen or cotton blouse protected by a colored, sleeveless bodice and a striped blue and white skirt covered by an apron, which she could gather by the ends and use to carry grain and other small items. Around her neck and over her shoulders she wore a scarf folded into a triangle and tied at the throat. On her head she wore a bonnet with a small puffed topknot and two gathered flounces that framed her face and protected her neck from sun and rain. On her feet she wore wooden shoes. If she were not too poor, she might have a pair of leather slippers, a more elaborate set of clothing made of finer fabric with an embroidered scarf, and a tall bonnet that either swept up in back or trailed lace below her shoulders for special occasions.[13]

Men wore shirts and knee-length blue pants with leggings, wooden shoes, and red or blue stocking caps. As cotton fabric became more and more available in the nineteenth century, men adopted a long overblouse, which they could belt at the waist and which protected their other clothing. Like the women, they might have a better suit of clothes in which

Figure 2.3. Peasant couple (*Source:* Marguerite Bruneau, "Le costume normand")

they were married and which they wore on special occasions. But a wool jacket and culottes, good shirt, necktie, hat, leggings, and shoes might cost more than a man could earn in a year, and only well-established peasants probably had such an outfit.[14]

The Caux was governed by a separate legal code (*coutume de Caux*) until the French Revolution and the Napoleonic Empire established a single legal code for all of France. The distinguishing feature of the *coutume de Caux* was that land inheritance was based on a strict primogeniture. In both noble and nonnoble families, the eldest son inherited the *masure* and two-thirds of the family's fields. The younger sons shared the inheritance of the remaining one-third of the land. Daughters inherited only if there were no male heirs. The practice contrasted starkly with the legal code of the rest of the Norman province, which required the equal division of inheritance among all sons.[15] It did not affect most of the residents of the *pays*, however, because less than one-fourth of the land belonged to the peasants who farmed it. The rest belonged to the nobility and bourgeoisie, who leased it for a money rent to *fermiers* (tenant farmers) on nine-year leases.[16]

Far more important for the peasants than the provisions of the *coutume de Caux* was the Rouen textile industry. From at least the beginning of the seventeenth until the middle of the nineteenth century, the Caux was a land of cottage industry as well as of agriculture. At first, peasants spun linen for themselves and wool for the drapers of Rouen. Then, at the turn of the eighteenth century, the Rouen merchants began to experiment with the spinning and weaving of cotton. Women switched from spinning wool and linen to the cleaner, better smelling, and more easily worked cotton, and men who had woven locally grown and spun linen (*toiliers*) began to ply their linen warps with cotton wefts and became *tisserands*. (Wool, by and large, had been woven by urban weavers.) By the middle of the eighteenth century, the Caux was one of the largest cotton-cloth producing regions in France.[17]

What made the Caux a *pays,* therefore, was not a clear set of geographical boundaries, but a uniform topography and climate, a unique language and legal code, shared cultural traditions, and a commonly shared, mixed economy based on cereal agriculture and cottage textile manufacturing for the Rouen putting-out merchants.

There was, of course, some variety within the region. Although most *cauchois* villages participated in the mixed economy, the balance struck between farming and manufacturing varied from place to place. Villages in the middle of the plain maintained the most even weighting of the two. Close to Rouen, where the demands of the putting-out merchants were most intense, agriculture began to take second place to cotton spinning and weaving, and villages were becoming industrial suburbs by the late eighteenth century. Villages along the Atlantic coastline, on the other hand, were far removed from Rouen and more oriented toward fishing, flax and hemp growing, and sail making than toward either grain farming or cotton manufacturing. A few villages, built near forests or rivers, were the homes of specialized artisan groups and produced more tanned hides, glass, or pottery than they did fabric. Even in these more isolated and economically idiosyncratic villages, however, the cotton merchants played a role, and the women, if not the men, worked for the Rouen textile merchants.

Villages varied in size as well as in economic structure. Some were tiny, out-of-the-way places rarely visited by anyone other than the putting-out merchants or their porters. Others were regional centers that housed hundreds of families and attracted traveling merchants and residents of nearby villages to weekly markets and annual fairs. There was, in short, no such thing as a completely typical eighteenth-century *cauchois* village. There were commonalities, however. Regardless of variations in size or economic interests, the residents of most villages divided their attention between producing cereal crops and manufacturing yarn and fabric for the Rouen merchants; they also shared in the cultural traditions of the region. In these regards, the village of Auffay, on which the demographic analysis of this study focuses, was a typical *cauchois* village.

The village of Auffay

Population

Located 36 kilometers north of Rouen and 26 kilometers south of Dieppe, along the fuzzy eastern edge of the Caux, Auffay was one of the larger villages on the plateau. By the middle of the eighteenth century, it had a large church served by three priests; it also had a doctor, pharmacist, and notary, and a large population of merchants, artisans, and farmers. Several inns (*auberges*) and taverns (*cabarets*) served the visitors and merchants who came to buy and sell at the thrice-weekly markets for cattle, grain, food, and tanned hides.[18]

Although it is clear that Auffay was a large village, it is impossible to determine the exact size of it or of any other *cauchois* village before the end of the eighteenth century. The French government during this period was concerned with the number of households (*feux*) in a given area, not the size of the population. Thus, both the tax records and independent counts like the one made by Dumoulin for the Généralité de Rouen in 1754 list households rather than individuals. Moreover, the tax roles list only taxable households, according to the standards determined for each tax, rather than all the households in a village. As a result, they undercount the actual number of households and never agree with each other. Counts made by individuals, on the other hand, are much larger than the tax roles and, when compared with later figures based on enumerated censuses, appear to be much too large. The *sel rôles*, for instance, list 164 households in Auffay in 1751 (157 taxable and 7 exempt), whereas the *taille rôles* list 181 households [164 taxable, 4 exempt, and 13 untaxable (*fugitifs et mendians*)], a difference of 17 households. Only three years later, Dumoulin listed the village as having 255 *feux*, 74 more than the larger of the two tax roles.[19]

Despite their shortcomings, when it comes to estimating the size of Auffay, the tax records do yield a picture of a growing community. The

Table 2.1. *The population of Auffay, 1751–1851*

Date	Central Village House-holds	Central Village Popula-tion	Hameaux House-holds	Hameaux Popula-tion	Commune House-holds	Commune Popula-tion
1751					164	656[a]
1754					255	1020[a]
1789					270	1080[a]
1796–1800					255	1149
1831	199	847	74	290	273	1137
1841	238	857	77	287	315	1144
1851	270	897	90	350	360	1247

[a]Based on the assumption of 4 persons per household. The question of what multiplier to use in calculating population from counts of households has been a subject of much debate among historians. Many use a multiplier of 4 or 4.5. LeParquier, however, considered even 4 to be too high a multiplier for the pays de Caux in the eighteenth century. (See LeParquier, *Cahiers*, p. lxvii.) In light of the fact that the *sel rôles* show a steadily increasing number of residents over the age of eight in Auffay households in the eighteenth century, and that the 1796–1800 counts of households and population yield a 4.5 ratio of residents per household, I have used a multiplier of 4 to estimate Auffay's population in this period. (See Bouloiseau, "La fiscalité du sel," p. 251, for a brief discussion of the problem of multipliers.)

Note: No meaningful distinction between houses (*maisons*) and households (*ménages*) was made until the 1851 census. In that year, there were 360 *ménages* but only 349 *maisons* in Auffay. All eleven houses with two households were in the central village.

Sources: ADSM 219BP364, L367, 6M1, 6M23, 6M83; E. LeParquier, *Cahiers de doléances du bailliage d'Arques,* p. 51.

sel rôles, for instance, show the number of taxable households increasing from 164 in 1751 to 197 in 1781, while the number of residents over the age of eight in these households increased from 2.4 to 3.0.[20]

The first surviving and reasonably accurate count of the population of the Seine-Inférieure was made in 1800. The enumerated lists for the Auffay section of the Caux no longer exist, but the summary sheets show the village as having a population of 1,149. When this count is combined with an extant census listing all residents of the village over the age of twelve, which was taken four years earlier, it appears that the turn-of-the-century village had a population of roughly 1,150, divided into 255 households with approximately 4.5 persons living under each roof.[21]

The term *village* is an ambiguous one in French history; the more appropriate term is *commune*. The population of a commune might be syn-

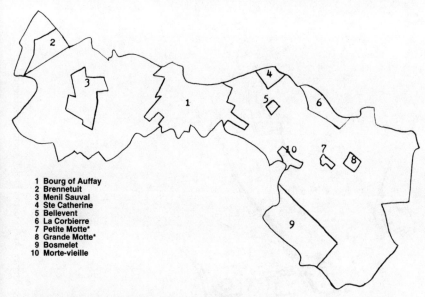

1 Bourg of Auffay
2 Brennetuit
3 Menil Sauval
4 Ste Catherine
5 Bellevent
6 La Corbierre
7 Petite Motte*
8 Grande Motte*
9 Bosmelet
10 Morte-vieille

* **By 1831, Petite Motte and Grande Motte formed one** *hameau.*

Figure 2.4. The commune of Auffay, 1800–1814 (Adapted from an undated map from the period of the First Empire, Service du Cadastre, Hôtel des Impôts, Dieppe)

onomous with the population of a village (or city or town), but, as was the case in the Caux, it might also include outlying *hameaux* (hamlets) and isolated farms. Communes were named for the central village, which contained a church and usually the largest agglomeration of houses and people in the commune. In this sense, Auffay was typical of *cauchois* communes. In the mid-nineteenth century, the central village contained roughly 75 percent of the commune's total population. The remaining 25 to 30 percent were divided among several small *hameaux*. Even though eighteenth-century tax records do not distinguish between village and *hameaux* residents, it seems safe to assume that the Auffay population was similarly divided between *hameaux* and the central village in the eighteenth century.[22] In this study, the name *Auffay* and the term *village* refer to the entire commune of Auffay, unless reference is made specifically to the central village of Auffay.

The village and the world

Auffay was founded around 1060 by a Norman knight, Richard d'Heugleville-sur-Scie, in an area formerly known as Isnelville. Richard

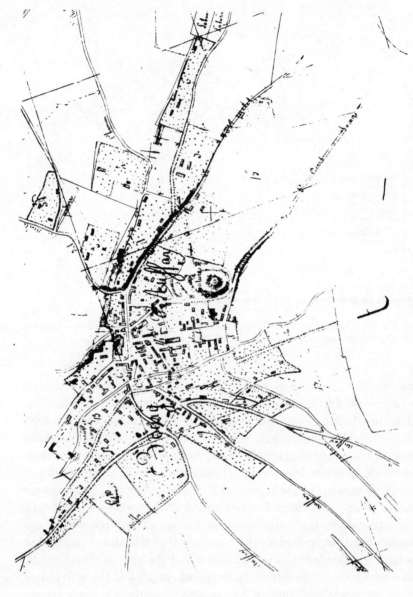

Figure 2.5. The central village of Auffay, 1800–1814 (*Source:* Service du Cadastre, Hôtel des Impôts, Dieppe)

named his new fortified village "the place planted with tall beech trees," or Altafagus, a name that underwent etymological transformation to become Alfagium, then le Haut-Fay, and finally Auffay. Richard's fortress and the surrounding cottages passed from him to his eldest son, Gilbert. On Gilbert's return from the battle of Hastings in 1066 and with the encouragement of his wife, Beatrix, he began construction of a church and donated it to the abbey of Saint-Evroult en Ouche. A priory was established and maintained at Auffay by twelve Benedictine monks from Saint-Evroult until the religious wars in the sixteenth century forced them to abandon it and retreat to Saint-Evroult. The monks did not abandon their right to collect the *grosses dîmes* in Auffay and its neighboring communes, however, and by the eighteenth century this was a serious bone of contention between the local priests, who were responsible for maintaining the churches and caring for the poor of the villages, and the absent monks.[23]

The Middle Ages were not an easy time in the Caux. Knights and soldiers returning from the Crusades brought leprosy with them. By the thirteenth century, it had reached epidemic proportions and virtually every large village had a *léproserie* to house victims of the disease. In Auffay, the priory, Clos-Jaquet, was converted into a refuge for lepers in 1139, a function it maintained until 1530, when the disease finally disappeared from the Caux.[24]

Leprosy, however, was not the most serious threat faced by Auffay. The Caux was a major battleground in the Hundred Years War between England and France and was overrun by the English in the early fifteenth century. Farmland was laid waste, and the regional population was devastated by repeated onslaughts of moving and marauding troops, pitched battles and seiges, and epidemics of contagious diseases including the plague.[25]

Barely recovered from the Hundred Years war, the Caux once again became a battleground in the sixteenth-century French Wars of Religion. Because of its *château-fort*, Auffay was the scene of repeated battles between Catholics and Huguenots. In 1589, the Catholics took control of Auffay and entrenched themselves in the *château-fort*. Later in the year, they were evicted by the Huguenots and the village was once again pillaged and left in ruins. The fortress was not totally destroyed, however, and when Henry IV was forced to give up his seige of Paris in 1591, he and his troops sought refuge at Auffay several times.[26] Although Henry IV's sojourns at Auffay brought the village some fame, at best they must have been a mixed blessing for the villagers. Armies, whether friendly or antagonistic to the people of a region, lived off the land, stripping the peasants, merchants, and artisans of resources if they stayed for any length of time. Having a fortress worth taking probably made the village more, rather than less, vulnerable to conquest and destruction during this period.

The conversion of Henry IV to Catholicism in 1593 and his admission to Paris the following year brought peace and a period of recovery to the Caux. But it was not to be a permanent recovery. When Louis XIV revoked the Edict of Nantes in 1685, there was a mass migration of Protestants out of Normandy. This migration, coupled with the drafting of men into the army to fight Louis' wars, stripped the region of many of its artisans, farmers, and merchants. A series of bad harvests in 1692, 1693, and 1694 further impoverished the region. Disease spread quickly through the weakened population, augmenting the already high death rate from the famines.[27]

The Caux badly needed the period of respite that the eighteenth century finally brought. During the reign of Louis XV, warfare ended, the economy began to recover, employment in cottage industry expanded, the regional population began to increase, and the amount of land under cultivation grew as the peasants cleared new or formerly abandoned land.[28] Attention shifted from the ravages of war, the drafting of young men, and the fear of religious persecution to local issues and daily life.

In the eighteenth and early nineteenth centuries, the central village of Auffay was rustic, if not ramshackle. From a distance, it looked leafy and green because there were as many trees as houses; viewed up close, it was merely pitiful and dirty. Narrow, twisting, dirt roads, filled with potholes, curved down from the hills and ran along the Scie River. Houses were partially embedded in the ground and covered with thatched roofs. Isidore Mars, a native son of Auffay who wrote two books on the village's history and customs, described the eighteenth-century village as a depressing place, filled with "an irregular agglomeration of low, damp, unhealthful houses, mean and shabby in appearance and distributed without taste."[29] In addition to houses, the village contained a large church begun in the eleventh century, a cemetery, a large pasture, and a relatively large marketplace for the thrice-weekly markets in grain, cattle, tanned hides, and foodstuff. The old *château-fort* no longer existed and the seigneurs no longer lived in the central village. In 1775, the market area was improved by the building of a new *halle* by the seigneur, Antoine-

Augustin Thomas du Fossé, and the merchants' huts that had lined the square were razed. Housing and roads continued to be of poor quality until well into the nineteenth century, however.[30]

One of the most frequented and least desirable areas of the central village lay to the northwest, along the banks of the Scie, where a large bark mill (*moulin à tan*) worked night and day to supply several tanneries with pulverized oak bark. The mill not only made a steady pounding noise that was audible throughout the village and shook the ground in the near vicinity but also produced a cloud of bark dust that covered the mill, the surrounding area, the men working in the mill, and any passers-by who lingered in the area. The tanneries supplied by the mill created their own, worse health hazards and annoyances. The air reeked with the smell of rotting carcasses and hides, and the tiny Scie River was polluted with waste from the tanneries' vats. Auffay itself was spared the worst of the tanneries' pollution because they were on the downstream side of the village, but one wonders about the effects of their waste on the communes that lay farther downstream to the north. The tannery section of the village, with its stench and bark dust, could not be avoided because it also contained the major bridge (*le pont du moulin à tan*) across the Scie, a major route to villages and *hameaux* lying to the west of the river.[31]

Auffay was more connected to the outside world than were smaller villages during the *Ancien Régime*. It had some administrative functions in the region and was one of eleven distribution centers for salt in the *arrondissement* of Dieppe.[32] More important to the average villager, however, was the fact that its size attracted itinerant merchants and hawkers who passed through the village on a regular basis. Some merchants, like the coppersmiths and tinkers, appeared annually. Others arrived three times a year to ply their wares or to combine begging with entertaining at the Auffay fairs. Still others appeared on a more regular basis to buy or sell goods in the weekly markets or to deliver flour or salt.

The itinerant coppersmiths set up shop in the public square when they came to town. After making the rounds of the village in search of pots with broken handles, holes, or broken spouts, they would build a fire, set up their bellows, prepare the copper to be used in mending the old pots, and set to work. Children thought the coppersmiths were a grand diversion and, following the example of the smiths themselves, made periodic forays up to the fire where they would attempt to cook potatoes and other vegetables when the smiths were not looking.[33]

Poorer than the coppersmiths, but skilled in the art of persuasion, tinkers traveled alone, carrying the tools of their trade – a large pot, two pairs of tongs, and a bellows. Making camp on the outskirts of town, the tinker would rove the streets, selling his services in a sing-song voice. "Have you nothing for the tinker? Spoons, forks, skimmers, half-pints, pints, warming pans? No, nothing at all. Casseroles, andirons, candlesticks, lanterns, teapots, lids, coffeepots? Nothing needed today? Dutch ovens, ladles, basins, trays, fireplace shovels, funnels, separators? No, no, nothing to fix." When someone appeared to listen to his song, the tinker would shift to making a deal, explaining how little his services would cost and how good the repaired articles would look. Eventually striking a bargain he seemed loathe to make, and leaving his customer convinced that she had gotten a good deal, he would move on in search of others.[34]

A more frequent visitor to the village than either the tinkers or coppersmiths was the porter who brought raw cotton to the spinners or warps to the weavers and collected yarn or fabric in return. The arrival of the porter was an important event in the region because of both his role in the economy and his flamboyant appearance and manner. Despite the terrible roads that forced most people to travel on foot or horseback, a porter arrived with a large wagon pulled by a team of four horses. Traveling through the night to reach the villages in the Auffay area, the sound of the bells worn by the horses and the crack of the porter's whip carried far and wide. Skill with the whip was the porter's badge of honor. He used different combinations of sounds to greet other porters as they passed and to send messages. One combination meant "All goes well," another, "Good evening, comrade." Still others signaled danger, called for help, or, according to one reporter from the period, commented on the looks of the women the porter passed.[35]

The millers' assistants (*chasse-mouttes*) also traversed the streets of Auffay, accompanied by pack animals (usually a horse and a mule), carrying sacks of grain and flour back and forth between customers and the mill. Unlike the tinkers, the *chasse-mouttes* did no bargaining because the mills were owned by the *seigneurs* and prices were not subject to negotiation. Traditionally, each villager chose a miller to grind all of his or her grain as there was no possibility of finding a better price elsewhere.[36]

In addition to these traveling artisans and merchants, a sizeable collection of peddlers passed through Auffay, attracted by the three weekly markets and triannual fairs. There were chimney sweeps, buyers and sellers of rabbit skins, wild beast tamers with small traveling zoos, bagpipers, basket weavers, mole catchers, medicine men, perfume salesmen, and buffoons and fools who performed at fairs and begged for pennies. Identified in the minds of the villagers with the provinces of Savoy and the Auvergne, the Hotel Nodin, in which this motley collection of itinerants stayed, was nicknamed the Hotel Saint-Flour, a play on names perhaps between a village in the Auvergne named St. Flour and the verb *"flouer"* meaning to cheat or to fleece (steal).[37] Among the most successful of the hawkers were the medicine men who sold concoctions to cure children of worms and to remove corns from the feet.[38]

The mixture of ridicule and contempt with which the people of Auffay regarded the down-and-out peddlers who passed through the village was a double-edged sword. Although they clearly felt superior to the vagabonds, their ridiculing of strangers must have fueled their own fears about how they would be treated if they, too, had to look for work in a place where they would be strangers and outsiders. These fears, which were ever present for people living near the subsistence line, became more and more realistic as the proto-industrial period progressed.

Education

Education in the Caux was primarily administered by the church and was segregated by sex. In Auffay, the presence of priests but no nuns in the first half of the century meant that many more boys than girls learned to read and write. In the early part of the century, girls may have learned to read and write only from their parents, and not many parents appear to have had the skill or inclination to teach their daughters even rudimentary skills. In the 1750s, more than six out of ten Auffay grooms could sign their names whereas fewer than three out of ten brides could do more than make an X on the marriage register.[39] The arrival of the Soeurs-Grises, an order of nuns devoted to teaching and caring for the poor, in 1765 (the will of the Duchesse de La Force provided funds to build a house for them)[40] had a profound effect on female literacy, however. By the end of the century, 70 percent of Auffay brides could print or write their names, and during the first decade of the nineteenth century, the percentage rose to almost 80 percent.[41]

The conditions under which children learned to read and write were far from optimal. Boys sat on rough wooden benches in a damp, unpaved room of the church. Girls probably fared no better under the tutelage of the Soeurs-Grises. And at the end of the century, when a Mademoiselle Benard opened a school for girls in Auffay, the house in which she taught was so wretched that water ran through it when it rained and she could

Table 2.2. *Literacy in Auffay, 1751–1850*[a]

	Brides			Grooms		
	Literate	Total	Percentage	Literate	Total	Percentage
1751–1760	12	43	27.9	28	43	65.1
1761–1770	12	32	37.5	21	33	63.6
1771–1780	19	42	45.2	28	44	63.6
1781–1790	33	59	55.9	44	58	75.9
1791–1800	50	71	70.4	48	71	67.6
1801–1810	31	39	79.5	28	39	71.8
1811–1820	47	81	58.0	54	81	66.7
1821–1830	39	71	54.9	49	69	71.0
1831–1840	46	82	56.1	54	82	65.9
1841–1850	35	56	62.5	40	56	71.4
Total	324	576	56.3	394	576	68.4
1751–1790	76	176	43.2	121	178	68.0
1791–1810	81	110	73.6	76	110	69.1
1811–1850	167	290	57.6	197	288	68.4

[a]Based on the ability to print or sign one's name. Whether eleven brides and ten grooms could sign is unclear in the registers. Only those cases in which the ability to sign is clearly indicated are included in this and subsequent tables. *Source:* ADSM Parish and Civil Registers, Auffay. First marriages only.

not hold classes.[42] Nevertheless, the children did learn to read and write, as the steadily improving number and quality of the signatures in the parish registers testify (see Table 2.2).

Peasants and nobles

In 1750, the Duchesse de La Force owned a large chateau built in the *hameau* of Bosmelet in 1640 (for which the *hameau* was named) and the full right to collect the seigneurial dues in Auffay. When she died ten years later, the seigneurial rights were split. The Bosmelet estate and half of the rights descended first to Antoine-Augustin Thomas du Fossé and then to his son, Jean-François. The other half of the seigneurial dues passed to Anne-Louis, the Marquis de Mathan.[43]

The Thomas du Fossé family viewed itself as the patrons of the village throughout the eighteenth century. They brought the Soeurs-Grises to the village in 1765, constructed a new market place in 1775, helped maintain the church, and employed many tenant farmers. They also held a festival for the villagers on the grounds of the Bosmelet estate every March.[44] The villagers saw things differently. Peasants, merchants, and artisans chafed under the seigneurial system and particularly hated the *droits de coutume de foire et marché* that required them to pay duty to the nobles for the right to display their goods in the Auffay marketplace, for the use of the scales to measure grain and other commodities, and for any goods actually sold. Particularly onerous to the people of Auffay were the fees levied on the sellers of cider in the market. Cider makers had learned to offset the *droits d'entrée* (fees for selling cider in the market) by adulterating it with water (it was the volume of liquid rather than the volume of apple juice that was the basis for the tax). The peasants and villagers who were forced to buy weak cider for the same price they had paid in earlier years for strong cider were far from pleased. In fact, the price of cider ranked third in Auffay's list of twenty-two grievances in 1789.[45]

Sixth place in the Auffay *cahier de doléances* was held by a complaint about the nobles' monopoly on the milling of grain (the *banalité de moulin*). The *cahier* declared that the millers charged such a high price for milling that more than one-eighth of the crop was ending up in their hands and the poor could not afford to have their grain milled at all. The peasants and merchants who drafted the *cahier* for the village were convinced that if the nobles' monopoly on milling was ended, the price would fall, and they suggested that the new millers would gladly grind the grain of the poor without charge. Whether the latter was likely to happen is questionable, but it was undoubtedly true that competition among millers would have reduced the price of milling grain.[46]

The Auffay peasants also resented the seigneurs' unrestricted right to keep pigeons who posed a menace to their crops during planting and harvesting, swooping out of the sky to consume grain broadcast on the fields or waving on ripened stalks. They also thought everyone should pay taxes, regardless of their estate, a demand directed particularly toward the nobles and clergy who were exempt from the *taille* and salt taxes.[47]

The relationship between the villagers and nobles of Auffay was not as bad as in many other places, however. The Thomas family was allowed to live peacefully at Bosmelet throughout the Revolution, and Jean-François Thomas played an active role in local politics in the early years of the Revolution, serving as mayor until the Revolution became more radical and he became a suspect of the local committee of public safety.[48]

Official religion and folk beliefs

Dominating the center of the village was a large church, begun in the eleventh century and almost constantly under construction or repair. By

Table 2.3. *Girls' names, Auffay, 1751–1760*

Name	Number	Percentage
Marie Anne	19	15.3
Marie Marguerite	19	15.3
Marie Catherine	17	13.7
Marie Madeleine	12	9.7
Marie Rose	6	4.8
Marie Elisabeth	5	4.1
Marie + (other)	25	20.2
Anne + (other)	6	4.8
Marguerite + (other)	4	3.2
Geneviève + (other)	4	3.2
Other saints or virtues	7	5.7
Total	124	100.0

Source: ADSM Parish Registers, Auffay.

far the largest church in this section of the Caux, Notre Dame of Auffay was a local attraction, and its construction accounts for the sizable number of masons, brickmakers, carpenters, and nailmakers who lived in the commune in the eighteenth century. The degree to which the Catholic church dominated the life of eighteenth-century peasants and artisans is not as clear, however, as the extent to which it dominated the physical space of the village. The depth of the religious beliefs of the average villager is impossible to determine, although there are many signs of religious sentiment and adherence to religious practices in the village. What is interesting is the degree to which Catholic beliefs were intertwined with folk beliefs and to which religious celebrations were the occasion for revelry and the release of tensions.

Everyone was married, baptized, and buried in the church. Baptism was so important that midwives were entrusted with the authority to baptize newborn infants who looked like they would not survive.[49] Marriage was discouraged during Lent and Advent, and very few people broke the tradition. Between 1751 and 1790, 141 couples were married in Auffay. Only five of them were married in March (Lent) and only four in December (Advent).[50] Without exception, children were named after saints or virtues. There was a heavy preference for girls' names beginning with Marie (83 percent). There was more variety for boys in the first given name, but the preference was for names beginning with Jean (27 percent), and Jean Baptiste was the single most popular male name. In the decade of the 1750s, only thirty female and thirty male names (in a va-

Table 2.4. *Boys' names, Auffay, 1751–1760*

Names	Number	Percentage
Jean Baptiste	13	10.9
Jean + (other)	19	16.0
Pierre + (other)	18	15.1
Nicolas + (other)	15	12.6
François + (other)	10	8.4
Jacques + (other)	10	8.4
Louis + (other)	9	7.6
Other saints or virtues	25	21.0
Total	119	100.0

Source: ADSM Parish Registers, Auffay.

riety of combinations) were given to children baptized in Auffay (see Tables 2.3 and 2.4).[51]

In the mid-eighteenth century, several confraternities dedicated to the veneration of saints were established in Auffay. There were confraternities for St. Mathurin, the patron saint of the Auffay weavers; Ste. Monique, the patron saint of the spinners; St. Crepin (Crispin), who was venerated by shoemakers; St. Eloi (Eligius), venerated by blacksmiths; St. Adrien, a Roman martyr who was often invoked against plagues and who was revered as having expelled *la peste* from the Caux; and, the holy savior (St. Sauveur), venerated by the tanners. The confraternity of St. Adrien was the most popular, and each year its members made a pilgrimage to a chapel dedicated to the saint on the banks of the Seine.[52]

To a large extent, village life was regulated and punctuated by the church. People not only did not marry during Lent and Advent, but they also celebrated a series of annual holy days and festivals. In addition to the religious significance, these celebrations helped release tension for people who lived close to the subsistence line and who could easily fall below it when the weather destroyed their crops or when changes in international relations or international markets interrupted the flow of raw materials or completed textiles. Among the most popular of the annual celebrations in Auffay were those of Twelfth Day (Epiphany), Mardi gras, patron saints' days, and Pentecost.

Twelfth Day was largely a children's festival in Auffay. Children were indulged in family circles and allowed to travel around the village with lighted candles, shouting "Bonjour, Les Rois," on the eve of the festival, and "Adieu, les Rois, for twelve more months," at the end of the celebration. The children's procession did not necessarily mark the end of the celebrating, however. Partying and drinking continued late into the night and, if it was not too cold or wet, ended with adults and children pouring out-of-doors to join hands around fruit trees (perhaps a symbol of fertility) and dance and sing until three or four o'clock in the morning.[53]

Mardi gras saw revelry that was even more boisterous than the dancing and singing on Twelfth Day. The day belonged to the young men, who wore costumes and entertained themselves and the villagers with mimicry and fake extortion. Some dressed as coppersmiths and went from house to house seeking work. Others pretended to be broom merchants and tried to sell their wares. Some sold "the Balm of Saturn" that, they said, would remove corns. And still others armed themselves with syringes full of water, entered houses offering various services, and, when they were refused, squirted water on the inhabitants as they made their escape. Late in the day, they climbed the hill where the old château had stood. There, amidst feigned mourning, they burned a straw effigy and then formed a funeral procession that wound through the village. The procession ended, they returned to laughter and practical joking.[54]

Good Friday, at the other end of the Lenten season, was, in contrast, a serious and somber day. Isidore Mars described the day as one on which "the poor, the mendicant, the infirm and the crippled" invaded the village, displaying their "nudity and their misery" to the eyes of the villagers and begging for charity in the public square, the cemetery, and from the porch of the church.[55] A wooden skeleton, known as La Mort d'Auffay, was exhibited in an open coffin in a faintly illuminated corner of the church that was hung with black drapery for the occasion. The skeleton was a graphic way of reminding the villagers of their mortality on the most solemn day in the Christian calendar.[56] Combined with the arrival of "the halt and the lame" outside the church, the entire day had a macabre tone, although it is impossible to tell what impact these displays had on peasants and villagers who were all too familiar with death. Parents regularly watched at least one of their children die, and everyone knew full well that a poor harvest would post a life threat for the old and the young.

Events that began as solemn religious rites sometimes turned into secular celebrations. One infamous day in Auffay's religious history (in the late 1760s), the pilgrimage of the confraternity of St. Adrien ended in ignominy and near disaster. As usual, the members of the confraternity set out from Auffay at two in the morning, carrying banners and chanting hymns. But by the time the procession reached the Seine, the "pilgrims" were more than a little inebriated. Enjoying themselves immensely, they attempted to commandeer the boats used to take them up the Seine to the chapel of St. Adrien, threatening everyone in the party, including the priest, with drowning.[57]

It was not just on special occasions that Catholicism was blended with secular celebrations and folk beliefs. In the stories of the villagers, werewolves stalked the countryside, and many were hesitant to venture beyond their homes at night.[58] Shepherds, who were readily identifiable by their long beards, sheepskin cloaks, and crooks, were held in awe and fear. Just as there was a tendency in many places in the sixteenth century to regard old women who lived alone as witches, in the Caux in the eighteenth century, the shepherds who lived on the margins of society were regarded as sorcerers capable of casting spells and conjuring up evil spirits. Having little in common with the more gregarious villagers, and being regarded by them as men with strange ways, they tended to keep to themselves when they came to the village on market days, behavior that merely increased the villagers' suspicions. People shunned them in town and avoided isolated paths that ran near the flocks for fear of encountering one of them.[59]

The church itself did not present a united front in the *cauchois* villages in the eighteenth century. Instead, it was torn with dissension over the collection of the tithe, a dispute in which the villagers readily chose sides, but which does not seem to have affected religiosity. The Benedictine monks who had maintained a residence at Clos-Jaquet until the Wars of Religion forced them to retreat to the monastery at St. Evroult, continued to collect a tithe on the grain crops (*grosses dîmes*) in Auffay and the surrounding communes. The *curés*, who were actually in residence in the communes and who were responsible for the upkeep of the local churches and the care of the poor, resented the collection of the *grosses dîmes* by the absent monks. As new land was cleared and cultivated in the eighteenth century, the *curés* attempted to collect what they called the "*dîmes novales*," that is, a tithe on new land. The monks, in return, claimed that their *dîmes* rights applied to new as well as old land.

The dispute over the *dîmes* raged until the Revolution, sometimes in the law courts and sometimes in the newly cleared fields. Probably typical of such disputes was one in 1763 between Nicolas Fécamp, the *curé* of Cent Acres (a commune to the north of Auffay) and his servant, Jeannot, on the one hand, and François and Robert Cahon, tenant farmers who had leased the right to collect the *dîmes* from the monks. Infuriated by the wealth and lack of religiosity of the monks, Fécamp took matters into his own hands and sent Jeannot to collect the *dîmes* on some new land. One day, as Jeannot was preparing to place the grain for the tithe in his wagon, the Cahon brothers appeared brandishing clubs and threatening to thrash him if he did not stop. Jeannot beat a hasty but outraged retreat and reported the episode to the *curé*. A few days later, he again tried to collect the tithe from the new fields of another peasant. This time, Jeannot succeeded in hauling one wagonload of grain to the barns of the *curé* without being stopped. But when he returned for a second load, he found that he had been observed by the Cahons as he left the field and that they had succeeded in hauling away the remaining grain. At this point, the *curé* took his case to the law courts, the outcome of which Mars, who reports the story, unfortunately does not tell us.[60]

In these disputes, the villagers sided with the *curés,* who were important personages and performed important functions in the village. They baptized, married, and buried everyone in the commune, held weekly religious services, and were responsible for dispensing money and food to the indigent. The monks, on the other hand, provided no services to the village and functioned like absentee landlords, collecting one-tenth of the peasants' crops out of their fields. To make matters worse, the tithe was collected not by the monks themselves, but by peasants to whom they leased the right to collect it. Such peasants were determined to collect every ounce of the tithe because their profit depended on their collecting grain worth more than what they were pledged to pay the monks. In Auffay, the right to collect the *dîmes* was leased to François Merlin in the 1780s for 3,600 *livres* a year; this was only one of several *dîmes* that the monks at St. Evroult collected. In contrast, the Auffay *curé*'s sole income was 700 *livres*, which he received from the monks (his *portion congrue*), and residence in the parish house.[61] It is small wonder that *curés,* peasants, merchants, and artisans alike resented the absent monks, who drained off a major portion of the village's revenue, spent no money in the community, and reduced the general standard of living by a tenth.

The harvest

The religious ceremonies and practices that marked the passage of time in Auffay were superimposed on the agricultural calendar, whose seasons annually brought marked changes in work, anxiety, and well-being. The agricultural year began in the fall with the preparation of the fields for the winter and the next round of planting and harvesting. A third of the fields always lay fallow. A second third was plowed and planted in the early autumn with wheat or rye or *meteil* (a mixture of the two grains), which lay in the fields through the winter until it began to germinate and ripen in the spring. The final third was plowed, but not planted, in mid-November. The peasants then retreated from the rainy, cold fields to their small, damp, and crowded houses.

During the winter, women prepared meals, cared for children and farmyard animals, and spun yarn for the putting-out merchants as they did year-round. The men repaired farm instruments, threshed the grain, helped their wives and daughters with carding or combing, or wove *siamoises* (cotton and linen fabric) for the Rouen merchants. In January and late February, the men plowed and harrowed the unplanted fields and then returned to the nonagricultural activities of the winter. Finally, at the beginning of April, a period of intense activity began. The fields were plowed and harrowed for the fourth time and planted with oats and barley, the spring cereals. The men anxiously watched the growing grain and the weather while the women weeded garden and flax plants, cared for newly born animals, and continued to spin for the textile merchants. At the end of the summer, the harvest occupied the entire community. Men, women, and children poured into the fields in late July for six weeks of work cutting, gathering, binding, and transporting the grain to the peasants' barns.[62] Harvesting was the most fatiguing of the peasants' work. It began before dawn and continued until after sunset in the hottest and longest days of the year. When poor weather threatened, work continued long into the night.[63]

After the harvest, the cycle began again. The fields that had contained the oat and barley crops rotated into fallow, the wheat and rye fields moved into the cycle of winter plowing in preparation for spring planting with oats and barley, and the fields that had been lying fallow the previous year were plowed and planted with wheat and rye, the winter cereals.[64]

Just as the seasons of the Christian year affected marriages so did the agricultural seasons, although not quite as dramatically. Between 1751 and 1790, 52 percent of all marriages in Auffay occurred in November, January, and February, the months when a good harvest created a period of respite and security for peasants and during which there was little agricultural work. (Very few marriages occurred in December because of the church's proscription of marriage during Advent.) (See Table 2.5)[65]

The agricultural calendar also determined the dates of two major commercial and social events in Auffay. Two of the three annual fairs occurred between the harvest and the spring planting. One was on the twenty-seventh of September, when the harvest and the planting of the winter

Table 2.5. *Distribution of marriages by month, Auffay, 1751–1850*

Dates	Jan	Feb	Mar	Apr	May	June	July	Aug	Sept	Oct	Nov	Dec	Total
1751–1760	11	5	0	5	2	7	5	3	3	1	15	2	59
1761–1770	6	9	4	2	5	1	5	3	5	7	11	0	58
1771–1780	9	12	0	4	2	4	6	3	1	2	13	1	57
1781–1790	11	14	1	1	4	5	6	6	2	5	11	1	67
1791–1800	7	8	3	5	2	11	9	8	9	12	14	9	97
1801–1810	3	6	3	0	4	6	2	2	5	4	10	3	48
1811–1820	14	6	4	6	10	3	12	9	6	8	8	10	96
1821–1830	11	8	5	6	9	3	4	6	7	10	8	3	80
1831–1840	9	5	2	3	10	13	13	4	5	9	11	5	89
1841–1850	8	5	2	6	5	12	7	2	10	5	10	4	76
	89	78	24	38	53	65	69	46	53	63	111	38	727

Source: ADSM Parish and Civil Registers, 1751–1850.

wheat and rye crops was finished, and the peasants had time, energy, and a little money to spend. The other was on the twenty-second of January, after the plowing of the unplanted fields and in the middle of the "dead" season. The third was linked to the church calendar and was held on the Friday after Pentecost.[66]

The grain harvest was the crucial element in the peasants' lives. The poor road system in all European countries in this era made it impossible to transport grain long distances. In terms of food supply, regions functioned as autonomous units, producing as much of their own food as possible and planting grain crops even when the climate and soil were poorly suited to their cultivation.[67] Everyone knew that if the harvest failed, hunger would stalk the land and the death toll would rise. Little or no help was to be expected from the outside, and peasants resented the shipment of grain out of their regions, even in years of abundant harvests, because the next year might bring a disaster that locally stored grain could help avert. As Steven Kaplan notes in his work on the eighteenth-century grain trade in France, "The dread of shortage and hunger haunted this society."[68]

The Caux was no different than other regions in this regard, although it was one of the largest grain-producing *pays* in France in normal years. The memory of a bad harvest lingered in the public mind for a long time, and everyone lived in dread of another bad year. Five times in the second half of the eighteenth century the *cauchois* harvest failed, the price of grain rose precipitously, and many people slid below the subsistence line. After a bad harvest, food shortages usually began in January. The worst period, both for the people themselves and for government officials concerned with maintaining law and order, was always the following spring and summer when grain supplies were very low and prices high.[69] In 1752, 1768, 1775, 1784, and 1789, complaints about hunger and high grain prices and charges that the shortage was artificial – that speculators and monopolists were hoarding grain to drive prices up – swept through the Caux, igniting disturbances in local markets and on the highways.[70]

The grain trade was tightly regulated in the *Ancien Régime*. To prevent the establishment of monopolies, bakers, merchants, and millers were forbidden to purchase grain in the early hours of the market. Millers could sell only the grain they received in payment for milling, not grain that they purchased. Noble landowners, *laboureurs*, and *fermiers* could purchase only seed grain. Farmers who had grain to sell were required by law to bring it to the market. They could not sell it from their farms nor could they bring only a sample of it to demonstrate its quality.[71]

After a bad harvest, the *laboureurs* and *fermiers* were in a tricky, albeit potentially lucrative, position. Rising prices increased their profit margin but inflamed the local populace. If they brought their grain to the market, the people might force them to sell it for much less than the going price, as happened several times in the late eighteenth century. If they did not bring it to the market, the people might invade their farms and barns and take what they could find. Without the facilities to store much grain, the *laboureurs* and *fermiers* were always forced to bring their grain to market sooner or later, and in the late winter and early spring after a bad harvest, they frequently found themselves facing an angry mob and failed to get the high price they and others were asking.

The events of 1775 in the eastern Caux were typical of the riots that food shortages and high prices could cause in this region, as in others. The larger villages in each section of the Caux alternated the days on which they held grain markets. Riots that began in one village were continued in another, gaining momentum and organization as people moved from place to place. In the eastern section of the Caux, riots usually began in Bacqueville on Wednesday, moved to Auffay on Thursday, and then on to other villages, as they did in 1775.[72]

On Wednesday, May 10, a woman at the Bacqueville market demanded that a *laboureuse* sell her grain for fifteen *livres* rather than for the thirty *livres* that she was asking. The woman's demand was backed up by the other customers at the market, and the argument grew more and more heated. The two cavaliers of the regional police (*maréchaussée*)

who were at the market to keep order quickly perceived that any attempts to arrest the woman or to support the *laboureuse* would result in
a full-scale riot and advised the *laboureuse* to sell the grain for fifteen
livres.

On Thursday, May 11, Auffay held the first of its two weekly grain
markets. A much larger number of people than usual attended the market
and made the same demand – that the grain be sold for fifteen *livres*.
(The selling price at the previous Auffay market had been thirty-three
livres a sack.) Order was somehow maintained, but on Saturday, May
13, at the second weekly grain market in Auffay, the demand was repeated once again, and this time the situation quickly got out of hand.
Many of the *laboureurs* had been frightened by Thursday's events and
had not returned to the Saturday market. When the crowd perceived that
there were only a few *laboureurs* present, they were infuriated. One customer informed a *laboureur* that "he should be happy to get even fifteen
livres" for his grain, and the threat of physical violence increased. Again,
the cavaliers at the market were seriously outnumbered and prudently
urged the *laboureurs* to sell the people the grain at the price they were
willing to pay, knowing that their bayonettes and muskets would be use-
less against a mob.

In the next few days, this scene was repeated in ten more villages in
the eastern Caux, resulting in a loss of 160 *livres* to the *laboureurs*. The
most serious loss occurred in Auffay, where the difference between what
the *laboureurs* were asking for their grain and the amount they were paid
added up to 122 *livres*. The government belatedly sent more troops to
the area who moved from market to market and prevented further rioting during the summer.[73]

Tension in the Caux following a bad harvet was exacerbated by the
density of the population in this region, where the possibility of summer
work in agriculture and winter work in cottage industry attracted immigrants and retarded emigration,[74] and by the continual movement of grain
toward Rouen and Paris. In the *Ancien Régime,* the supplying of grain to
urban areas (especially Paris) always took precedence over the supplying
of villages because urban riots posed a more serious threat to the government than did rural riots. In particularly bad years, the government imported foreign grain to feed Paris. Arriving by ship at Dieppe or Le Havre
to travel by wagon or barge to the capital, the passage of this grain through
the Caux or along the Seine aroused local citizens, aggravated their sense
that the shortage was artificial, and undermined any faith they might
have had that the government would help them.[75] Attacks on the wagons

and barges, and even on the grain as it was transferred from ships to wagons, accompanied the attacks on local markets and urban granaries as the hungry people of the Caux took matters into their own hands, offered what they regarded as a fair price for the grain, and took by force what they regarded as theirs by right.[76]

Living conditions

Life in eighteenth-century Auffay was difficult. Because agricultural work alternated with spinning and weaving, work was constant for most people. So was the fear that the harvest might fail, bringing hunger and destitution. Little could be done about illness, and families had no alternative but to watch children and the elderly die in periods of famine or epidemics or even in relatively good times. Most families lived near the subsistence line, and their lives included few, if any, luxuries. Houses were small, damp, and dark. Heated by poorly ventilated fireplaces, the walls were blackened with smoke, and it was often impossible to see across even small rooms. Visitors frequently had to call out to see if anyone was home even if they had already come in the door. Pictures and curtains were unheard of luxuries, and furniture was sturdy but in short supply.[77]

Fermiers and *laboureurs* who lived in farmhouses surrounded by *masures* were much better off than the *journaliers* whom they hired by the day, although the wealth and resources they controlled varied considerably.[78] In 1789, for example, Pierre Ursin, a *fermier*, worked 30 acres of land and paid 58 *livres* in *taille*. Jean Joseph Lenoir, another *fermier*, farmed 60 acres and paid 123 *livres* in *taille*. Charles Jullien, a *laboureur*, owned 100 acres and paid 282 *livres* in *taille*. The number of farm buildings and the size of houses depended on the family's resources. All houses and barns were built with frames of wooden beams, however. The beams were left exposed and the space between them was filled with clay mixed with straw. In large houses, bricks were sometimes used in place of wood at the corners and around the door and window openings.[79]

These were not ideal building materials for the *cauchois* climate. The exterior walls on the west and south had to be protected from the prevailing winds and rain by embedding pieces of wood or slate in the clay. Floors were usually bare earth, and roofs were thatched with straw. In the winter rains, the latter leaked, the former turned to mud, and the interiors of houses were cold and damp. The thatched roofs also deteriorated rapidly, and *fermiers* who rented their *masures* frequently had to replace part of the roof every year. The wooden beams and clay contracted as they dried, leaving cracks and openings in which mice nested and through which winds blew and rain seeped. The kitchen fireplace, the only source of heat in these drafty houses, could not keep the occupants warm in the winter. The combination of fireplaces, straw roofs, exposed wooden beams on the interior of the house, and wool, linen, and cotton hung to dry from the ceiling posed a serious fire hazard, as many families learned tragically.[80]

Most houses had only one floor and two or three rooms. The largest room with the fireplace was the kitchen. Strings of apples, pears, onions, beans, and peas were suspended from the beams of the ceiling to dry. Muskets and household utensils also hung from beams because there were no cabinets to hold them. The warmest place in the house was the ledge above the fireplace, where people and cats perched on cold winter evenings. A shelf set into the wall contained eating utensils, dishes, and cooking pots. One corner of the kitchen was occupied by a dispenser that held the precious and highly taxed salt. The center of the room was filled by a table on which the family's usual meal of bread, butter, salt, and large radishes (in the summer) was set. Several heavy chairs, one of which was occupied by a sack of flour, and a kneeding trough completed the kitchen's usual furnishings, although peasants who had managed to get a little ahead might have a grandfather clock in the corner – a symbol of wealth in Auffay as throughout Europe.[81]

The second room was the sleeping chamber. It contained an *armoire,* the most expensive part of a woman's dowry, in which the family's clothes and any extra linens were stored. There were beds and, if space permitted, looms and spinning wheels.[82] Sleeping was segregated by seniority, not by sex. If there were two sleeping rooms, the larger one was for the *laboureur* or *fermier* and his wife, and the smaller one was for the children and servants, although male servants sometimes slept in the stables with the animals.[83]

One-story houses had an exterior staircase leading to the roof, built on the side of the house least exposed to the winds and rain. (In most cases, this was the east side.) The roof extended over the top of the staircase to protect it, and firewood was stacked against the side of the house under the staircase.[84]

Rudimentary as such houses were, they were a good deal better than the cottages in which the *journaliers* and their families lived. In fact, *cottage* is too pleasant a name for the hovels described in 1805 by the unnamed author of a handwritten book about the Seine-Inférieure:

The dwellings of the laborers are damp and unhealthy. They often consist of a dwelling where a well-to-do man would hardly believe it was possible to keep animals. The little light that they receive is scarcely able to penetrate the dark window panes.

These dwellings, blackened by the smoke from the leaves and vegetable matter that the poor burn in the winter, [and] low and damp, resemble a foul dungeon more than a house inhabited by useful and honest citizens. In the winter the smoke is suffocating. In the heat of the summer it is impossible to breathe. If a contagious disease attacks someone in the house, all the inhabitants rapidly fall victim to it.[85]

It would not take much to push such families below the subsistence level. And yet, the peasants and villagers in the Caux were better off in the late eighteenth century than they had been in earlier centuries and than their contemporaries were in many other regions. Agricultural work alone would not have kept most families above the subsistence line. However, the availability of work in agriculture and cottage industry made it possible for families to remain in the Caux and even attracted migrants from other, more purely agricultural regions where there was no winter work in spinning and weaving. Most families not only stayed above the subsistence line, but also in good years had some money to spend on alcohol and entertainment at village fairs and at the cafés and taverns that appeared in the wake of the putting-out merchants.[86] Why these merchants came to the Caux and how their search for workers affected life on the plain are the questions to which we now turn.

3

~·~

Proto-industrial theory and the pays de Caux

In 1971, Charles and Richard Tilly identified three processes they thought deserved further investigation by European economic historians in the decade of the seventies. The first was "industrialization before the factory system, or protoindustrialization."[1] They had adopted the term *protoïndustrialization* from Franklin Mendels's dissertation, "Industrialization and Population Pressure in 18th-Century Flanders."[2] The term had been used before, most notably by E. J. T. Collins, E. L. Jones, and S. J. Woolf in analyzing the interplay between labor supply and agricultural advance in the eighteenth and nineteenth centuries,[3] but Mendels was the first to define it systematically and to suggest that it should be viewed as a stage in the industrialization process.

In 1972, Mendels's first published work on proto-industrialization appeared. In it, he described proto-industrialization as "the rapid growth of traditionally organized but market-oriented, principally rural industry," accompanied by regional specialization in agriculture and paving the way for industrialization proper (factory production of goods for national and international markets) by creating "capital accumulation, market connections, entrepreneurial skills, and agricultural progress," and he analyzed its demographic effects in Flanders.[4] Mendels's work captured the attention of economic historians and touched off what the Tillys had called for — an investigation of industrialization before the introduction of the factory system. In addition to Mendels, a host of historians have increased our understanding of the proto-industrial process and its impact on particular regions.[5]

Research on cottage industry did not, of course, begin with Franklin Mendels. In the early twentieth century, Henri Sée and E. Tarlé, among others, wrote important works on French rural industry;[6] in the 1960s, Joan Thirsk, Rudolf Braun, Eric Jones, Jan de Vries, and Herbert Kisch directed their attention to the development of large-scale cottage industries in Europe and England.[7] Mendels's definition and use of the term

38

proto-industrialization focused attention on rural industry in a new way, however. What had appeared to be a common and undifferentiated preindustrial phenomenon – the coexistence of agriculture and cottage manufacturing – now came to be seen as a complex process with distinct stages, the last of which – large-scale cottage manufacturing organized by urban merchants in subsistence farming regions for export to national and international markets – might shed light on two of the major issues in European economic history – the location of industrial centers and the link between economic development and demographic behavior.

In his 1972 article, Mendels was primarily interested in identifying proto-industrialization as an economic process with clear demographic consequences, at least in Flanders, and not in analyzing the specific circumstances that would lead regions to adopt large-scale cottage industry. Mendels's interests have been shared by most of the historians who have worked on proto-industrialization. Analyses of demographic patterns have been sophisticated, although the general conclusions drawn from them are not entirely correct. Analysis of the pre-requisites for the spread of a proto-industry into a region and of the factors that ultimately determined where proto-industrialization occurred has, however, remained contradictory and off target, even though Mendels has turned to this aspect of the problem in his most recent published writings on the subject.[8]

The prevailing explanations of proto-industrialization

A variety of theories about the economic conditions that triggered the proto-industrial process and determined its locations have emerged in the last decade. Forming a backdrop for all of these theories is the understanding that virtually all eighteenth-century agriculture had strong seasonal variations in labor demand. The major exceptions to this rule were the viticulture regions, where the vines demanded year-round attention from the agricultural work force. All cereal crops were highly seasonal in their labor demands, as were most of the new crops introduced during the eighteenth and early nineteenth centuries. Potatoes and flax, whose cultivation was spreading, simply intensified the swings in labor demand by augmenting (and only slightly lengthening) the period of peak labor demand. The same was true of the enclosure movement and the replacement of fallow fields with such root crops as clover and legumes. Although these crops (as well as the hedges used as fences) provided more year-round jobs in agriculture than had the old system of fallow farming and open fields, they did little to solve the seasonal unemployment problem because they also increased the amount of labor needed during the harvest period.[9]

This alternation of intense work seasons with dead or no-work seasons in agriculture made cottage industry and agriculture compatible for centuries. The questions for proto-industrial historians are why these cottage industries grew dramatically in scale in some regions and not in others and why this happened when it did. Answers to these questions have revolved around analyses of regional agricultural conditions, legal systems, competition for markets, the size of the rural labor force, and land distribution.

Regional specialization

In a 1968 article, "The Agricultural Origins of Industry," Eric Jones developed an hypothesis that continues to be accepted by proto-industrial historians. He argued that interregional competition for shrinking or stagnating agricultural markets between 1650 and 1750, as a result of a diminution in English demographic growth and the outright decline of the western European population, resulted in regional specialization in cereals and husbandry and hence in regional interdependency. The adoption of better farming techniques (enclosure, the planting of forage crops, and the creation of artificial pastures) in the areas most suited to grain production increased their output of cereals and allowed them to squeeze less easily plowed areas of heavy clay and less fertile regions out of urban markets. Peasants in these areas were forced to rely on a combination of husbandry and cottage industry for income. This growing regional specialization made the two types of regions mutually dependent: the technically progressive, commercial agricultural areas sold their grain and meat surpluses to the relatively infertile areas whose agriculture was now confined to subsistence farming and animal grazing; the subsistence farming regions, in turn, sold some of their manufactured goods to the commercial agricultural regions.[10]

Mendels's research on Flanders supports Jones's argument. In the maritime regions, large commercial farms produced wheat, butter, and cheese for foreign and domestic markets. In the interior regions, peasants eked out a living on small plots planted with flax, potatoes, and grain and supplemented their small incomes with earnings from winter work in cottage industry.[11] Like Jones, Mendels regarded this not as a long-standing differentiation but as a phenomenon with recent origins. Unlike Jones, however, Mendels spoke not in causal terms but in terms of simultaneous developments.[12] Many regions, he argued in 1972, which "had previously engaged in agricultural production *cum* part-time industry, now shed their industries and began to purchase industrial products in other regions while they became specialized in commercial agriculture. Neighboring regions, meanwhile, experienced growth in their rural handicrafts."[13]

By 1980, Mendels had come to regard proto-industrialization as a process that not only accompanied regional specialization in agriculture but which also was most likely to occur in regions where commercial and subsistence agricultural zones were in close proximity. The juxtaposition of the zones, he argued, would have been mutually beneficial and would have allowed the subsistence agricultural area to concentrate more and more on cottage manufacturing because its residents could buy surplus food from the nearby cereal-producing region. Moreover, the peasants in the subsistence zone could supplement their earnings from cottage industry with harvest work in the commercial zone. Meanwhile, farmers in the commercial area would have benefited from the existence of a large harvest labor force located only two or three days away. Workers could easily adjust to variations in the date of the harvest from one year to the next, and harvest wages would be lower than if workers had been in shorter supply or had had to travel longer distances. In addition, some of the surplus crops would have found a ready and conveniently located market in the subsistence zone.[14]

The compactness of the small-farm zone and its location adjacent to a large-farm zone were the keys to proto-industrialization in Mendels's view. If the zone was too large or not easily reached by the putting-out merchants, it would not experience proto-industrialization; nor would homogeneous regions consisting of small (subsistence) farms interspersed with large (commercial) farms because "the difficulty and cost of controlling and coordinating the craft production and transporting its output to a central place" would be prohibitive.[15]

Subsistence and pastoral agriculture

The central aspect of the theories of Jones and Mendels regarding proto-industrial areas is that the process occurred in poor, subsistence farming, or pastoral regions, not in commercial agricultural regions. In general, according to Jones, it was "relatively infertile areas, uncompetitive in cereals" that took up cottage manufacturing.[16] Mendels's research on Flanders proved to be a case in point. The maritime region was much more fertile than the rest of the country and was more suited to cereal production than was the less fertile land in the interior, even though the heaviness of the soil in the maritime region made a costly investment in plows and horses necessary.[17] And it was in the interior of Flanders, not in the fertile maritime region, that the cottage linen industry flourished.

Jones and Mendels are not the only historians to have identified proto-industrialization with noncommercial, subsistence farming or pastoral regions. In 1910, Tarlé argued that the principal cause of the peasants' acceptance of work in cottage industry was "the poverty of the soil" that made it impossible for them to survive on agricultural work alone.[18] More important, perhaps, a variety of recent case studies has supported Jones's and Mendels's view that proto-industrialization occurred in regions of pastoral or subsistence farming and not in regions of commercial agriculture.

In his pioneering 1960 work on cottage industry in the Zurich highlands, parts of which appeared in English in 1966 and 1978, Rudolf Braun discovered a large-scale cottage textile industry in a steep and sparsely settled "back country with discrete zones of settlement, wood glens 'of forbidding aspect,' inconceivably bad communications, and a rude climate." In contrast, the flat, more fertile, and more easily cultivated region between the city of Zurich and the highlands had no cottage industry.[19]

In England, David Levine discovered that Shepshed, the poorest of the villages in his study of Leicestershire, England, had a large proto-industry, whereas other, slightly better off villages did not. In Shepshed, where much of the land was "rocky and stony, yeelding fruit not without great labour and expences," cottage framework knitting was widespread. In neighboring Bottesford, where the land was of higher quality and peasants were less poor, there was no framework knitting.[20] Similarly, Pat Hudson found that the worsted branch of the West Riding, England, textile industry, which existed in a region of upland pasture, developed into a proto-industry whereas the woolen branch, located in an area of valleys and hills, where the soil was better and farms produced a variety of crops, did not.[21]

In France, James Lehning found a large textile industry in the Stephanois mountains outside Saint-Etienne, France, in the late eighteenth and early nineteenth centuries. Until the decline of the Saint-Etienne ribbon industry in the late nineteenth century, this was a classic proto-industrial region. Peasants combined subsistence cereal farming, sheep herding, and dairying with ribbon weaving for the putting-out merchants of Saint-Etienne, who sold the ribbons in national and international markets.[22]

Attempts to explain why proto-industrialization occurred in these poor agricultural regions and not in others (and not in wealthier agricultural regions) have focused on manorial and communal controls. Braun, for instance, argued that the development of large-scale cottage industry was only possible in poor agricultural areas where communal norms regarding crop rotation and the grazing of animals had never existed or had begun to break down. The Zurich highlands were an example of the former. In this forbidding region, survival was difficult, at best, and called for individual initiative, not collective planning. As a result, people were free to divide their time between agriculture and manufacturing according to their own needs, and, being poor but having the "economic values and spirit of the entrepreneur," they welcomed the earning opportunities provided by the putting-out merchants. In the fertile flatlands between the city and the highlands, field rotations, the timing of planting and harvesting, and even building permits were determined collectively. "In such a firmly articulated and close-knit collectivity," Braun argued, "industry had little play. Industrialization would have destroyed not only the material but also the human bases of such a community."[23] Sensing this, the community took steps to keep cottage industry out. The Zurich merchants who undoubtedly would have preferred the closer, more accessible flatlands to the mountainous highlands as a putting-out region, had no choice but to seek cottage workers in the pastoral, mountain area.

Although Bottesford peasants worked better land than their Shepshed counterparts, the difference between the two villages was not great, and Levine's major explanation of why the former did not develop a proto-industry is manorial control. Suggesting that the Bottesford peasants might have welcomed a by-employment in industry in the seventeenth and eighteenth centuries, when the village was being squeezed out of the grain market by the lighter, sandy soil regions in southern and eastern England and was being forced to turn to pastoral farming, he argued that such a development was prevented by the duke of Rutland, who owned 54 percent and controlled an additional 25 percent of the land in Bottesford.[24]

As Braun's and Levine's works suggest, the relationships among manorial or communal controls, subsistence or pastoral agriculture, and proto-industrialization were complex. Strong controls could prevent the putting-out merchants from entering both relatively rich farm lands and relatively poor villages. Research by Lutz Berkner has similarly shown that a strong manorial system that restricted the sale of land and the building of cottages could also make a subsistence farming region with locally organized cottage industries inhospitable to the putting-out merchants.[25] Herbert Kisch has shown that strong feudal lords who, in one era, en-

couraged the development of cottage textile production for local markets
might later prevent the expansion of that production, not by controlling
population growth, but by preventing merchants from acquiring the kind
of centralized control that was necessary if the industry was to compete
effectively in the national and international textile markets of the nineteenth century.[26]

The strength of the manorial or communal system thus has come to be
regarded as an important factor in determining the location of proto-
industries. Nevertheless, when it comes to looking for such industries,
historians continue to focus on the quality of the land. Strong manorial
or communal systems simply explain the absence of proto-industries in
regions in which one might otherwise expect to find them; poor soil and
subsistence or pastoral agriculture explain their presence.

Land fragmentation and population growth

In an article that predates the proto-industrial literature, Joan Thirsk suggested that partible inheritance combined with peasant ownership of land
might have encouraged children to stay in Suffolk villages and to marry
at younger ages than was usual elsewhere in the fifteenth and sixteenth
centuries. The resulting population growth and land fragmentation may
then have provided the impetus for villagers to take up the manufacture
of woolen cloth.[27] Following her lead, historians have argued that demographic growth, the fragmentation of landholdings, and, hence, the
existence of a large land-poor population were major factors in determining which regions would proto-industrialize. Hans Medick, in fact, felt
that the relationship between population density and cottage industry
was so strong that he argued that a "numerous, under-employed class of
small peasants or landless rural dwellers" was an essential precondition
for proto-industrialization.[28]

Following closely in Thirsk's footsteps, Pat Hudson recently argued
that partible inheritance combined with an open market in land fostered
proto-industrialization in parts of the West Riding by creating a large,
landless or virtually landless class of laborers whose survival in the countryside depended on work in cottage industry.[29] Mendels's study of Flanders provides the clearest evidence for the theory, however, although it
was not partible inheritance and peasant land ownership that created
population growth and land fragmentation in that region. Most of the
land in the interior was owned by city dwellers and rented to the peasants
who worked it. Some of the rented land was held in large parcels, some
in small, and the land actually owned by the peasants was almost inevitably divided into very small plots. As a result, many peasants were land

poor long before the eighteenth century. In that century, however, the introduction of the potato allowed the population of the interior to double. Seeing the possibility of obtaining higher rents from several small holdings rather than from one large one, the absentee, city-dwelling property owners subdivided their land as population increased, thereby increasing land fragmentation and reducing the possibility that a family could support itself from the land it farmed. Only the expansion of the cottage linen industry allowed this growing (and increasingly land-poor) population to remain in the countryside.[30]

Problems

There are several problems with the current explanations of why proto-industrialization occurred when and where it did. In the first place, only Flanders conforms to Mendels's regional model of adjacent and mutually dependent zones of subsistence agriculture/cottage industry and commercial agriculture. The Zurich highlands were not connected to the kind of cereal-producing zone for which the model calls because the nearby flat regions were still areas of relatively unproductive, traditional subsistence farming, relying primarily on family labor. In fact, far from supplementing the earnings of people who worked as migrant harvest laborers in these or other cereal areas, Braun argues that proto-industrialization in the highlands allowed men to cease working as migrants.[31] The extent to which Shepshed was involved in a process of geographical specialization, and whether it was adjacent to a cereal surplus-producing region, is not indicated in Levine's work. Nor is it clear that the model fits the Suffolk villages studies by Thirsk or the Stephanois mountain villages studied by Lehning.

Second, although all the current studies identify proto-industrialization with subsistence or pastoral agriculture, they do not explain why the process did not or could not have occurred in a commercial cereal-producing area. They simply assume that the two were incompatible. The reasons for the assumption are not clear, however, especially since the demand for labor in cereals was highly seasonal.

Third, although the availability of cheap labor was clearly an important factor in the spread of cottage industry, neither population growth nor the fragmentation of landholdings through partible inheritance or the subdivision of leaseholds was a universal characteristic of the proto-industrial regions that have already been studied. Medick's claim that population growth was an essential precondition for this development is overstated. In proto-industrial Shepshed, demographic growth followed rather than preceded proto-industrialization.[32] In the Zurich highlands, neither population growth nor land fragmentation preceded the region's adoption of cottage weaving. The highlands could not have supported a dense population before the diffusion of the cotton industry, and it was the marginality of the land rather than lack of land that created the poverty that made the region receptive to the urban merchants' search for labor.[33]

Fourth, little attention has been devoted to the role of the urban merchants in determining the location of proto-industries. Like the seasonal nature of agricultural work, their role in the process is largely taken for granted. The merchants put work out into the countryside and collected it for finishing and sale. References to their decisions to do this are inevitably based on the assumption that they were rational, economic-decision makers. Jones and Tarlé, writing in different periods, both argued that the merchants chose to use rural workers because they could be paid less than urban workers.[34] One of Mendels's arguments for his regional model is that the merchants preferred compact, densely populated, and easily accessible regions so they could minimize transportation costs.[35] Other aspects of the merchants' decision making, such as the size of the urban work force, sexually segregated labor markets, and geographical constraints, have not been systematically explored.[36] Finally, although the studies often indicate that women and men performed different tasks in both agriculture and cottage industries, a systematic analysis of the sexual division of labor in proto-industrial regions has not been included in the examination of the size of the rural work force and its role in determining the location of proto-industries.

The proto-industrialization of the Caux highlights the problems in the current explanations because the region fails to meet most of the suggested criteria for the location of a proto-industry: it was not a region of subsistence farming or animal husbandry; nor was it an area of fragmented landholdings or of demographic growth at the time when cottage manufacturing spread into the region on a large scale. Instead, it was a commercial cereal-producing region of large farms and a stable population. Thus, the decision of the merchants to put large quantities of cotton out into this region for spinning and weaving raises serious questions about the ability of current theories to explain the location of proto-industries and provides a basis on which to revise those theories.

Agriculture and cottage industry in the Caux

Arthur Young, the English agronomist, traveled through the pays de Caux in the late eighteenth century and judged it to possess "one of the richest soils in the world,"[37] a judgment with which virtually all twentieth-century historians have agreed. Jules Sion called the Caux a "*bons pays,* a region where nature recompenses man for his work."[38] Marc Bloch thought that "from the twelfth century onwards the fields of the Caux and those of Lower Normandy were the richest in all France."[39] And E. LeParquier, in his study of the *cahiers de doléances* from the northeastern section of the Caux, pointed out that the peasants of the Caux did not complain about the quality of the soil or the size of the harvest in ordinary years as the peasants of the neighboring pays de Bray did.[40]

Only Tarlé, writing in 1910, ventured a different opinion. Tarlé was well aware that the Caux was one of the most fertile regions in France in the late nineteenth and early twentieth centuries, but he thought this might have been a recent development and that perhaps the region had not been as fertile in the eighteenth century.[41] His suggestion arose from the fact that he was already working with the notion that cottage industry spread in areas of poor soil and subsistence farming, not in areas of rich soil and commercial farming. Knowing that there was a large cottage textile industry in the Caux in the eighteenth century, he was hoping that its land might somehow have improved and that the putting-out system had penetrated the area "because the soil procured the means of subsistence so badly."[42] Tarlé was forced to adopt this opinion or otherwise admit that the Caux was an exception to his thesis that cottage industry spread in poor agricultural regions. He was not prepared to deal with the threat that such an exception would pose to his thesis and left the question of the fertility of the Caux unexplored. His dilemma is crucial to an understanding of the causes of proto-industrialization, however, and must be explored.

Unfortunately for Tarlé and the later proto-industrial theorists, all indications are that the Caux was as fertile in the eighteenth century as in the twentieth. The chalk foundation of the plateau was covered with a bed of lime that was (and is) loose enough to support the cultivation of cereal crops. In various places, the lime rests on a subsoil of thick clay that retains enough moisture to support pasture land and hence cattle rearing. The only natural handicap for agriculture is a shortage of water. Precipitation is plentiful, but streams and natural ponds are rare. A large part of the rainfall passes through the porous soil and sinks into the underlying bed of chalk, where it can be tapped only by wells. First ponds and then wells were dug in the *masures* to provide water for animals and farmhouses, but in dry summers, the lack of water for crops as well as for animals was and still can be a serious problem.[43]

The Caux was classified among the first rank of grain-producing regions in the *Ancien Régime*. Between 70 and 80 percent of the land was under cultivation throughout the eighteenth century. (In the canton of Auffay, 79.2 percent was under cultivation in 1798. Twelve percent was contained in *masures*, 1.9 percent in meadows, and 7.0 percent in woodland.)[44] Wheat, rye, oats, and barley were the region's principal crops, although flax and hemp were grown along the coast, and rapeseed (*rabette* and *colza*) began to appear as the demand for oil increased in the eighteenth century.[45] Not all of the land was of equally good quality. In the eighteenth century, 38.9 percent of the plowed land was classified as being of good quality, 31 percent was of mediocre quality, and 30.2 percent was of poor quality.[46] Although these figures apply to the department as a whole, they can be viewed as approximating the percentages for the Caux alone because the Vexin normand and pays de Bray were approximately equal in size and on opposite ends of the land-quality spectrum.

Except for years of dearth, grain production remained fairly constant and was high for France. At the end of the eighteenth century, the *pays* produced 17 hectoliters of grain per hectare. In 1840, the department still was one of only four in France that produced as much as 18 to 20 hectoliters per hectare and was outproduced only by the department of the Nord.[47] The Parlements of Paris and Rouen fought for years over the grain rights to the Caux and the Vexin normand, and the region regularly exported grain to the cities of Rouen, Le Havre, and Paris, although it frequently also had to import food before the harvest year was over in order to feed its own large population.[48]

Despite the relatively high grain yields for France, the productivity of the region was not overwhelming given the descriptions of its soil, and whether the state of cultivation was in keeping with the fertility of the land is a separate question that has been debated ever since Arthur Young declared in 1789 that agriculture in the Caux was in a wretched condition:

... the Pays de Caux, possessing one of the richest soils in the world, with manufactures in every hut and cottage, presents one continued scene of weeds, filth, and beggary; a soil so villainously managed, that if it were not naturally of an inexhaustible fertility, it would long ago have been utterly ruined.[49]

Young's criticism is especially interesting because of his inference about the relationship between agriculture and cottage industry. He believed that in the pays de Caux, as in Ireland, the widespread employment of the populace in the cottage textile industry had destroyed agriculture:

... when the fabrics spread into all the cottages of a country, as in France and Ireland, such a circumstance is absolutely destructive of agriculture . . .[50]

Young's analysis runs counter to that of most observers, who have argued that cottage industry spread into areas of subsistence farming, not that it caused subsistence farming in places otherwise suited to commercial farming. It was this aspect of Young's argument that particularly alarmed Tarlé and led to his conclusion that the land might have been infertile (rather than poorly managed) in the eighteenth century.

But Young's criticisms of cultivation in the Caux were exaggerated. He was observing the results of unusually bad weather conditions in 1788 and 1789 and not the typical state of *cauchois* agriculture. In June 1788, severe hail storms damaged the crops and seriously reduced the harvest. This disaster was followed by an exceedingly cold winter. Part of the grain froze in the ground; the rest was exposed during the thaw and similarly destroyed.[51] It is quite possible that Young assumed that the situation he was observing was the ordinary state of affairs in the Caux, rather than an extraordinary exception to the general rule of good harvests.[52]

Young's criticism also reflected his strong opposition to open-field cultivation and fallow farming. It was customary at the end of the eighteenth century for agronomists like Young to regard open-field agriculture as backward and static by definition. The Caux was a prime target for his contempt. In the eighteenth century, the region was covered by open, irregular fields, and the fields of large landowners and tenant farmers were not contiguous but scattered throughout the area of a commune or several communes.

The peasants used a triennial rotation of crops and fields. Each field was planted with wheat and rye during the first year, with oats and barley the second, and left fallow the third. Before the discovery and adoption of complementary cropping, the fallow was indispensable to the cultivation of cereals, especially wheat, because they exhausted the soil more than other crops. While they lay fallow, the fields were fertilized by grazing cattle and fortified for another round of crop bearing.[53]

Leaving one-third of the cultivable land unplanted seriously limited the crop yield of regions like the Caux. The most important agricultural discovery of the seventeenth century was the planting of fields during the normal fallow period with root crops, which not only did not deplete the soil of nutrients needed by the cereals, but also replenished the nitrogen extracted by the cereal crops and increased the yield of fields when they were subsequently planted with cereals. This was the basis of the agricultural revolution in the eighteenth and early nineteenth centuries. Instead of rotating into fallow, fields were planted with legume or root crops (especially clover and turnips) that simultaneously improved the soil and produced crops that could be fed to animals after they were harvested.[54]

During the late eighteenth century, the Caux gradually adopted artificial meadows and eliminated fallow farming. Clover was the most important of the new crops to be introduced into rotation. Agronomists continuously praised the properties of the turnip as fodder for animals and as a boon to the soil, but the peasants of the Caux, where they accepted the new agriculture, did not consider turnips a proper food for animals and preferred to plant clover.[55]

In general, the three-field, three-crop rotation system continued to be used, although complicated variations on it also appeared. In the first year, a field was generally planted in wheat. In the second, it was planted with alternate rows of clover and oats. Oats grew quickly and protected the young clover from the winds on the plateau. After the oats were harvested, the clover was allowed to continue in the field for the third year. Then the cycle began again.[56]

The new agriculture was adopted only gradually in the Caux for a variety of reasons familiar everywhere in France. The peasants were suspicious of change, fearing that the new crops would usurp the place of cereals and lead to grain shortages.[57] The importance of wheat and other bread cereals to the peasants and villagers of the Caux cannot be exaggerated. Bread was the principal food in their diet, and, because the road system in France was so poor, any shortfall in the harvest meant deprivation and hunger for many. Anything that threatened the production of grain was to be resisted. This included new crops of all kinds, as the *cahier de doléances* from the commune of Luneray clearly demonstrates. Luneray's inhabitants feared that increased cultivation of colza would lead to a shortage of grain:

... a farmer, who cultivates 100 acres of land, should only entrust four acres each year to rape-seed and colza. The high price of this commodity, occasioned by the large number of street lamps in the cities, has caused an intolerable abuse in the cultivation of this plant; several farmers entrust a tenth, sometimes even an eighth of their land to its cultivation: this results in less land for wheat. ... and from this, the scarcity of wheat follows.[58]

Communal obligations and the system of open fields made it difficult for individuals to introduce change by themselves. Groups of fields rotated together from fallow to wheat and rye to oats and barley, and, while they were fallow, everyone could graze animals on them. Unless individual peasants had the means to enclose their individual fields, it was impossible for them to break with this system and to plant artificial meadows.[59]

Poverty also prevented many peasants from adopting the new agriculture. The planting of artificial meadows required not only fences (unless a communal decision was made to plant an entire block of fields with clover) but also more seed and cattle for fertilizer. If a peasant had enough money to purchase the cows and seed demanded by the new system, he or she entered an upward economic spiral. The yield-per-acre of land that was planted periodically with legumes or roots was higher than the yield-per-acre of land that rotated into fallow. And, although the new system demanded more cows and fertilizer, it also made it possible to feed cows better. As a result, they produced more milk products and brought more on the beef market. Thus, with the same amount of land, the peasants' incomes would increase if they could only afford the initial outlay for more cattle and seed. The problem, of course, was that many peasants could not afford the initial investment.[60]

Tenant farming on nine-year leases in the Caux sometimes discouraged even wealthy peasants from adopting the new agriculture because there was no certainty that they would benefit from the improvements. Instead, they might only face higher rents, a particularly unattractive prospect if the innovations required additional labor input on an annual basis, as these changes did.[61]

Finally, the village *curés,* in their continuing search for new sources of revenue, tried to collect the *vertes dîmes* (a tithe intended to apply only to land permanently planted with legumes and clover) on the fodder crop from fields that rotated into artificial meadows, thereby further reducing the peasants' incentive to plant the new crops.[62]

Despite the obstacles, agriculture did improve in the Caux. The system of open, irregular fields was less resistant to change than were the systems of open and elongated fields that existed elsewhere in France, especially elsewhere in the north. In the latter system, each strip of property was so thin that the practical obstacles to branching out on one's own were insuperable. The irregular shape of the *cauchois* fields made enclosure of individual fields somewhat more feasible.[63] The existence of natural pastures and woods (which by the eighteenth century were assumed to have been closed to grazing from "time immemorial") and the practice of deep plowing the fallow in the early spring (which involved closing the fields

to cattle much earlier than in many areas) meant that enclosure was not
a totally alien concept.[64] This, plus the existence of natural pastures, which
provided some grazing options for peasants who did not have sufficient
land for their own animals and who, in other areas, vehemently opposed
enclosure because it made it impossible for them to keep animals, facilitated the spread of enclosure and crop rotations.[65]

Artificial meadows began to appear in the *pays* in the middle of the
eighteenth century.[66] They were adopted most readily near large urban
centers and in the middle of the region where the population was the
most dense. By the end of the century, one-sixth rather than the traditional one-third of the land was rotating into fallow, and in some cantons
as little as one-tenth of the fields still rotated into fallow. In the canton
of Auffay, located on the eastern edge of the Caux approximately halfway between Rouen and Dieppe, progress was slower and only one-third
of the land that normally rotated into fallow was planted in clover in
1801.[67]

In short, although agricultural progress in the Caux may have been
slow in comparison with parts of England, the region was far from being
as backward and ill-managed as Arthur Young claimed. Instead, it was
one of the most advanced grain-producing regions in France. There is no
way that the pays de Caux of the eighteenth century can be made to fit
the hypothesis that proto-industrialization occurred in regions of poor
soil and subsistence or pastoral agriculture.

The question is, Why did the cottage textile industry spread in this
region of prosperous agriculture? An important part of the answer is that
many peasants needed a supplementary source of income. Before the introduction of the mechanical reaper in the late nineteenth century, the
harvesting of cereal crops demanded a large, seasonal labor force. There
was not enough agricultural work, however, to keep this work force occupied during the rest of the year. The enclosure of fields created some
new year-round farm jobs, but it also augmented the seasonal demand
for farm labor by increasing the amount of land in need of harvesting
and was not, therefore, a solution to the agricultural labor problem.[68]

In an area like the Caux, where farmers relied on an indigenous labor
force to harvest the crops, the seasonal character of agricultural work
created problems both for landowners (*laboureurs*) and large tenant farmers
(*fermiers*) and for small holders and day laborers (*journaliers*). For *laboureurs* and *fermiers,* the problem was to keep the harvest labor force
in the countryside, that is, to prevent urban migration.[69] For small hold-

ers and *journaliers,* the problem was chronic unemployment. There simply was not enough work in agriculture to occupy them year-round. Women especially were underemployed because virtually all of the off-season agricultural labor demand was met by men, and women could find work in the fields only during the harvest season.[70] The tradition against women working in the fields other than during the harvest was so strong that in 1796, when many adult men were serving in the army (and hence absent from the commune), only three Auffay women worked as *journalières.*[71]

By the mid-eighteenth century, the need for cash was high in the Caux. Virtually everyone needed money to purchase food, firewood, clothing, shoes, and candles, to pay a variety of taxes (the *gabelle* or salt tax, the *taille* if they owned or rented any land, the *vingtième,* and the occasional *capitation*), and to pay the rent on a house and perhaps a garden plot or *masure.* For the *journaliers* and their families, harvest earnings, although relatively high, did not come close to covering these expenses. Adults earned between twenty-five and thirty *livres* for six weeks work on the harvest. In normal years, the price of bread in the Caux was two *sous* and two or three *deniers* per pound.[72] (Twelve *deniers* equaled one *sol;* twenty *sous* equaled one *livre.*) At this price, thirty *livres* would have purchased 275 pounds of bread. Assuming that an average adult consumed two pounds of bread a day (and nothing else), harvest wages would have fed an adult for 137 days.[73] Clearly, individuals and families could not survive simply on harvest earnings, even if children as well as adults worked during that period. Without a supplementary source of income like that provided by work in cottage industry, many families would not have been able to survive in the region, and the *fermiers* and *laboureurs* would have been forced to rely on migrant labor to harvest the crops.

The *fermiers* needed money not only for food, clothing, shelter, and taxes, but also to pay the rent on their land, rent that increased steadily in the eighteenth and nineteenth centuries.[74] Less than one-fourth of the land belonged to the peasants who farmed it. The rest belonged to the nobility and bourgeoisie who leased it for a money rent. In Auffay, a high percentage of the land was owned by the Dufossé family and its descendants. In 1822, when a cadastre was made of the commune, Jean François Thomas de Bosmelet owned almost 50 percent of the total land surface (551 out of 1129 *arpents*) and 22 percent of the arable (124 out of 564 *arpents*).[75] His estate alone constituted the *hameau* of Bosmelet, and his land covered most of the southeastern part of the commune. The other eight large landowners were bourgeois, five of whom did not live in the commune. (One hundred ninety-four *arpents* of arable were owned by nonresidents of the commune.)[76]

In many communes, an even higher percentage of the land was owned by the bourgeoisie. Bourgeois landownership began with the wars of the fourteenth and fifteenth centuries that decimated the ranks of Norman nobility. Many families lost their male heirs and sold the family estates. Others suffered such severe financial losses from pillaging and the refusal of peasants to pay feudal dues that they were forced to sell their land.[77] Because landownership was a sign of social status and a path to nobility in the *Ancien Régime,* members of the bourgeoisie were always eager to purchase it. In the Caux, their desires had been more easily satisfied than in many regions. They were further satisfied during the Revolution, when the land of *émigré* nobles was auctioned off. If Jean François Thomas de Bosmelet's father had not remained on his estate throughout the Revolution, the land would have been in the hands of the bourgeoisie (and perhaps of a few wealthy peasants who might have been able to purchase some of it) by the time of the cadastre. As it was, the cadastre of 1822 probably reflects the pattern of landownership in Auffay for the eighteenth as well as for the early nineteenth century.

The need for rent money forced small *fermiers* to sell part or all of their crops immediately after the harvest, when the price of grain was low, and then to purchase grain or flour late in the season, when the price was high. Such a system benefited the wealthy *laboureurs* and *fermiers,* who could afford to withhold their grain from the market until prices had risen, but clearly disadvantaged small holders, providing them with a strong incentive to engage in cottage industry.

The size and distribution of landholdings fostered the development of large-scale cottage industry in the Caux as much as the system of tenant farming did. At the top of the economic ladder in virtually every commune were a few wealthy peasants who owned or leased large farms. At the bottom were peasants who owned or leased no land at all. In between were peasants with small farms and artisans who, in some cases, also owned a small piece of property. In some communes, there were very few families between the large landowners and the day laborers or very small landholding peasants. In Belleville-en-Caux, for instance, there were one hundred households, but there were only four large farms (one with 28 acres and three with 18 acres each). The middle rungs on the ladder were occupied by an additional eight families with small farms. The remaining eighty-eight households were headed by men and women who worked as day laborers, weavers, or spinners.[78] Ventes d'Eawy was much larger than Belleville-en-Caux, but the range and description of wealth was the same. Only 38 of the 358 taxable households held arable land. The rest of the population was essentially landless and earned a living as day laborers, cottage textile workers, artisans, or merchants.[79]

In the region as a whole, almost 80 percent of the land was contained in farms with at least 10 acres, and more than 50 percent was in farms with 40 or more acres.[80] Auffay was no exception. At the top of the ladder in 1787 were ten families who owned or rented between 30 and 100 acres of land. At the bottom were the families of sixty-seven male day laborers, weavers, and poor artisans, and of nineteen women (mostly widows) whose property consisted solely of a rented shelter (*couvert*). *Couverts* are clearly distinguished from houses (*maisons*) in the tax roles and were cottages, built partially below ground level, surrounded by hedges (hence "covered"), with no farmyard (*masure*) or cultivable land.[81] In between these two groups were 137 families whose property holdings ranged from houses without *masures* to houses with *masures* and a few arable acres, to houses and places of business (boutiques, tanneries, mills, inns, and forges).[82]

The *vingtième rôle* for 1770 gives a much fuller picture of the landholding patterns in Auffay than the *taille rôles* do, although they are not a perfect record of land division because they do not include the property owned by the Marquis Dufossé and rented to eight tenant farmers.[83] (The 1787 *taille rôle* shows Dufossé as owning 190 acres that he leased to 3 wealthy peasants. He probably owned a similar number of acres in 1770 because his descendant, Jean François Thomas de Bosmelet owned 124 *arpents* or 181 acres of arable in 1822.)[84] The *vingtième rôle* indicates clearly, however, that many Auffay peasants who leased or owned land had parcels that were too small to support them and were in serious need of another source of income. These small holdings of a garden, *masure,* or small planted field were common throughout the Caux, but they constituted only a small percentage of the arable land. In Auffay, almost 60 percent of the families who owned or leased any land had less than one and a half acres of arable for a sum total of only 3.1 percent of the arable land.[85]

The owners or leaseholders of these very small plots were either peasants, who earned their livings primarily by hiring out as day laborers for other richer peasants, or rural artisans, who survived primarily on their earnings from weaving or other crafts. In the eighteenth century, they provided one of the major sources of workers for the cottage textile in-

Table 3.1. *Property designations in the taille*
rôle, Auffay, 1787

Type of property	Number
Couvert	88
House	15
House and *masure*	47
House, *masure* and land	18
House, *masure* and boutique	4
House and boutique	28
House, boutique and garden	3
House, boutique and land	1
Inn (1 with land)	5
Ferme	9
Land	6
House and land	2
Tannery or forge or mill	5
Unspecified	4
Total	235

Source: ADSM C1730.

dustry. Almost as desperate for an additional source of income as families who only had a *couvert,* they had enough interest in the land to want to remain in the village but not enough land to survive without an additional source of income. Spinning and weaving for the putting-out merchants allowed them to remain in the village and to continue farming on a small scale.

Peasants who worked farms of one and a half to ten acres were better off than the smaller landowners or tenant farmers, but their existence was also precarious. They did not have the means to purchase a plow and plowteam or the work to justify it, and yet the use of a heavy plow and at least two horses was necessary four times a year if a peasant was going to plant cereals in this region of heavy clay soil. Those who farmed such small holdings had to lease a plow and plowteam, thereby adding to their expenses and the precariousness of their economic situation.[86]

Only *fermiers* and *laboureurs* who owned or leased more than ten acres of arable could absorb the cost of maintaining a plow-team and still run a profitable operation. Consequently, almost 80 percent of the land was contained in farms with at least ten acres of arable, and more than 50 percent was in holdings of forty or more acres.[87] In other words, the majority of the land was owned or leased by a small minority of wealthy peasants who could maintain their own plowteams. (See Table 3.2.) They

Table 3.2. *Size of landholdings, Auffay, 1770ᵃ*

Size of holdings	Holdings		Arable Acres	
	Number	Percentage	Number	Percentage
Garden plot only	29	23.8		
masure only	18	14.8		
Less than 1.5 acres	26	21.3	24	3.1
Subtotal	73	59.9		
1.5 to less than 10 acres	33	27.0	116	14.8
10 to less than 40 acres	10	8.2	164	20.9
40 or more acres	6	4.9	479	61.2
Total	122	100.0	783	100.0

ᵃDoes not include property owned by Dufossé and leased to eight tenants.
Source: ADSM C537.

employed domestic servants on a year-round basis, day laborers during the heavy work periods of plowing, planting, harvesting, and threshing, and small-holding peasants, cottage workers, and others during the six weeks of the harvest. For this group of landowning peasants, the advantage of the cottage textile industry was not that it supplemented their income from farming but that it enabled them to use local rather than migrant workers to harvest the grain crops.

This pattern of landownership and use – vast portions of the land owned or leased by a small minority of the population, with the majority owning or leasing little or no property at all – produced a situation similar to that found in areas of partible inheritance and population growth: the majority of the population was land poor. In the pays de Caux, however, the situation was not the result of partible inheritance; the *coutume de Caux* specified that the eldest son was to inherit two-thirds of the landed property and had the right to purchase the other one-third from his siblings at reduced rates.[88] Nor was it the result of population growth because most of the demographic growth in the Caux came after, not before, the introduction of the cotton industry.[89] On the contrary, landlessness in the Caux was a consequence of heavy soil and cereal agriculture. The effect of the concentration of land in the Caux was the same as that of fragmentation in Suffolk, Flanders, and Shepshed. To survive in the region, many families needed a supplementary source of income. The result was a pliable labor force for the putting-out merchants.

As the number of peasants employed in the cotton industry expanded, the wealthier *fermiers* and *laboureurs* worried that it would jeopardize their labor force. The harvest was so important that anything threatening to reduce the number of *valets* and *servantes d'aoust,* was strongly resisted. In 1789, the communes of Ancourt and Blosseville in the northeastern section of the Caux complained about the drafting of young men because they thought it would leave the farmers without enough workers to harvest the crops.[90] As early as 1722, the Parlement of Rouen heard complaints that the carding, spinning, and weaving of cotton were making it impossible for the farmers to find enough labor. The complaints were the source of a 1722 decree by Parlement forbidding the putting-out of textile work into the countryside between July 1 and September 15.[91] The decree was clearly intended to ensure that peasants who worked in cottage industry would participate in the harvest. The law was unenforceable, however, and the landowners continued to worry about the effects of the textile industry on their ability to recruit harvest workers, fears that resulted in the renewal of the law in 1744 and 1747.[92]

There is little evidence that the farmers' fears about harvest labor were justified during the eighteenth century. Cartier, the Sub-prefect for the arrondisement of Dieppe during the First Empire and the early years of the Restoration, reported a very large transference of labor from cottage industry to field work during the harvest period, and there is no reason to believe that this was a new behavior pattern.[93] Moreover, there is good evidence that the population of the Caux grew steadily throughout the second half of the eighteenth century, as births exceeded deaths, and immigrants, attracted by the possibility of combining work in agriculture and cottage industry, arrived in the region.[94]

In the Caux itself, population density varied according to the availability of cottage work, with the heavily agricultural communes having the lowest density. Nevertheless, the population of the entire region far exceeded the labor needs of agriculture, and no farmer should have had to go farther than a few kilometers to find numerous harvest workers. Compared with their counterparts in the Vexin normand, where there were large grain crops to harvest but no cottage industry, *cauchois* farmers were very well off. Overall, the population density of the Caux was 99 inhabitants per square kilometer by 1806, whereas in the Vexin it was only 53.9.[95]

A more serious question than the effects of cottage industry on the availability of harvest workers is whether cottage industry interfered with agricultural work during the rest of the year. Were the fields being neglected as Arthur Young claimed? There certainly were complaints to this effect. In 1722, farmers lamented to both the Parlement and the Municipality of Rouen that their farms were becoming "deserted of animals" because they could not find workers to repair barns or to work as herdsmen and shepherds.[96] As proof of their problems, they claimed that the wages of plowmen had risen from forty to fifty *livres* a year to more than 150 *livres,* and that *journaliers* and threshers who had formerly earned seven to ten *sous* a day now wanted twenty to thirty *sous* plus food, which they even wanted prepared "to their taste."[97]

There may have been some truth to the complaints. The coexistence of cereal agriculture and cottage industry in this region might have reduced the off-season agricultural work force and retarded enclosure and the introduction of artificial meadows because both of these developments demanded more year-round labor (as well as more harvest labor) than the old system. Even so, the Caux was regularly regarded as one of the most advanced of the French regions in the eighteenth century, and some progress in enclosing fields was made during the second half of the century. Conflicts over the labor force were probably exaggerated by the *fermiers* and *laboureurs,* whose genuine fears about their labor force were exacerbated by their distaste for paying higher wages.

By and large, the labor needs of agriculture and cottage industry in the Caux were complementary in the eighteenth century. The *laboureurs* and *fermiers* wanted to hire men to work in the fields and barns, whereas the cottage textile industry hired primarily women. The reliance of the textile industry on female labor was the result of a traditional sexual division of labor in textile production and an imbalance in the labor relation of spinning to weaving. In the Caux, as throughout Europe, spinning was considered women's work and weaving men's. The work of children was not segregated by sex, and young boys as well as girls were taught to spin by their mothers.[98] Because men knew how to spin and the looms used in the Caux were small enough for women to use, there probably was some informal sharing of work by adult family members also. In terms of formal occupations (those listed on tax records and in the parish registers), however, no women were weavers and no men were spinners. Because six to ten spinners were needed for every weaver, this sexual division of labor meant many more women than men (including many women who were not related to male weavers) were employed by the putting-out merchants.[99]

This sexual division of labor in the cottage textile industry meshed nicely with the sexual division of labor that existed in *cauchois* agriculture. The employment of women in spinning posed no threat to the year-round agricultural work force. Only the possibility of the withdrawal of men from day laboring to cottage manufacturing alarmed the *laboureurs* and *fermiers*. In the early eighteenth century, the danger (in their eyes) was that men would work as carders, not as weavers. By midcentury, however, it appears that carding as well as spinning had become the work of women and children, and the threat of a labor shortage for agriculture was largely illusory.[100]

In the nineteenth century, cottage industry and agriculture may have competed more for the same labor force as the demand for cottage weavers (following the mechanization of spinning) and year-round farm workers (as a result of enclosure) increased simultaneously. Between 1796 and 1851, the size of the weaving labor force in Auffay doubled (increasing from thirty-three to seventy-one weavers), while the year-round agricultural work force (*journaliers* and farm domestics) almost tripled (increasing from 71 to 207).[101]

Even the harvest labor force may have been in some jeopardy in the nineteenth century because the merchants who employed the weavers preferred not to have their labor force disappear periodically to work in the fields now that the mills produced yarn year-round. As a result, interaction between agriculture and cottage industry lessened. Young weavers continued to follow the old pattern and left their looms to participate in the harvest, but older, highly skilled weavers withdrew entirely from the agricultural work force.[102] The intimate union of agriculture and cottage industry that had existed in the eighteenth century was breaking down, and the two work forces were becoming mutually exclusive.

The large landowners renewed their complaints about the cost of farm labor and began to search for labor-saving machines. Wages were increased. In 1789, plowmen earned between 100 and 130 francs annually. By 1805 (*an* XIII), they were earning 200 to 250 francs. The wages of the *valets de cour* doubled, going from 100 francs before the Revolution to 200 francs in 1805. Female farm servants (*servantes de basse-cour*), who had earned 60 to 70 francs before the Revolution, now earned 140 to 150.[103] Confronted with high wages and scarce labor supplies (at least in the eyes of the *laboureurs*), the search for an inexpensive threshing machine began. Threshing with a flail was the major winter occupation of farm workers. Replacing them or at least some of them with an efficient machine would reduce the labor demand in the nonharvest season. Machines were invented, but they remained too expensive for most farmers until after midcentury.[104]

Sion reported in 1909 that he constantly had the sense when he was studying nineteenth-century agricultural documents that there was a serious shortage of men in the fields, despite the fact that the villages in the region were overpopulated from the standpoint of agricultural needs. He attributed this situation to the expansion of cottage weaving.[105] Although Sion might have been right about the lack of men in the fields, women workers were not in short supply. The mechanization of spinning had created a serious unemployment problem for village women, and, as the demand for agricultural workers and weavers increased, they moved into these traditionally male occupations. In Auffay, sixty-three women were working as day laborers in 1851, compared with only one in 1796.[106]

What the nineteenth century documents reported may be precisely what Sion said – a shortage of men rather than a shortage of labor. The *laboureurs* and *fermiers* who were accustomed to hiring women to work in the fields only during the harvest may not have felt that it was appropriate or satisfactory to hire them in other seasons, despite the fact that they could and did pay them less than male day laborers.[107]

But any difficulties that proto-industrialization created for agriculture in the early nineteenth century were over-shadowed by the problems created by its demise in the 1870s. As the mechanical loom came to dominate weaving, a mass exodus from the Caux began, and the region began to suffer from a real shortage of labor. The irony of this situation was remarked by Paul Hohenberg in 1972. "French landowners," he noted, "found themselves short of labor paradoxically just because rural people had *lost* other work."[108]

In the long run, then, the advantages of cottage industry to commercial agriculture in the Caux clearly outweighed the disadvantages. Because of the highly seasonal demand for labor in cereals, rural exodus would have begun much earlier if work in cottage industry had not been available to supplement harvest wages. Peasants with large landholdings would have been forced to use migrant labor, as they did in the maritime region of Flanders, or to limit production and agricultural progress, as they did in the lowlands of Zurich.

The seasonal nature of agricultural work in the Caux made it compatible with a cottage industry that men and women could abandon during the harvest. The use of a local harvest labor force, combined with the concentration of property in the hands of a few wealthy farmers, made the presence of such an industry necessary. And the sexual division of labor, which reserved non-harvest agricultural work for men, made a

rural industry that employed primarily women, as the Rouen textile industry did, particularly desirable. Commercial cereal agriculture and large-
scale cottage industry clearly were compatible.

The Rouen merchants and proto-industrialization

Despite its compatibility with agriculture in the Caux, proto-industrialization might not have occurred if the region had been less favorably located. The wealthy *laboureurs* and *fermiers* might have relied on migrant
labor as their counterparts did in some other commercial agricultural
regions, and the concentration of land in the hands of a few wealthy
farmers might have led peasants to abandon the countryside, regardless
of their ties to place and people. But the Caux was located just north of
Rouen, a major textile center; and when the urban merchants wanted to
increase production, they looked to the Caux for workers.

Connected to both the urban markets of Paris and the export markets
of England and Spain by short water routes, Rouen had become an important port by the seventeenth century. In the Middle Ages, it was a
major wool-producing city, importing fine wool from Spain that its drapers
wove into high-quality woolens. For a variety of reasons, the Rouen wool
industry was in decline by the sixteenth century; however, as France acquired colonial markets and sources of raw cotton in the West Indies, the
city (again well-placed to take advantage of the Atlantic trade), turned to
the production of cotton and linen goods.[109]

As early as 1534, Rouen *passementiers* (silk weavers) experimented
with weaving cotton and linen into heavy fustians and lightweight, checked
dimities. These fabrics were not popular, however, and were produced
only in small quantities. The cotton fabric used in the region for women's
bonnets, aprons, and handkerchiefs and for the linings of men's clothing
continued to be imported from India.[110]

In 1694, an important Rouen merchant (*négociant*) named Delarue
found himself unable to dispose of forty bales of raw cotton to the *passementiers*. Wanting to avoid serious financial loss, he convinced two
toiliers (linen weavers) to have the cotton spun and to weave it on looms
strung with silk. The resulting fabric, reminiscent of the oriental fabrics
imported into Normandy since the 1670s, was called *siamoise*. The early
siamoises were used to make women's skirts and petticoats, but it was a
weak fabric and had a limited market. Sensing correctly the possibility of
a wide market for lightweight but strong cotton fabric, Delarue substi-
tuted stronger linen thread for the soft silk warp threads, and what came

to be known as the "rouennerie" was born. Delarue's *siamoises* were so successful that many Rouen textile merchants, following his lead, imported raw cotton and put it out to be spun and woven with linen warps.[111]

Production in the cotton industry increased rapidly. By 1750, the Rouen *halle* was the biweekly scene of frantic and active trading in thread and fabric. Some observers thought it was the most flourishing of the textile markets in France.[112] Whether this was true is hard to judge, but the figures compiled by the market, although they should be viewed as estimates rather than as precise counts, reveal dramatic increases in production. Before 1717, no more than 60,000 pieces of cotton cloth passed through the official *halle*. By 1731, the figure had risen to more than 150,000 pieces; by 1743, it was more than 435,000. By midcentury, the period of steady increase had ended and production began to vacillate between 300,000 and 500,000 pieces per year.[113] In addition to the fabric that passed through the official marketplace, there was a secret and illegal textile market that may have handled as much as half of the fabric produced in the pays de Caux.[114] When the two markets are considered together, it is clear that a truly impressive amount of fabric was being produced for the Rouen merchants.

The success of the Rouen cotton industry was the product of several factors. In the first place, production was fueled by a rising demand for cotton fabric. Second, the Rouen merchants were masters of imitation, copying the popular fabrics of India, England, and the Netherlands, and even scenting some of them with spices to confuse the purchasers about their origins and selling them as the real thing. Third, the merchants initiated a search for a solid red dye that would not fade with repeated exposure to the sun and rain. In the late 1760s, such a dye was produced. Much of the popularity of the Rouen textiles came from their bright colors, especially Turkish red. Finally, the peasants and villagers of the Caux took readily to the work, enabling the merchants to increase their labor force without much difficulty and without increasing wages.[115]

As production expanded, the merchants turned to the Caux for more and more spinners and weavers. Several factors lay behind this decision. In the first place, as the production of *siamoises* increased, there simply were not enough spinners and weavers in the city to meet the labor demands of the merchants. Although Rouen was a relatively large city by eighteenth-century standards, its midcentury population of fifty to sixty thousand was not nearly large enough to meet the needs of the textile merchants. (By 1782, there were more than 188,000 spinners and weavers working within a fifteen-league radius of Rouen.)[116]

Putting work out into the countryside also saved the merchants money. Differential wage structures were established for urban and rural textile workers. Rural spinners and weavers were paid less than their urban counterparts yet maintained a higher standard of living because harvest wages and the produce from garden plots supplemented their industrial wages. In 1782, urban weavers earned twenty-five *sous* per day; rural weavers twenty.[117] In addition, putting work out into the countryside enabled the merchants to avoid guild regulations and government taxes, which also saved them money. When cotton was first introduced, the large wool and linen houses in Rouen feared that putting work out into the Caux would undermine their control of production and petitioned the Parlement to forbid the spinning and weaving of cotton outside the city. Fearing, in turn, the effects of large-scale urban immigration if such a law were passed, the Parlement refused.[118] The corporations' fears were well-placed. By midcentury, they were no longer able to control production, and, in 1762, the King's Council of State recognized the *fait accompli* of the putting-out merchants and formally gave peasants the right to manufacture cloth without joining the corporations of crafts.[119]

Government inspection of all cloth at the *halle de Rouen* and its regional branches continued to be required by law, but the law was unenforceable. As much as half of the fabric produced in the Caux may have passed through the textile black market, escaping the quality control of the *halle* and government taxes, making it impossible to determine exactly how much cloth was being produced in the region, and enhancing the ability of the merchants to produce inexpensive, mass-marketable goods.[120]

It is clear from government records that the putting-out merchants could reap considerable profits from the fabric produced in the Caux. Subprefect Cartier reported in 1809 that cottage weavers produced approximately one and a half pieces of fabric a month. Merchants paid weavers fifteen francs for each piece and sold them for approximately 120 francs.[121] Even taking into account the merchants' costs for spun yarn, warps, transportation, and porters' wages, it is clear that the putting-out system was highly profitable.

The Caux's terrain and proximity to Rouen was also in its favor when it came to choosing a putting-out region. All putting-out systems involve transportation expenses and time lost while raw materials and finished goods are transported between workers and markets. The shorter the distance between them, the better for the merchants. The pays de Caux was immediately adjacent to the city of Rouen, and transportation on the plateau was relatively easy in the late eighteenth century. Although travelers complained bitterly about its condition, the highway leading across the plateau from Rouen to Dieppe was one of the best roads in France because it was part of the major route from Paris to England. The smaller roads connecting the villages on the plateau were in the usual poor condition associated with eighteenth-century roads. Travel was not difficult, however, compared with hilly or rocky areas like the pays de Bray, and it was relatively inexpensive to transport raw and spun cotton and woven fabric between Rouen and the villages of the Caux.[122] In addition, the damp climate of the Caux was well-suited to the manufacture of cotton cloth. Weaving did not have to take place in cellars, as it did in some regions, to keep the yarn from becoming dry and brittle.[123] For a variety of reasons, then, the Rouen merchants looked to the Caux for a labor force, and there they found women, men, and children who were willing to work for low wages.

Redefining the causes of proto-industrialization

The case of the pays de Caux shows that the link historians have been pursuing between subsistence agriculture and cottage industry is exaggerated. Proto-industrialization may have occurred more often in subsistence farming or pastoral regions, but, as the expansion of the cottage textile industry in the fertile and well-farmed Caux demonstrates, large-scale cottage industry could and did spread in regions of commercial cereal agriculture. This fact suggests that seasonal unemployment and landlessness, not poor land, were the distinguishing features of proto-industrial regions.[124]

Writers on the subject have underestimated the link between seasonal unemployment and cottage industry because they have examined proto-industrialization in subsistence farming regions alone and have contrasted them with two types of commercial agricultural regions: those that relied on migrant labor (maritime Flanders, Zurich lowlands) and those that introduced enclosure (especially the light-soil regions of England). The migrant regions had no need for cottage industry because the seasonally unemployed agricultural workers lived elsewhere. These workers needed industrial work in their home subsistence regions, not in the commercial regions.

Whether the agricultural day-laboring families in the enclosed regions could have benefited from the presence of cottage industry is unclear. Enclosure did increase the number of year-round jobs in agriculture, and women as well as men worked in the fields in these regions. But there still was much more work available for men than for women on a year-round basis, and there was more work available for both sexes during the summer than during the winter.[125] It seems likely that a cottage industry with flexible labor demands, which employed primarily women, would still have been very desirable in these regions from the point of view of the day-laboring families, and perhaps especially from the point of view of female day laborers who performed some of the most back-breaking tasks in the new agriculture – transplanting young plants, hoeing root crops, weeding, digging potatoes, and pulling turnips.[126]

Farmers, on the other hand, probably regarded any alternative to agricultural work as a threat to both their labor force and their low pay scale for women and children.[127] And the merchants would have found such regions less attractive than areas in which there was less year-round agricultural work for women and, hence, more women available to work for them on a full-time basis. Consequently, enclosed commercial agricultural regions were unlikely candidates for proto-industrialization, not because day-laboring families did not need jobs, but because neither the wealthy farmers nor the putting-out merchants regarded it as worth their while.

By contrast, in traditional commercial agricultural areas like the Caux, where little enclosure had occurred by the mid-eighteenth century and where an indigenous labor force harvested the crops, there was a definite need for off-season employment in cottage industry. Such regions could and did experience proto-industrialization without harming agricultural production, especially when the proto-industry employed primarily women. (Textiles, which traditionally employed many more women than men, was the quintessential proto-industry because its labor demands were opposite those of most agricultural systems that, like the one in the Caux, relied exclusively on men for labor outside the harvest season.)

The importance of landlessness as a causal factor in proto-industrialization has also been obscured by a focus on mechanisms that either created population growth (especially partible inheritance customs in areas of peasant land ownership) or linked it (through rising rents) to the fragmentation of landholdings. Landholding patterns in the Caux point to a third source of landlessness. To plant cereal crops in small plots was an inefficient use of capital in a heavy-soil area like the Caux that required heavy plows and large plowteams. In consequence, large farms dominated the Caux, and most peasants were land poor and needed a supplementary source of income. Cottage industry provided it and, in fact, allowed the size of the landless or land-poor population to increase steadily. The major point here is that the existence of a large land-poor population, regardless of its cause, increased the desirability of cottage industry in any region in which the demand for agricultural labor varied seasonally.

The complementarity of urban and rural needs has also been underemphasized in studies of proto-industrialization because they have focused on the rural side of the putting-out system. That the *cauchois* peasants' need for off-season work complemented perfectly the Rouen merchants' need for a large, cheap labor force was a major factor in the development of the Caux into a proto-industrial region. Such complementarity of needs was at work wherever the process of proto-industrialization occurred.

The proto-industrialization of the Caux thus suggests that the conclusions usually drawn about the relationship between agriculture and cottage industry need revision. Proto-industrialization did not occur only in subsistence farming or pastoral areas. On the contrary, the seasonal nature of most traditional agricultural work created a need for cottage industry as a supplementary source of income in commercial grain regions, which relied on an indigenous labor force to harvest crops, as well as in subsistence agricultural regions. In commercial grain regions, large-scale cottage industry could and did satisfy both the desire of the wealthy farmers to keep their harvest labor force in place and the need of poor peasants for supplementary work. The latter need was especially acute in areas with a large land-poor population. Landlessness had several sources: population growth, partible inheritance customs, and the technical needs of agriculture. What is important in determining the location of proto-industries is the landlessness, not its cause. Given certain characteristics of the rural population, what ultimately determined the choice of proto-industrial regions in the eighteenth century were factors unrelated to agriculture, such as the closeness of urban markets, the ease of transportation, and the demands of local merchants for a large labor force. In short, proto-industrialization was most likely to occur where urban and rural needs complemented each other.

4

~~~~~~

The golden age of spinning

When Delarue and his fellow merchants began to put cotton out into the Caux for spinning and weaving, their efforts were eagerly embraced by the peasants and villagers, much to the dismay of the wool merchants and wealthy *laboureurs* who feared the loss of their work force to what they regarded as the "soft occupation" (*molle occupation*) of carding and spinning cotton.[1] The wool merchants' fears were, of course, well placed. Given a choice between wool and cotton, carders and spinners readily chose the cleaner, better-smelling, and more easily worked cotton. By the 1730s, the master drapers in such cities as Rouen and Bolbec were having difficulty recruiting spinners despite their decision to increase wages, and, by the 1760s, the industry was in a full-scale decline.[2] Wool and cotton spinning competed directly in a way that spinning and agricultural work did not, however, and the fears of the *laboureurs* were not as well founded as those of the wool merchants. Throughout the eighteenth century, rural workers alternated spinning and weaving with agriculture on a seasonal basis, and, in the nonharvest season, agriculture employed only men and the cotton industry employed primarily women.

Most of the cotton fabric produced in the Caux was woven with linen warps and was called *siamoise*. Some pure cotton cloth was produced, but the cotton fibers produced by hand spinning were generally too weak to withstand the pressure applied to warp threads in the weaving process. *Siamoises* came in several varieties: Some were solid colors – white, red, or blue; some were blue and white or red and white checks; and, some were blue and white or red and white stripes. The best white *siamoises* were sent to *teinturiers* in Rouen to be imprinted with designs before they were sold.[3] Most *siamoises* were not of high quality, however, and their major purchasers were peasants, urban workers, and colonial planters who bought them to clothe their slaves.[4]

Before the introduction of spinning machines at the end of the eighteenth century, textile production could only be expanded by increasing the number of workers. It is impossible to determine the exact number of *cauchois* women, men, and children who were employed in the cotton industry, but it was a substantial and ever-increasing number. Based on the number of looms operating in the region, Pierre Dardel estimated that 56,992 persons were employed in producing fabric (cotton, linen, and silk) in the généralité of Rouen in 1732.[5] Using the same technique, M. Goy, an Inspecteur des Manufactures à Rouen in the eighteenth century, estimated that by 1782 the number had grown to 188,207, most of whom were in the pays de Caux.[6] (The total population of Upper Normandy in the 1780s was approximately 590,000.)[7] The percentage of adults in the Caux who were employed in the industry was considerable, so considerable that Arthur Young, traveling through the Caux in 1788, recorded in his diary that he saw "farm-houses and cottages everywhere, and the cotton manufacture in all."[8] This may have been hyperbole on Young's part, but inventories of possessions made after death support the basic thrust of his statement. Spinning wheels, distaffs, and looms commonly appear in the inventories, regardless of the official occupation of the deceased.[9]

The numbers of spinners and weavers in the Caux were far from equal since spinning constituted a serious bottleneck in the production process. Estimates of the number of spinners (and carders) necessary to keep one weaver working full time vary from observer to observer and historian to historian, but eight to ten seems to be a likely number. Goy figured that there were 9.5 workers per loom to arrive at his 1782 figure of 188,207 cotton workers (approximately eight spinners to one weaver).[10] Spinning had long been regarded as women's work in Europe, and the expansion of demand in this field did not really alter that fact in the Caux, despite the *laboureurs'* fear that men would be drawn into this soft occupation. Instead, the sexual division of labor was maintained (at least on a formal level), and the expansion of cotton production came about primarily through an expansion in the number of women employed in spinning.

The extent to which an informal breaking of the sexual division of labor occurred in textile production is, unfortunately, an unanswerable question. Because boys as well as girls helped their mothers with carding and spinning, it is obvious that most adult men knew how to perform these tasks. In the village of Auffay, seven boys (average age 13.3 years) were listed as spinners in the 1796 census. Because children under the age of 12 were not listed in this census, there may have been many more boys who earned money for their families by spinning alongside their mothers.[11]

It is usually assumed that the unrecorded transfer of male labor between agriculture and cottage industry consisted of seasonal movements from day laboring to weaving. The assumption is partially born out by the inventories of possessions, such as the one made after the death of Jean Hebert, a *journalier,* in Auffay on October 31, 1778. Hebert had lived with his second wife, Marie, and a son by his first marriage. Among other items, the house contained two *siamoise* looms and a spinning wheel. The wheel belonged to Marie, a linen spinner, who had brought it to the marriage in 1762 as part of her dowry. One loom was in use and one was standing idle, perhaps an indication that illness preceded Jean Hebert's death. In any case, Jean Hebert and his son clearly alternated agricultural work with weaving, as many men did.[12]

Many *journaliers* may have worked during winter months, not as weavers but as carders or spinners, because the demand was so much higher for them. There is nothing to indicate whether this was the case, however, except the fears of the *laboureurs* and the remonstrance of the Parlement of Rouen in 1722 that "there is almost no village in the province of Normandy, above all in the pays de Caux, where a mill for dyeing cotton has not been built, almost no men (*hommes*) who are not occupied with carding and spinning."[13]

There also is no way to determine the labor relationship between carding and spinning because all of the preparatory tasks were defined as the work of spinners (*fileuses*) in this region. Neither women nor men are listed in the tax records or parish registers for Auffay or its neighboring villages with the occupation of carder (*cardeuse/cardeur*) in the eighteenth century.[14]

Although raw cotton was much cleaner than fleece, it still had to be cleaned and combed before it was spun. Cleaning involved pulling pieces of the raw cotton from the bale, laying them out on a screen or tightly stretched ropes, and beating them with switches to remove the dirt. After it was beaten, the cotton was soaked in water to make the fibers cling together. If it was intended for fine spinning, it was washed as well as soaked and then hung up to dry, adding to the already serious fire hazard posed by the vegetables and fruits hanging from the open wooden beams in *cauchois* houses.[15]

After it was soaked or washed, the cotton was carded. This was done by placing a piece of cotton on a flat, rectangular brush (card) that had several parallel rows of metal teeth protruding through a heavy piece of leather attached to a piece of wood. The cotton was then brushed or combed with another card until the fibers lay straight and parallel to each other.

After combing, the cotton passed to the spinner, who first twisted it lightly to create rovings and then spun it a second time to make yarn that was ready for weaving. Most spinners in the Caux used a large spinning wheel that they turned by hand. A spinner held the combed cotton or rovings in her left hand and fed it onto one or two small bobbins, which she rotated by turning the wheel with her right hand. The key to spinning was to maintain a steady balance between the amount of cotton fed through the spinner's fingers and the speed with which the wheel was turned. If a spinner fed the fiber too quickly, the spun yarn would be coarse and heavy. If she fed it too slowly, it would be thin and might break in the weaving process. Variations in tension resulted in uneven yarn, which produced uneven fabric. Thick yarn was called *ploc,* and it was a deadly insult to a spinner to accuse her of being unable to spin anything but *ploc.*[16]

A few spinners used a foot-powered wheel that enabled them to feed cotton to the bobbins with both hands. The advantage of controlling the cotton with two hands was offset, however, by the difficulty of keeping the wheel turning at a steady pace. Foot wheels tended to advance in spurts rather than slowly and smoothly, and the yarn they produced was less even than that of hand-powered wheels.[17]

Some women continued to spin with the distaff rather than with the wheel because it produced a finer thread. The distaff was a stick about a meter in length on the top of which the combed fibers or rovings were placed. The spinner held the distaff under her left arm and drew a continuous strand of cotton from it with her left hand. With her right hand, she twisted the fiber between her forefinger and thumb. The end of the strand was attached to a spindle that dropped toward the floor as the twisted thread or yarn lengthened. When the spindle reached the floor, the spinner picked it up, wound the yarn onto it, and began the process again.[18]

Once the raw cotton was spun it had to be measured. This was done either by the spinner herself or by another woman called a *dévideuse* working with a simple machine called a *dévidoir.* The *dévideuse* took the bobbins from the wheels, or the spindles from the distaffs, and unwound them onto the *dévidoir* by turning a small handle. The handle rotated four or six rods placed parallel to each other around the circumference of a circle. The yarn was wound into loose skeins. When the *dévideuse* had turned the set of rods sixty times, a bell sounded. After three hundred turns (five rings of the bell), a complete skein of 375 *aunes* had been produced. Called a *pièce,* this was what the spinner sold back to the *marchand de coton.*[19]

It is difficult to determine how much spinners earned because they were paid by the piece rather than by the day, and piece rates varied according to the quality of the yarn. Lighter, more finely spun yarn received a higher price than heavy yarn. Inspecteur Goy estimated that *fileuses* earned between ten and fifteen *sous* per day, depending on how many hours they worked. Arthur Young, the traveling agronomist, reported that spinners (both male and female) earned nine *sous* a day but, to the eternal frustration of historians, did not indicate his source of information. And E. Tarlé examined records that said Norman spinners earned around twenty *sous* per day in the late 1780s.[20] Only very skilled spinners could have earned such high piece rates in the eighteenth century, however, and most *cauchois* women probably never earned more than twelve *sous* per day. This may, in fact, be a high estimate because there is no way to tell whether the time spent cleaning, carding, and washing the cotton is included in the estimates of how much yarn a woman could spin in a day. If this work was done by women but not included in time estimates for spinning, then Arthur Young's figure of nine *sous,* the lowest of the eighteenth-century estimates of average daily earnings for spinners, may be the most accurate.

Trying to move from daily earnings to annual earnings simply compounds the problems of accuracy. There is no way to know how many days a year a woman spent at her wheel or with her distaff. In general, spinning stopped during the harvest, although women's work certainly did not. In the *Ancien Régime,* harvesters earned between twenty-five and thirty *livres* for six weeks of work in the fields. Assuming that women were on the lower end of the harvest wage scale (which is probable, given their lower wages in every other rural occupation), and that harvesters worked seven days a week, then women earned 11.9 *sous* per day on the harvest, enough to draw any woman earning less than twelve *sous* a day as a spinner away from her wheel and into the fields.[21]

Outside of the harvest season, it is impossible to know how many hours a day or how many days a week women spent spinning, although it is clear that their work did not end at sundown. In Auffay, women and girls gathered together in each others' houses to spin and talk during the long winter evenings.[22]

The spinners of the Caux were not generally known for their fine yarn, perhaps partially because work conditions in the crowded, dirty, and smoky cottages of the Caux were far from ideal, and partially because spinning was frequently interrupted by other tasks – preparing meals, caring for children, feeding barnyard animals, and more. In addition, women were operating on very tight budgets and had to produce yarn quickly, another circumstance that led to low-quality yarn. Spinners who did not have the money to purchase the raw cotton from the *marchand de coton* received it on credit, a system that allowed them to work but further reduced their already low earnings.[23] Especially for these women, fast production (hence, the spinning of coarse yarn) was crucial; obtaining the day's food ration depended on completing a *pièce* of yarn for the merchant.

Spinners who were not working on credit would not necessarily sell their yarn to the same merchant who sold them the raw cotton. In Auffay, the *fileuses* rose in the middle of the night to carry their skeins of yarn in leather backpacks to the textile market in Bacqueville, where trading began at dawn. The trip to the market was an exclusively female pilgrimage. Neither men nor children were allowed to accompany the women on their weekly treks.[24]

The *marchands de coton* sold the yarn to another group of merchants called *marchands toiliers, marchands siamoisiers, marchands siamoisiers fabricants*, or simply *fabricants*. These men had the thread washed and dyed. (Colored, checked, and striped fabric was woven with colored threads, not printed after weaving.) Some of it was then twisted and wound onto warping beams; the rest was wound onto bobbins for the weft shuttles. Some weavers had the tools for making their own warps, but many purchased them from porters who brought them from Rouen in their wagons.[25]

The dampness of the *cauchois* climate made weaving relatively pleasant compared with areas where looms had to be set up in cellars to ensure a humid atmosphere and prevent the fibers from becoming brittle and breaking. Like Jean Hebert's house, the homes of weavers often consisted of three rooms: a kitchen, a sleeping chamber, and a work or weaving room.[26] The work room usually had space for two looms, one operated by the father/husband of the family and the other by a son or nephew. It is likely that women took turns at the looms when the men were ill or tired or working in the fields, but in Auffay, at least, the sexual division of labor was strictly maintained for public purposes, and, before the beginning of the nineteenth century, no woman was listed in tax roles or parish registers as being employed in weaving.

Whereas carding and spinning were regarded as soft occupations, suited not only to women but also to children and the elderly of both sexes, weaving was not. Both strength and skill were necessary. Many weavers preferred to mount their own warps on the loom, even though this required two or three people. The warp had to be wound with just the right tension. If it was too tight, the threads would break in the weaving process; if it was too loose, the fabric would be crooked.[27]

Once the warp was mounted and bobbins wound for the shuttles, the weaver was ready to begin. Latapie, who recorded the stages of textile production in the Caux in the late eighteenth century, described weavers' passing the shuttle from one hand to the other rather than using the flying shuttle that operated by means of a pulley system.[28] The flying shuttle, invented by John Kay in 1733, came into general use in England in the 1760s.[29] It was slow to catch on in France, however, and Latapie's failure to refer to it probably means it was not in use in this region, or was being used by only a few weavers.[30] The advantage of the flying shuttle was that it increased a weaver's speed, but as long as the bottleneck in carding and spinning existed, increased weaving speed was hardly necessary.

The weaver raised and lowered combinations of warp threads with foot pedals, passed the shuttle back and forth through the warp, and beat the weft threads together with a bar called a beater. If he did not push the pedals down firmly, the weft threads could not be properly beaten into place; if he beat the threads too hard, the fabric would be brittle; if he beat too lightly, it would be flimsy and weak.[31] The average weaver beat between fifteen and twenty thousand times a day.[32]

Boys began to learn weaving between the ages of twelve and fifteen. Some worked as apprentices for six months, but weavers' wages were so low that they often could not afford to keep an apprentice, and many boys simply learned the craft from their fathers. They were set to work at the second loom to augment the family's income as soon as they had acquired minimal skills. Weaving required strong legs to operate the pedals and strong arms to beat the cloth. Weavers reached their peak between twenty-five and forty. After forty, their strength and, hence, the quality of their work began to decline. Although tuberculosis and other diseases associated with dampness were not as much of a problem for weavers in the Caux as they were where men worked in cellars, weavers universally suffered from chest and neck ailments, varicose veins, and fatigue in the legs.[33]

In keeping with the greater skill and strength requirements and the greater health hazards involved in weaving, as well as with its designation as men's work, weavers were better paid than spinners. Like spinners, they were paid by the piece. Rates varied according to the size of the piece, the difficulty of the work, and the fineness of the weave.[34] Average wages again are difficult to determine because we know nothing about the weavers' hours and days of work on either a weekly or an annual basis. It is clear, however, that experienced weavers earned more than beginners because they worked more quickly and with greater skill. It is possible that highly skilled weavers earned as much as thirty or forty *sous* in a day.[35] But, according to Inspector Goy, the average *cauchois* weaver earned only twenty *sous* per day, five *sous* less than weavers who lived in the city of Rouen.[36] The differential reflects, at least in part, the greater cost of living in the city, where food and lodging prices were higher (and the quality lower) and where it was impossible for weavers to supplement their earnings with produce from a garden plot or seasonal earnings in agriculture.[37] Although it is impossible to be precise about the earnings of men and women in cottage industry, it is important to note that whenever a range of wages is cited, the lowest wages paid to men are higher than the highest wages paid to women. Moreover, when wages for female and male spinners are distinguished, those of male spinners (*fileurs*) fall between those of female spinners and male weavers.[38]

Determining the hours and days worked by weavers and hence their earnings is further complicated by the fact that most of them alternated weaving with work in the fields. The most skilled weavers left their looms only during the harvest season when Parlementary decrees made it illegal for the merchants to distribute work in the countryside. It was probably tradition and the importance of the harvest rather than the law that determined their behavior, however, because the law was unenforceable and more and more ignored as the century progressed. Less skilled weavers may have spent as much as half of the year working in the fields, a work pattern stimulated by the difficulties weavers periodically experienced in obtaining warps and shuttle yarn. Downturns in the textile market were passed along to the weavers in the form of reduced work, and, in January, merchants with backlogs of fabric often slowed the distribution of yarn and warps so they could reduce their inventories.[39]

Children began to work in cottage industry around the age of six.[40] As young children, their work was not segregated by sex, and both boys and girls helped clean and comb cotton and then learned to spin. Middle-class observers considered the employment of children (and of the elderly) in carding and spinning enormously beneficial to society because they otherwise would be dependent on other people. In particular, both observers and merchants thought carding and spinning were admirable occupations for orphans and the residents of hospitals, even though their work was not of the highest quality.[41]

Children's wages varied according to their age, sex, the kind of work they did, and the regularity of the yarn they produced (if they were spin-

Table 4.1. *Female literacy by occupation, Auffay,*
1751–1800

Marriage occupation	Total	Illiterate	Percent illiterate
Spinner	122	82	67.2
Servant	23	17	73.9
Seamstress	34	5	14.7
Merchant	12	1	8.3
Cultivator	6	0	0.0
Miscellaneous	6	3	50.0
Unknown	44	13	29.5
Total	247	121	49.0

Source: ADSM Parish and Civil Registers, 1751–1800. First marriages only.

ners). Historians place the potential earnings of children in textile factories in the late eighteenth century at between three and five *sous* per day.[42] Children working in cottage industry must have earned approximately the same, although children who were working away from home in a factory or for another family were paid wages on a regular basis, whereas those who worked for their own parents were not paid in the literal sense of the term. Instead, their wages were realized in terms of the increased output of the parents, especially of the mother.

Historians have generally found that children from textile families who were engaged in productive tasks on a year-round basis (unlike farm children, who might not have winter work to do unless their mother was a spinner) were among the children least likely to receive any education. François Furet and Jacques Ozouf's study of literacy and industrialization in the Nord, for instance, has found higher literacy rates, especially for men, in purely agricultural regions that had a slack work season than in regions where work in agriculture and industry alternated seasonally.[43]

In Auffay, however, the literacy pattern was somewhat different. Many textile workers were illiterate. Two-thirds of the spinners and two-fifths of the weavers who married in the village could not sign their names. But the men and women identified as agricultural workers (*journaliers,* male farm domestics, and female farm servants) were much more illiterate than the spinners and weavers, and female literacy improved dramatically as the second half of the century progressed, despite the employment of

Table 4.2. *Male literacy by occupation, Auffay, 1751–1800*

Marriage occupation	Total	Illiterate	Percent illiterate
Weaver	35	14	40.0
Day laborer	41	30	73.2
Domestic	22	13	59.1
Merchant or artisan	109	17	15.6
Cultivator	13	0	0.0
Miscellaneous	26	4	15.4
Unknown	3	2	66.7
Total	249	80	32.1

Source: ADSM Parish and Civil Registers, 1751–1800. First marriages only.

virtually every able-bodied woman and girl in carding and spinning.[44] For whatever reasons, textile manufacturing and at least rudimentary education were not totally incompatible in Auffay.

In this era of the family economy, the wages women, children, and men earned in cottage industry and agriculture were spent not by them as individuals but were contributed to the family. Husbands and wives formed economic partnerships to which children were added as soon as they were old enough to work. Retirement from the work force was virtually unheard of except for those who were too feeble to work, and then the inability to earn money meant severe economic hardship.

At the family level, the textile industry was extremely important. In Auffay, 80 of the 154 women who married in the village between 1751 and 1786 were spinners at the time of their weddings (52 percent). (See Table 6.5.) An additional 24 of these women are known to have worked in spinning sometime during their married life, placing the percentage of married women with a known tie to the putting-out industry at 67.5.[45] Although women earned less than men, their wages were crucial to their families. They helped the families survive the seasonal fluctuations in the demand for farm labor; paid the rent on small parcels of land, cottages, and workshops; and made it unnecessary for men to look for work as urban laborers during winter months. Without women's earnings from spinning, many families would have been forced to choose between sending sons and daughters away from home to work, making the husband/father a seasonal migrant, and moving out of the region. None of these survival strategies was necessary in the Caux. There is no evidence of seasonal migration by adult men, and children, especially daughters, remained at home until they married. Women's earnings thus helped keep the family together and, in good years, provided for small luxuries like an evening in a café for the men.[46]

At the individual level, spinning allowed some single and widowed women to support themselves without the assistance of an adult male wage earner. Although eighteenth-century tax roles do not list the occupations of most of the women who headed households (and never list them for other women), given the predominance of spinning in the occupations of women, it seems likely that most of the women who headed households were spinners. Their earnings from this, combined, perhaps, with the produce from a garden and a few chickens and sometimes with the earnings of their children, allowed them to live in their own homes rather than board with relatives or neighbors. Throughout the second half of the eighteenth century, between 10 and 15 percent of the households in Auffay were headed by women, a fairly high percentage for an eighteenth-century village.[47]

Although spinning was by far the most important occupation for women in the Caux, it was not the only one. Women also worked as seamstresses, domestic servants, merchants, and farmers. Like spinning, dressmaking was an occupation pursued by both married and unmarried women. Judging by the social status of the husbands of seamstresses (they married primarily merchants, artisans, and *laboureurs,* not weavers or day laborers), and by their high level of literacy (between 1751 and 1800, 85 percent of them could sign the marriage registers compared with only 43 percent of spinners), dressmaking may have been a more desirable occupation than spinning, at least in Auffay. The reasons for this are unclear, however, because in most places the wages of seamstresses were pitifully low.[48]

Domestic service, on the other hand, was a less desirable occupation than spinning. Unlike spinners, who generally remained at home until they married, servants worked for and lived with other families. They were the least likely of all young women to learn to read and write in the eighteenth century (only 16 percent of them could sign the marriage registers), and their husbands tended to come from the ranks of the poorly paid weavers, day laborers, and farm domestics. Marriage almost inevitably entailed a woman's leaving her job as a servant, although she could return to this work as a widow. After marriage, most servants appear to have turned to spinning to contribute to the family's income. Marie Marquerite Pallier, who worked as a servant on a fifty-acre farm before her marriage in 1771 to Augustin François LeGras, a tailor, is typical. After her marriage, she appears in the parish registers five times, each time with the occupation of spinner, the last being the time of her death in 1811.[49] She is one of seven servants who married in Auffay and appears in later records with the occupation of spinner. Two other servants married *laboureurs* and became *laboureuses*. (For the remaining nine servants who married in the village, there are no entries in the parish registers after their weddings and consequently no information about their marital occupations.)

The women in the potentially best social and economic positions were those who married wealthy farmers or master craftsmen. Generally speaking, these women were the daughters of *laboureurs* or artisans. As widows, they frequently were able to carry on their husbands' work. The widow of Pierre Poulet, for instance, ran a farm of 60 acres with the aid of three employees from 1751, when her husband died, until her own death in 1768. Marie Laurence ran the family masonry business from the time of her husband Joseph Eustache Gibert's death in the 1740s until her own death in 1763, at the age of sixty-six. The widow of Louis Nicolle and her children lived at the flour mill and, one suspects, continued to run it after Louis's death, although the tax records are unclear on this point. Other widows ran large and small farms, operated inns and cabarets, and managed artisan businesses like shoemaking.[50]

When a widow controlled a large farm or ran an important local business, she acquired both the income and the social status that accrued to men in these positions. Marie Laurence, for instance, was regarded as the head of the masonry business and of her household even though her son, who lived with her, was clearly a mason and at least participated in running the business from 1758 to 1763.[51] The occupations held by widows varied from year to year, however, and well-situated widows were always an anomaly in the village. The majority of women were left in very precarious circumstances when their husbands died and were more likely to end up as mendicants than as community leaders. (See Table 4.3.)

The imbalance in labor demand between spinning and weaving, combined with the sexual division of labor in this and other rural occupations, made cottage industry much less important as an employer of men than of women. In Auffay, weaving employed only 13 percent of the male heads of households in the late eighteenth century and was the occupation of only twenty grooms, compared with eighty brides who were spinners.[52] (See Tables 6.5 and 6.6.) There were as many merchants as weavers (indeed, one more in 1771) and many more artisans and day laborers. Although their relationship to the land ranged from that of

Table 4.3. *Women's marriage occupations, Auffay,*
1751–1786

Occupation	Number	Percentage
Agriculture:		
Cultivators	4	2.6
Day laborers	2	1.3
	6	3.9
Nonagriculture:		
Domestics	18	11.7
Spinners	80	52.0
Weavers	0	—
Seamstresses	19	12.3
Merchants	8	5.2
Artisans	0	—
Miscellaneous	2	1.3
	127	82.5
No occupation	0	—
Unknown	21[a]	13.6
Total	154	100.0

[a]Fourteen of these women married between 1751 and 1755 when the recording of female marriage occupations was erratic.
Source: ADSM Parish Registers, Auffay.

wealthy landowner or tenant farmer to that of landless day laborer and farm domestic, one-third of the men were employed in agriculture for most or all of the year.

Many men alternated between weaving and farming, but it is impossible to tell how frequently they moved back and forth, or even what a typical pattern was. Some alternations may have been seasonal; others may have been determined by the availability of work in cottage industry or agriculture in particular years or even by a man's age. In general, the older the men, the less we know about them. Before 1796, when an enumerated census was taken, occupations were recorded only at the time of marriage, the birth of children, and death. For many men, the gap between the birth of their last child and their own death was considerable, and we know nothing about them during these years. Records of the events in the life of Jacques Recher amply illustrate the problem. We know Recher's occupation at five different points between 1773 and 1777. In April 1773, when he married Marie Magdeleine Linot, he was a *jour-*

nalier. One month later, when his first child was born, he was a weaver. In May 1774, he was again listed as a weaver; in January 1776 and March 1777, he was a *journalier.* We do not know why he alternated between day laboring and weaving or how long he stayed in each occupation, but we do know that he was changing jobs frequently. After 1777, however, we know nothing about him until his death in September 1800, when his occupation was again listed as *journalier.*[53]

It is also impossible to tell what criteria were used in listing occupations on church and state records. We do not know, for instance, whether a man listed the occupation that he pursued for most of the year or the one he currently held. Nor is it clear that the man himself made the decision. A man might have been known as a weaver even if he had been working in agriculture for awhile, or vice versa. Even in a village as large as Auffay, most men were known by the record keepers who may simply have listed them by their "known" occupations. The occupational patterns that emerge from the parish registers leave us with many questions. But they do tell us clearly that many men moved back and forth from weaving to agricultural day laboring.

The reasons men moved from one of these occupations to the other also remains obscure, but upward movement was rare. Unlike the occasional skilled weaver who moved up into the ranks of the merchant weavers (*marchands toiliers* or *marchands siamoisiers*) who bought spun yarn, had it washed, and made the warps for other weavers,[54] the men who moved into and out of weaving and day laboring remained at the bottom of the economic ladder.

Artisans and merchants had radically different occupational patterns from those of weavers and day laborers. They held positions that necessitated specific skills (including literacy) and rarely changed occupations, other than to move through the ranks from apprentice to journeyman to master craftsman. Those who acquired a skill clearly acquired a fairly high degree of job security in a village like Auffay in the eighteenth century. The unskilled had to change jobs with the seasons or the vicissitudes of life.

Artisans were more numerous in Auffay than in many villages because of the tanneries. They provided work not only for tanners and curriers but also for leather-working craftsmen – harness makers, glovemakers, and shoemakers. Except for the latter group, these craftsmen would not have been present in most villages, and even shoemakers were scarce in this region because the peasants wore wooden shoes (*sabots*) made by *sabotiers* rather than leather shoes made by *cordonniers.* In addition to the leather crafts, Auffay artisans worked in construction and farm-related crafts (as carpenters, nail-makers, masons, blacksmiths, brickmakers, etc.) and in general artisan crafts, supplying goods that people could not manufacture for themselves (candles, guns, barrels, metal tools, furniture, etc.). Almost one-third of the male heads of households in Auffay were skilled artisans, a substantial percentage of the adult male population and far more than worked at anything other than farming.

Although there were fewer merchants than artisans, there were still more of them than would have been found in smaller villages. Auffay had its own butchers, bakers, millers, grocers, and fish merchants, as well as innkeepers and small textile merchants (linen and cotton). The village still depended on the services of traveling tinkers and coppersmiths to repair its pots, pans, kettles, and andirons, however. Finally, a handful of men constituted a small group of village professionals – doctors, priests, the parish clerk, and the local notary or lawyer. (See Table 4.4.)

Men's jobs were not only more diversified than women's jobs, but also were less dependent on external employers and markets. Some goods produced by the artisan craftsmen, especially those of tanners, were sent to markets in Dieppe and Rouen. Large farmers were partially dependent on markets outside the region for the sale of their crops. Weavers were dependent on the *fabricants* of Rouen for their raw materials and the sale of their cloth. However, like much of the grain, the vast majority of the goods produced by artisans and merchants in such villages as Auffay was consumed locally.

When one examines the economy of the Caux as a whole, however, it becomes clear that this picture of a relatively self-contained male economy is false. Many male jobs depended on the wages women earned in spinning and therefore on the cottage textile industry. Without women's earnings in cottage industry, either the number of families living in absolute poverty would have been much higher or the population of the region would have been much smaller, and wealthy farmers would have had to rely on a migrant labor force to harvest the grain crops. Reliance on migrant labor, in turn, would have reduced the need for artisan and merchant crafts, further reducing the area's population. Thus, in many ways, the work of women in cottage industry was the linchpin both of the family economy and of the overall economy of the Caux. Without the spinning industry, or some other large female employer, the economic structure of the entire region would have been vastly different.

Thus, the involvement of women in spinning formed the primary link between the villages and the larger regional and national economy. Their

Table 4.4. *Occupations of male heads of households
in 1771 and Auffay grooms, 1751–1786*

Occupation	Heads of Households		Grooms	
	Number	Percentage	Number	Percentage
Agriculture:				
Cultivators	9	5.9	11	7.1
Day laborers	32	21.0	31	20.1
Domestics	0[a]	—	9	5.9
	41	26.9	51	33.1
Nonagriculture:				
Artisans	48	31.4	41	26.6
Merchants	18	11.8	19	12.3
Weavers	17	11.1	20	13.0
Tailors	7	4.5	6	3.9
Professionals	9	5.9	5	3.3
Miscellaneous	7	4.5	9	5.9
	106	69.2	100	65.0
Unknown	6	3.9	3	1.9
Total	153	100.0	154	100.0

[a]Domestics never headed their own households. Hence, the tax records underreflect the percentage of adult men employed in agriculture.
Source: ADSM 219BP364; Parish Registers, Auffay.

employment in the cotton industry gave the villages an important stake in the state of the French textile industry. Fluctuations in that industry, like those following the Anglo – French treaty of 1786 and the trade embargoes of the Napoleonic period, affected the region primarily through their impact on women's jobs, not through their impact on men's jobs. As Chapter 5 demonstrates, the families of the Caux became all too familiar with unemployment and low wages through their female members, and slumps in the industry had a devastating effect on the well-being of entire villages.

The importance of women's earnings to the regional economy and to a majority of the families in the region raises the question of their status in this region. Hans Medick has argued that in proto-industrial regions, where a sexual division of labor was maintained and there was more work for women than men, household tasks previously designated as women's work were assumed by men as the family strove to maximize income and women began to participate in status consumption alongside their men.[55] His argument supports the findings of social historians that the status of women was higher in the eighteenth century, when women produced goods for sale as well as for family consumption, than it was in the nineteenth century, when rising male incomes, combined with the movement of textile work into factories, led married women to withdraw from the paid labor force. Although the family lived better and children were healthier when women devoted their full attention to homemaking and childcare, women's status declined as they began to be regarded as spenders rather than earners of money.[56]

The status of women might have been higher under the conditions of full female employment that existed in the Caux in the eighteenth century than it would be in the nineteenth century, but this was far from an egalitarian era. Compared with men, women had few job options, none of which paid well. The highest wages women earned in spinning were usually lower than the wages paid to male weavers and day laborers, the two most poorly paid male occupations. Only after her husband's death could a woman become a skilled artisan, although her ability to do so at that point indicates clearly that she possessed the required skill long before she had any authority or status in the craft.

Women did exercise some power in the family when it came to spending the money they earned. The Auffay spinners walked seven miles to the textile market in Bacqueville to sell their yarn and make purchases. Men never accompanied them on these trips and had no control over how women spent their part of the family's earnings. Women congregated in each others' homes during long winter evenings to work and talk. Again, men were not present.[57] Such occasions for female community may have strengthened individual women when it came to dealing with their husbands or children.

While the women were gathering to work, their men were gathering in the local cafés to drink and bet small sums on dominoes. Judging from the *cahiers de doléances* of 1789, the cafés were male enclaves. The complaints in the *cahiers* about the cafés appear to be directed toward their deleterious effects on the behavior and morality of young men, not young women.[58] Ironically, it was the earnings of women in cottage industry that allowed the cafés and taverns to spread and on which they depended for their existence. Women had no comparable gathering place. They gathered to work, not to relax.

Women also were not the equals of men legally in the Caux. They did not inherit land from their fathers unless they had no male siblings, and although they ran farms and artisan businesses after their husbands' deaths, they did not truly own these businesses unless they had no sons. They merely had a lifetime right to the income from one-third of their deceased husbands' property. Such matters concerned only a small minority of *cauchois* women, however. For the majority, life was a matter of incessant work; small, damp, crowded houses; worry about the harvest or the availability of raw cotton for spinning and weaving; and fears about childbirth, illness, and death. For most women, the death of a husband meant increased misery, not improved social status and independence.

Women's status may have been higher in the Caux than it was in regions in which there were fewer jobs for them, but there is no evidence that Medick's argument about the effects of proto-industrialization on women's status holds for this region. Both the level of female employment and the level of male employment and wage differentials are important in determining the status of women. Although women were fully employed in the Caux, so were men, and the lower wages earned by women made them the logical ones to take time from work to care for children and prepare meals. Even though women's wages provided the cushion that allowed some money to be spent in cafés, women did not participate in this status consumption. At least by the nineteenth century, the subordinate position of women was reflected in the names given to individual dominoes. The double six (the most valuable domino for scoring purposes) was the big daddy (*le gros papa* or *le gros père*); the double blank was the laundress (*la blanchisseuse* or *la blanchinette*).[59]

As is true for most places, the evidence regarding female status is very slight for the Caux, and the position of women undoubtedly varied from family to family. The existing evidence does not point toward increased egalitarianism or the sharing of nonproductive tasks and public recreation areas by men and women in the eighteenth century, however. Instead, the evidence reveals a culture that valued male work more highly than female work and provided more leisure and status consumption for men than for women, despite the importance of women's earnings to their families and to the entire region.

5

~.~

Crisis and change in the Caux

Revolution

By the winter of 1788–89, the French monarchy was in serious financial trouble and embarked on a series of fateful decisions. Having failed to convince the *parlements* to register edicts that would have levied taxes on the nobility, the king ordered a meeting of the Estates General, announced procedures for electing delegates, and requested people meet by village, order, and occupation to compile lists of grievances. The peasants, artisans, and merchants of Rouen and the Caux held meetings, elected representatives to regional assemblies, and wrote their *cahiers de doléances*. The major concerns of the *cauchois* peasants and artisans were not, however, the kingdom's finances and the struggle taking shape over the national government, but their need for economic aid. Unfortunately for Louis XVI, as well as for the Caux (at least in the short run), the government was rapidly losing its ability to help itself, much less anyone else.

The problems in the Caux had begun earlier in the decade, when English textiles began to eat into the foreign market for French textiles. They did not become truly serious, however, until 1786, when an Anglo–French commercial treaty allowed English fabric to be sold in France itself. Commonly called the Eden Treaty after the chief English negotiator, William Eden, whose preparations for the meetings allowed him to outmaneuver the French at every step, the treaty was greeted with dismay by French manufacturers. Reaction was particularly acute among textile merchants because English cotton cloth was both higher in quality and lower in price than French fabric, factors that would hardly be offset by the 12-percent tariff provided by the treaty.[1] Reductions in work and wages began immediately as merchants nervously anticipated the coming drop in sales.[2] By July of 1788, a year after the treaty took effect, the quantity of English merchandise imported into France had more than doubled, and many French textile merchants were facing bankruptcy.[3]

Among cottage workers, unemployment was rampant. Workers who

86

could still find work continued to spin and weave, but for greatly reduced wages. Spinners who had earned eight to twelve *sous* per day before the treaty, now worked much longer hours to earn only three *sous*.[4] Even when they doubled the number of hours they worked, spinners and weavers earned less than half of what they needed in order to survive in the best of times when food prices were stable and low.[5]

Families in which the women spun and the men wove were devastated by the lack of work, as were widows and unmarried women who depended solely on the textile industry for income. Families in which the men were farmers, day laborers, or artisans were slightly better off, but they, too, usually depended on the earnings of women in spinning to supplement the men's earnings and to pay necessary expenses. *Cahier* after *cahier* lamented the "stagnation of commerce" in cotton and pleaded for a resumption of work. The small commune of La Heuze exemplified the common plight:

Commerce, especially the cotton branch, which employes the women and girls in this area, has entirely fallen into ruin; they can no longer find the means to subsist in this part despite their vigilance and continual work because of the paltry price they are paid for their labor; . . . .[6]

To make matters worse, the crisis in the cotton industry coincided with a series of bad harvests in the Caux. In 1788, hail and rain storms ruined the ripening grain. In 1789, an exceptionally cold winter destroyed the wheat and rye crops as they lay in the fields.[7] The price of grain rose precipitously. By March of 1789, bread was selling for four *sous* a pound, almost double its usual price of two *sous* and two or three *deniers*.[8] Spinners who earned three *sous* a day for endless hours of work could not afford even a pound of bread a day.

Not all the villages in the Caux experienced the same degree of unemployment and hardship. Those with a portion of the population employed in an artisan craft or other manufacturing process fared the best, but even they were in trouble. Ventes-Saint-Remy reported that even though its men were still able to earn money by cutting wood for the two local glass factories, its women could earn almost nothing from spinning and "most of the inhabitants are dying of hunger."[9] Even Auffay, which had a relatively large number of artisans in comparison with weavers, reported in 1789 that "public misery is at its height because of the dearness of bread and the stagnation of commerce, and the number of poor is multiplying daily."[10]

Communes with large numbers of male weavers as well as female spinners were in an especially precarious position. Saint-Martin-de-Veules, one such commune, reported in its *cahier* that the textile workers were no longer able to support their families and were "forced to seek their livelihood at night."[11] Whereas the writers of Saint-Martin-de-Veules' *cahier* shied away from explaining what these unemployed workers did at night, the residents of La Chapelle-sur-Dun had no such inhibitions. They reported that unemployed textile workers had two options – "a sack on their shoulder or a club in their hand," that is, begging or stealing.[12]

The simultaneous onset of inflation, unemployment, and reduced wages created many more poor than the villages of the Caux were able to assist. Public disorder became a serious threat both to property and to personal safety. By the spring of 1789, the poor were roaming across the plateau in bands, stopping grain shipments on the highways, rioting in market-places, and raiding peasants' homes at night.[13]

As the harvest neared, the situation deteriorated further. Groups of hungry people waited by the roadsides and stopped wagons carrying grain to Rouen and Paris. The local mounted police were not numerous enough to prevent or even to stop these attacks, especially as the size of the groups increased.[14] On market days, women and men invaded the villages and forced farmers to sell their grain for half the price the sellers wanted, that is, the price of grain in normal years.[15] At night, the bands directed their attention to the farms, demanding food and drink from the farmers and their families, sometimes beating the residents of the farm and threatening to burn the houses and crops if their demands were not met.[16] Given such threats and the number of poor on the roads, it is amazing that there was no *grande peur* in the Caux.

By the summer of 1789, the region was close to anarchy. Belleville-en-Caux, located just to the west of Auffay, reported that four to five hundred mendicants passed through the village every week.[17] As the deadlock between the King and the Estates General (now the National Assembly) worsened, and the people of Paris prepared to storm the Bastille in search of weapons and ammunition, the government in Normandy attempted to restore order and to alleviate the worst of the hunger problem by provisioning marketplaces. By this time, however, their efforts were doomed to failure. On July 8, nine hundred bushels of grain were sent from Rouen to the market in Bacqueville. The government intended to sell the grain at the going rate of forty-eight to fifty *livres* per sack. (Each sack contained six bushels or approximately three hundred pounds of grain.) A large crowd (numbered at three thousand by government reports, but surely exaggerated) demanded that the grain be sold for twenty-four *livres* instead. Troops stationed at the market tried in vain to keep order. Sacks were opened and grain was sold at the people's price. When the guards tried to intervene, people pelted them with rocks from the rooftops and rolled stones under the feet of their horses, tactics that forced the troops to retreat and regroup. Finally, the troops cleared the market-place by firing their guns and threatening violence. On the same and succeeding days, other markets in the Caux were invaded by bands of two to four hundred people, and similar scenes transpired.[18]

No grain shipment was safe. On July 11, nine wagons carrying grain were hijacked outside of Rouen, and all of the grain was lost. On the twelfth, a convoy of twenty-five wagons guarded by the *maréchaussée* was stopped several times on its way to Rouen. In the end, only two of the wagons made it into the city.[19]

In Rouen, attacks on grain depots, grain merchants, and flour millers began on the night of the twelfth and continued throughout the next two days. As the attacks continued, their targets broadened. On the four-teenth, the abbey of Saint-Ouen was pillaged by a hungry and angry mob searching for food. Textile merchants who had installed spinning ma-chines faced angry mobs. People were hungry not only because the price of food was high, but also because they were unemployed. Those mer-chants who had introduced machines after the Eden Treaty took effect appeared to threaten the few jobs that were left rather than to offer hope for the future. Once some of the people's need for food and their anger at the "monopolists" believed to be profiting from the high prices had been assuaged, the machines became a prime target of their rage, fear, and frustration.

During the riots of July 12 to 14, a spinning mill in Saint-Sever was systematically destroyed. On the nineteenth and twentieth, *ateliers* with the hated machines were attacked in Rouen itself. The machines were broken, tossed out the windows into the street, and set on fire. The best the government could do was to put out the fires and haul the broken pieces to the courtyard of the Hôtel de Ville for safekeeping. Not until mid-August was calm restored in Rouen and government reform be-gun.[20]

Machine breaking was peculiar to Rouen and its suburbs because they were the only places to receive spinning and carding machines before 1790. If there had been *ateliers* with spinning machines in the Caux, they probably would have been the target of attacks. As it was, however, the unemployed *cauchois* weavers and spinners directed their attention to the price of bread and the inadequate provisions for aiding unemployed workers. The basic antagonism that ran through the Caux was between the producers and consumers of grain, not between unemployed cottage workers and the textile merchants.

The *cahiers* from the Caux generally conceal the antagonism because they were written by the wealthier artisans, merchants, and farmers. In Calleville, a small commune just to the west of Auffay, however, the wealthier citizens were unable to impose their will on the unemployed weavers, and two *cahiers,* differing only in one article, were submitted. The disputed article reveals the rift in the community. The farmers and merchants viewed themselves as overburdened, harassed, and well-intentioned. In their version of the *cahier,* they complained that they were forced to sell their grain for less than market value by mobs in the marketplace, were hounded by "numberless mendicants who come, even at night, to importune and menace them," and, despite all of this, were expected to help the poor of the village.[21] Altogether, they felt it was an unfair burden.

The weavers, on the other hand, viewed themselves as trapped in a hopeless situation from which they could not escape, no matter how hard they worked. They complained that the price of grain was so high that it was impossible for "the best worker, responsible for two or three children, to be able, even with the work of his wife, to succeed in providing them with bread," and predicted morosely that "if the entire year remains this bad, everyone who is obliged to buy grain, and who has no resource other than the work of his hands, will need to receive charity."[22] Both groups knew who would be called on to provide help, and neither liked it very much.

Occupying a kind of middle ground between the weavers and cultivators were the small farmers, who were both producers and consumers of grain. With rent and taxes to pay, they were forced to sell their grain immediately after the harvest, when the price was lowest, and then to purchase grain for their own needs later in the season, when the price was higher. Like the weavers, they depended partially on women's earnings from spinning. With the loss of these wages, many of these families found it impossible to pay the rent on their land and homes without charging high prices for what little grain they had to sell, even though later in the season they too would suffer from grain shortages and high prices. In a sense, they had a foot in each camp.

The situation of the small farmers clearly illustrates the intimate relationship between cottage industry and agriculture in the Caux. Many families depended on employment in both branches of the economy;

moreover, the weavers and spinners who were faced with high grain prices knew the farmers from whom they purchased grain because they worked for them during the harvest. Resentments about farmers' work demands and low or grudgingly paid harvest wages found a natural outlet during periods of inflation in complaints about the price of bread, especially because the destitute spinners and weavers knew what they had been paid to harvest the crops they now could not afford. The *laboureurs* and *fermiers* had grievances of their own about cottage workers who sometimes chose to spin or weave rather than harvest and thresh, who demanded higher wages than their employers wanted to pay, and who may not have worked as hard during the harvest as the farmers wanted.

The grievances on both sides were highly personal in these small villages and were bound to surface during periods of grain shortages and high prices. The 1789 commercial crisis intensified these old antagonisms much more than it created a new enemy. If anyone was to blame for the unemployment in spinning and weaving, it was, in the eyes of the villagers, the government that had signed the commercial treaty with England, not the merchants.[23] (The merchants liked the treaty no better than their unemployed workers did.)

The antagonism between the producers and consumers of grain continued throughout the Revolutionary period and exploded in market riots and raids on grain shipments and wealthy farmsteads, whenever grain was low in supply or high in price. Following the traditional pattern, riots that began in one market traveled to others. In the Auffay region, they began at the Bacqueville market on Wednesday and carried over to the Auffay market on Thursday and Saturday. In 1791, one of these riots was large enough to be called the "Insurrection of the pays de Caux" by the *Journal de Rouen*.[24] First in Bacqueville and then in Auffay, a large group of people took control of the market, set the price of grain, and "mistreated those who wanted to oppose them." The Bacqueville disturbance was put down by locally stationed troops, but the Auffay affair required the government to dispatch two hundred troops from Dieppe. When they arrived, they were confronted by a crowd of "three to four thousand inhabitants of the countryside, armed with guns and rifles" who demanded that the shipment of grain be more closely regulated, that grain be sold at a fixed price, and that the troops of the line be removed from the canton.[25] The complaints, as well as the market riots, point to the severe food shortages the region was facing as grain continued to be shipped out to provision (and calm) Paris and as massive numbers of army troops lived off the local population.

None of the records of the period reveal the occupational or sexual composition of the crowds that invaded marketplaces and stopped grain shipments in the Caux, making it impossible to determine to what extent spinners and weavers were active in these demonstrations. Earlier in the eighteenth century, it is clear, however, that women were prominent in provoking confrontations with *laboureurs,* and women as well as men were active in the 1789 bread and machine-breaking riots in Rouen.[26] Because women suffered the most from the decline in the cotton industry and the periodic increases in grain prices in these years, and because women were traditionally both leaders and participants in collective action in this region, it seems likely that they continued to play major roles in the battle over grain prices during the Revolution.[27]

As the revolutionary governments of France became increasingly radical and decrees affecting village politics and religion were issued, political divisions grew up alongside the preexisting economic divisions. What is interesting is that the Caux did not experience a counterrevolution, despite the presence of the cotton industry and tenant farming, two features of rural life that have been identified as sources of opposition to the Revolution in other parts of western France. Charles Tilly, for instance, has argued that the weaver/peasants of the Mauges region of the Vendée (whom he calls "industrial artisans") felt a "venomous enmity" for the wealthy merchants on whom they depended. When the Revolution provided the latter group with the opportunity to seize both land and power, they became strong supporters of the new government. The textile workers, who gained little or nothing from the Revolution, turned to counterrevolution in opposition both to their old enemies and to legislation on the Church and conscription laws, which seemed to rob the rural community simultaneously of its identity and its men.[28] T. J. A. LeGoff and D. M. G. Sutherland, in contrast, have argued that it was not early industrialization but the predominance of tenant farming in western France that made the entire region peculiarly prone to counterrevolution. Unlike landowners in other regions, tenant farmers were hurt rather than helped by the economic legislation of the Revolution. In 1791, the Civil Constitution of the Clergy provided them with a "focus and justification" for their grievances and led to counterrevolution. The poorer peasants and cottage workers eventually followed their lead.[29]

Had the wealthy farmers and merchants supported the revolutionary government wholeheartedly in the Caux, the poorer peasants and unemployed textile workers might have turned to avowedly counterrevolutionary activities, as their counterparts did elsewhere in western France. Until at least 1795, however, peasants and cottage workers supported the Revolution more strongly than did the local elite of landowners, tenant farmers, and wealthy merchants. There are a variety of reasons for this. In the first place, the *cauchois* merchants and cultivators benefited little from the Revolution and did not strongly support it. Little land changed hands because much of it was owned by the bourgeoisie, and many nobles who were substantial property owners, like Thomas de Bosmelet in Auffay, remained on their estates, preventing their sale. Wealthy *fermiers* (the renters of land) were no better off than they had been under the *Ancien Régime* because they could not purchase property, and they acquired no strong loyalty to the Revolution. The same was true of the textile merchants, many of whom were, in fact, hurt by the disruption of trade created by the war with England.

Although not firmly tied to the Revolution, the innate cautiousness of the merchants and cultivators (witness the textile merchants failure to adopt spinning machinery before the Eden Treaty forced them into it, and the cultivators' reluctance to institute enclosure and crop rotation), kept them from much overt counterrevolutionary activity. Instead, along with ex-nobles like Thomas de Bosmelet (now Citoyen Thomas), they used their economic power and political skills to manipulate the new system and to mitigate the effects of governmental decrees.

In Auffay, the first major hint of opposition from the more established members of the community arose with the arrival of the constitutional priest in September 1791. Three of the Auffay priests had refused to sign the constitutional oath pledging allegiance to the revolutionary government. Until the new priest arrived, these men continued to say Mass at the usual hours, and the village remained calm. The new priest instituted a new order, however, and trouble began. He "relegated" the refractory priests to an "isolated and obscure altar," refused to give them the bread, wine, candles, and vessels necessary for the celebration of the Mass, prevented them from announcing the hour of their Masses by sounding the church bells, and permitted them to celebrate Mass only between five and six in the morning, an inconvenient hour from everyone's point of view.[30]

In May of 1792, a hundred members of the Auffay church wrote and signed a letter protesting these practices. The letter was hardly a model of religious piety. Its authors were not concerned with religion but with the effects of the new priest's actions on their businesses. The concern was great enough for them to threaten the departmental government with revolt if the refractory priests were not allowed to say Mass "at hours convenient for the public, like seven in the summer and eight in the winter."[31] The major thrust of the letter was that

... the interests of the commune have suffered considerably. The number of masses has always attracted a large number of people to Auffay on Sundays and holidays. If the non-juring priests are forced to say their masses before six o'clock in the morning, the residents of neighboring parishes will not come to Auffay and the merchants and innkeepers, who are numerous, will be deprived of the sale of their food and merchandise, *which might give rise to discontent.*[32]

The protest met with some success. The constitutional priest was directed to provide the other priests with the necessary items for saying Mass and to allow them to say Mass between six and seven in the summer and between seven and eight in the winter, an hour earlier than requested, but an hour later than the constitutional priest had condoned.[33]

Although the roots of the 1792 protest over the hours of Mass appear to have been more economic than religious, Thomas and some of the major merchants in Auffay continued to support the priests and religious traditions long after there was any economic gain to be won from such a position. By the fall of 1797, with the Vendée in revolt against the Revolution, the central government was seriously concerned about the loyalty of the Caux, and especially of its leading citizens. There were reports of armed "brigands" circulating in the area, forcing people to donate to the royal and Catholic army, and placards with anti-Revolution statements appeared on trees throughout the canton. In Auffay, the resistance to changing the days of local markets and fairs to conform to the revolutionary calendar was so strong that they continued to be held on traditional days, despite repeated attempts to impose the new calendar on the village.[34]

Jacques Pierre Truffier, a wealthy merchant and cantonal official, was regarded as a fanatic who opposed the principles of the government because he had rung the bells in the Auffay church to announce the hours of the religious offices. Much to the dismay of the departmental government, the ringing of the bells in Auffay had been followed by the ringing of bells in the neighboring villages.[35] Thomas, president of the canton, was regarded as equally suspicious for a variety of reasons. He had taken in an old priest in 1796 (*an* IV) and allowed him to say Mass in the chapel on the grounds of his estate. As president of the canton, he had prevented or retarded the enforcement of laws he did not like. He had not forced the sale of the property of *émigré* priests but had allowed it to remain in the hands of their families. He had prosecuted no one for the ringing of the church bells. Moreover, his large property holdings meant many tenant farmers depended on him for their leases and were in no position to oppose his politics, even if they wanted to.[36]

Despite the suspicions, Thomas managed to ride out the Revolution without going into exile. In the late 1790s, the canton of Auffay submitted a list of inhabitants who manifested antirepublican sentiments. Nine residents of Auffay were on the list: Thomas, two wealthy cultivators (Louis Bertrand and Pierre Roussel), and six merchants. Bertrand and Roussel eventually fled into exile, but Thomas remained on his estates, depending on his economic power to protect him, as it appears it did.[37]

Unlike the merchants and cultivators who were never more than lukewarm toward the Revolution, the peasants and cottage workers fervently supported it at various points. After the dechristianization decrees of 1793, the Auffay church was ransacked and converted into a temple of liberty and a storehouse for saltpeter. The statues were broken; prayer books and vestments were carted out into the cemetery and burned; the organ was dismantled and the parts sold; and all but one of the bells were broken.[38]

In June 1794 (*Prairial an* II), a Committee of Public Safety was established in Auffay to root out antirepublican activity. It heard denunciations of Thomas and the other moderates or conservatives and received reports of activity ranging from the cutting down of a liberty tree to the illegal baptizing of infants by refractory priests, to interference with the production of saltpeter.[39] There was no shortage of people willing to testify about these matters and about the hoarding of grain by farmers.

How committed the *cauchois* peasants, weavers, and spinners were to the Revolution, however, is impossible to say. In large part, it may simply have given them an opportunity to wreak a little vengeance on their traditional enemies, the wealthy landholders. In any case, poor peasants and textile workers were unlikely to oppose the Revolution in any open fashion because they would have had to join forces with the farmers, and this was an unpalatable alliance. The counterrevolutionary activity by the poor in Auffay and other *cauchois* villages was, therefore, limited to market riots and attacks on wealthy farmers whenever grain was in short supply and prices high, activity that was counterrevolutionary only in the sense that it impeded the government's attempts to maintain order and a steady flow of provisions to Rouen and Paris. Even the Civil Constitution of the Clergy was not a counterrevolutionary rallying point for them because the wealthy *laboureurs* and *fermiers* championed the refractory clergy and protected the goods of *émigré* priests.

The enmity that Tilly found between textile workers and putting-out merchants in the Vendée also had no counterpart in the Caux. The merchants were not regarded as outsiders who paid inadequate wages and provided too little work. Instead, cottage workers saw their interests as allied to those of the merchants. The lack of work, not the merchants, was their problem, and the merchants' control of the Revolution in cities like Rouen was not likely to turn them into counterrevolutionaries.

In short, old alliances and old antagonisms in the Caux continued to flourish in the new circumstances of the Revolution, just as they had under the *Ancien Régime,* and neither side gained or lost enough during the conflict to produce counterrevolution. The *laboureurs, fermiers,* and merchants remained in control of the economy and the villages, while the day laborers, spinners, and weavers continued to eke out a living and to suffer through periods of unemployment, low wages, and high prices, just as they had before the Revolution.

Mechanization

Until the Eden Treaty of 1786, the Rouen merchants had almost completely ignored the technical progress in spinning and carding that was taking place in England. They continued to put cotton out into the cottages of the Caux to be carded, spun, and woven by hand. Quality remained constant, and production could not be increased without large increases in the number of workers, because ten or more spinners and carders were employed for every weaver. In England, meanwhile, a series of inventions was dramatically increasing the speed of production, decreasing the size of the labor force, and improving the quality of cotton fabric. These were developments that the Rouen merchants ignored to their peril.

The advances in England began in 1765 with James Hargreave's invention of the spinning jenny.[40] The jennies had multiple advantages over spinning wheels. The increase in productivity per worker was enormous. With a small jenny, one woman could produce what it had previously taken twelve to fifteen women to produce. Fabric quality improved because the jennies produced a finer, more even yarn than spinning wheels. The introduction of jennies did not entail a change in the location of work because they were small and could be set up in spinners' homes.

The jennies did not produce cotton yarn that was strong enough for warp threads, however, and looms continued to be strung with linen or (occasionally) hand-spun cotton. The problem of producing cotton warp threads was solved a few years after the introduction of the jenny by Richard Arkwright's invention of the water-frame. It operated on the principle of rollers rather than wheels and spindles and produced strong cotton yarn that could be used for warps. Combined with weft yarn produced by the jennies, the water-frame allowed the large-scale production of pure cotton cloth for the first time in European history. Unlike the early jennies, however, the frames could not be set up in people's homes because they could not be powered by hand. (The use of water to power Arkwright's early machines was such a distinctive change in the production of yarn that it became attached to the machine's name.)[41] Thus, with the water-frame, spinning began the transition from cottage to factory, although in the early years, cottage spinning with jennies and factory spinning with water-frames increased together.

Work on a carding machine proceeded alongside that on the spinning machine. The major development came in 1775, when Richard Arkwright took out a patent on a series of machines that would perform all of the preliminary steps in the spinning process – carding, drawing, and roving. By 1790, Arkwright's machines were spreading rapidly through the textile-producing regions of England, and carding as well as spinning was moving into factories.

In 1779, the third of the successful spinning machines was invented by Samuel Crompton. It was a hybrid that combined the features of the jenny and the water-frame and, in a move that reflected the rural nature of English society in the late eighteenth century, was called a "mule" (*"mull-jenny"* in French). The mule produced cotton yarn that was stronger than that of the jenny and finer than that of the water-frame and made possible the production of fine muslins on a large scale. By the 1790s, the mules were too large to be set up in cottages and powered by hand, and the final transition to factory spinning began. Cottage spinning declined rapidly as more and more merchants built small factories along running streams, and spinners who could not find jobs in the new mills found themselves unemployed.

Like their English counterparts, a few French merchants experimented with spinning and carding machines. Some of these men were Rouen merchants, most notably, John Holker, whose father had been an Englishman. The government tried to stimulate inventions by offering prize money to merchants who developed successful machines. The French merchants did not have the success of the English inventor – merchants, however, and there were no mechanized mills in the Caux or Rouen before the signing of the Eden Treaty.[42] The treaty provided the motivation that had been lacking. Faced with competition from the higher-quality and lower-priced English fabric made with machine-spun yarn, the merchants were forced to introduce machines or to abandon textile production altogether. Attempts to invent their own machines were abandoned as the merchants introduced the English machines. By 1789, several *ateliers* with spinning machines (especially mules) had been built in and around Rouen.[43]

Jennies were simultaneously introduced into workshop and cottage production, and the rural cotton industry began to revive. By 1805, the General Council of the Seine-Inférieure reported that "the spinning machines for cotton replace the spinning wheel in a multitude of small houses."[44] The spread of the jennies combined with other developments to slow down the advance of factory spinning in the Caux. Repeated attacks on *ateliers* with spinning machines in the Rouen area, in 1789, made the merchants leary of investing heavily in the new machines, even though they increased their profits. The annulment of the Eden Treaty in 1793 and France's return to a policy of protectionism reduced the threat of bankruptcy for merchants who did not mechanize production and, hence, the incentive to mechanize quickly.[45] Finally, the war between France and Britain made it difficult for the merchants to acquire English technology and craftsmen who could build and repair the new machines.[46]

The slowness with which mechanization proceeded in the Rouen region allowed hand spinning to revive partially, and, for awhile, it appeared that the spinning machines would not seriously disrupt work patterns and employment levels for women in the Caux. In 1796, ten years after the Eden Treaty was signed and factory building begun, spinning was still the major female occupation in the Caux. The percentage of adult women (aged twelve and over) in the canton of Auffay who were spinners ranged from 97.6 percent in the commune of Sevis to 60.5 percent in St. Maclou de Folleville. Auffay itself was at the lower end of the spectrum, with only 61.1 percent of its women earning money from spinning. None of the women in the canton were working in mills, although some of them may have been using small jennies in their homes.[47] In other sections of the Caux, small mills powered by small rivers or by horses began to appear. In 1801, a small mill employing twenty-two women and children was built on the Scie River in St. Victor l'Abbaye. Later it employed sixty workers.[48] Like the St. Victor mill, the early mills employed women and children to operate the small mules and jennies. They

Table 5.1. *Female spinners, canton of Auffay,* an *IV (1796)*

Commune	Spinners	Women	Percentage
Auffay	223	365	61.1
Bazomesnil	41	50	82.0
Bracquetuit	117	179	65.4
Cressy	114	149	76.5
Cropus	98	107	91.6
Etaimpuis	59	66	89.4
Fresnay le Long	87	122	71.3
Heugleville sur Scie	228	292	78.1
Montreuil	148	215	68.8
St. Denis sur Scie	78	85	91.8
St. Hellier	77	108	71.3
St. Maclou de Folleville	112	185	60.5
St. Sulpice	74	89	83.1
St. Victor l'Abbaye	173	206	84.0
Sevis	120	123	97.6
Totes	61	71	85.9
Varneville	102	133	76.7
Vassonville	99	177	84.6
Total	2011	2662	75.5

Note: Three communes – Biennais, Loeuilly, and Nôtre Dame du Parc – recorded very few female occupations and are not included in the table. Bracquetuit probably undercounts the number of spinners because it did not record the occupations of the seventeen wives and fourteen daughters of the *cultivateurs*.
Source: ADSM L367.

had little trouble finding workers because it was often the only alternative for unemployed cottage spinners, and entering the mill workforce allowed women and children to continue contributing to the family income without moving.

By the end of the century, jennies had spread throughout the Caux. Their exact cost is impossible to determine from existing records, but their rapid dispersion is generally attributed to their low cost. A government report on commerce in Rouen claimed in the year IV (1795–96), for instance, that their spread was "hardly surprising because they are so inexpensive that workers, with a little economy, can easily procure one."[49] Whatever their exact cost, the jennies were more expensive than spinning wheels and distaffs, however, and many poor women must have been unable to practice the "little economy" necessary to procure one, regardless of what the government thought.[50] These women were forced either

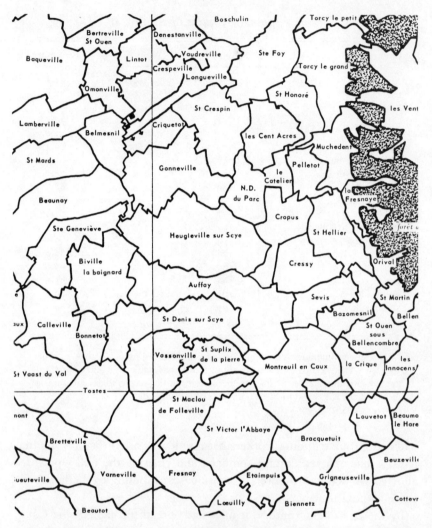

Figure 5.1. Auffay region of the pays de Caux (*Source:* Pierre Gouhier, Anne Vallez, Jean Marie Vallez, *Atlas historique de Normandie*, vol. I [Caen, 1967].)

to seek work in a spinning mill or to abandon spinning as a means of livelihood, because hand spinning could not compete with jenny spinning.

Jenny spinning, however could not long compete with factory spinning, and the dispersal of jennies into cottage production provided only a temporary respite for the cottage spinners who could afford them.[51] The small *cauchois* mills did not last long either. Rivers like the Scie were too small to provide much power for the machines, and a lack of coal and wood prevented the use of steam to power machines. By 1815, the mill in St. Victor l'Abbaye, like many other small factories in the Caux, had closed, and machine spinning was concentrated in mills lining the tributaries of the Seine River, where the volume of water was greater and its descent from the plateau to the Seine River Valley provided far greater power than the streams of the Caux. By the early years of the Restoration, cotton spinning was no longer a viable occupation for village women, and the economy of the Caux and of rural families was in the midst of a major transition.[52]

The owners of mills on the tributaries of the Seine did not find it as easy to hire workers as had the local mills. They were built in isolated, hilly locations where there was little or no work for men, even in agriculture. If a family chose to move to the site of the new mills when the women could no longer find work in cottage spinning, it might simply reverse its unemployment problem. Now the women might be employed and the men unemployed, since the early mills hired far more women than men. Such a prospect hardly made the break with family and community entailed by work in the mills desirable, and most families preferred to stick things out in their home villages.

For better or worse, people were known in their local communities. Their families lived near them. Moreover, they were accustomed to working either in or near their homes and to alternating work in cottage industry and agriculture on a seasonal basis. The regimentation of work and the inflexibility of hours in the new factories did not appeal to them, and they resisted entering the mills as long as possible. Single women who worked in the mills often left at the approach of the harvest to return home and help their families. Mill owners were infuriated by such behavior. Given their new investment in machines, they were no longer content with a labor force that disappeared during the harvest. But in the early years of factory building, the difficulty of recruiting workers left them in no position to stop the seasonal migration of their workers. In fact, some mill owners found it so difficult to recruit workers that they tried to hire state orphans (*enfants assistés*), who would have become indentured servants.[53]

For a while, many women were able to resist moving to work in the new spinning mills by combining flax spinning with harvest work. In 1811, Sub-prefect Cartier estimated that there were ten thousand flax spinners in the Dieppe area who worked at their spinning wheels for only six months of the year. For the other six months they worked in the fields.[54] This was much more than the six weeks of harvest work that was usually available for women in the Caux and reflects the absence of men from the region as a result of conscription. By the turn of the century, seventy-four men from the commune of Auffay alone were in the army, and the number continued to rise as the war between France and the other European nations continued. (Absent soldiers constituted 13 percent of the total male population of the commune.)[55] Women took up some of the slack, working in the fields far beyond the harvest season, and this work, combined with flax spinning, allowed them to resist moving to the factories. Women's resistance to the offers of mill owners is particularly interesting because they could have earned three or four times more money in the mills than they earned in cottage spinning and agriculture,[56] and provides clear evidence of the degree to which women and their families preferred a familiar and traditional, albeit poor, life style to higher wages and the regulated hours and confinement of the factory.

The transition to factory spinning continued, however, despite the reluctance of the *cauchois* peasants to move, and it became more and more difficult for women to find cottage work. This was especially the case during the second decade of the nineteenth century, when the British blockade of the continent interrupted France's Atlantic trade and repeatedly threw the textile industry into depression. The decade between 1808 and 1818 was particularly bad. Periods of high wages and full employment alternated repeatedly with those of low wages and unemployment rates that could go as high as 50 percent. The spinning mill at St. Victor l'Abbaye frequently cut its work force in half (it employed sixty women and children at its peak), and, during the slump of 1813, the number of weavers in the Dieppe region fell from a high of 7,000 to 3,600. Although the government reports from this period fail to include them, the number of cottage spinners undoubtedly rose and fell with those of the factory spinners and hand weavers.[57]

Wages varied along with employment. In bad economic periods, those who were lucky enough to continue working did so for reduced piece rates. Female factory spinners in St. Victor l'Abbaye earned 1.00 franc a day in good periods and probably half that in bad periods. The piece rates for hand spinners must have varied similarly, although they probably began at a lower level. Weavers' earnings ranged from a high of 1.80 to 2.50 francs per day in 1814 to a low of 60 to 75 centimes in 1816. During bad economic periods, their problems were exacerbated by having to wait for the delivery of warps from Rouen (in good periods, they kept a supply of warps on hand) and by being forced to work with poor quality yarn that broke and required repair, thus slowing the rate at which they produced fabric.[58] For a while, the manufacturers hoped that the restoration of a Bourbon to the throne in 1814 would result in the stabilization of trade and economic recovery. Instead, it led to renewed competition with English fabric, and the textile industry entered another period of severe depression that lasted until 1818.[59]

Linen spinners and linen and *siamoise* weavers were even worse off than their counterparts in cotton, although the linen industry, as a whole, probably benefited from the difficulties of the cotton industry. Flax was grown in the Caux, and its supply was not affected by the Revolution and war. When cotton was in short supply, linen was usually still available. Wheels, looms, and spinning machines could not convert from one fiber to the other, however, and although linen workers may have been more steadily employed than cotton workers, they were always paid less than the latter. Between 1810 and 1818, the wages of linen weavers ranged from a high of 1.50 francs per day to a low of 75 centimes (compared to a range of 2.50 to 0.60 francs for cotton weavers during the same period). The earnings of flax spinners varied from a high of 35 to 40 centimes to a low of 15 centimes (compared with a high of 1.00 franc per day for factory cotton spinners).[60]

When slumps in the textile industry occurred in the summer, work in the fields alleviated some of the unemployment and misery.[61] But agriculture never employed all of the unemployed and underpaid textile workers during these periods, and the frequency of work shortages, combined with the overall decline in employment in cottage spinning, forced more and more women to seek new jobs either in the mills near Rouen or in something other than spinning.

Generally speaking, weavers were in a very different position than spinners. Spinning had been the bottleneck in the production process, and speeding it up had been the focus of the inventors' and merchants' attention. Mechanizing weaving was a more complicated and less urgent problem, and weaving continued to be done at hand looms until well into the nineteenth century. Ironically, weavers who watched the new machines eliminate the jobs of their wives and daughters, also found that the jenny, mule, and water-frame increased the demand for their work, a demand they could not meet even when they worked year-round rather than only part of the year at their looms. Whenever supplies of raw cotton were available, the merchants competed for the weavers' labor, raised their wages, and tried to keep them out of the agricultural work force, much to the dismay of the *fermiers* and *laboureurs* who found themselves forced to increase wages for harvest workers and domestic farm help just when their own demands for labor were increasing because of enclosure and the planting of artificial meadows.[62]

By the beginning of the nineteenth century, the number of cotton weavers in the Caux was steadily increasing. Some men abandoned agriculture, others switched from linen and *siamoise* to cotton weaving. In Auffay, the number of weaver grooms in the thirty-five years preceding the Eden Treaty (1751–86) was twenty, or 13.0 percent of all grooms who were marrying for the first time. During the transition to factory spinning (1787– 1817), the number increased to thirty-seven (19.2 percent). At the same time, linen weavers almost completely disappeared from the village. Seven of the weavers marrying between 1751 and 1786 were linen weavers (*toiliers*), compared with only one of those marrying between 1787 and 1817.[63]

Aside from periods of economic decline in the textile industry, *cau-chois* men found themselves in the enviable position of full employment and relatively high wages. Jobs in agriculture and weaving were increasing, and those in the merchant and artisan crafts remained constant. Men could not easily change occupations (merchant and artisan crafts required literacy and training; weaving required skill in stringing the loom and beating the fabric, etc.), but jobs remained plentiful in all the traditional male occupations and young men had some choice.

Women, on the other hand, faced a serious unemployment problem and low wages. As an employer of female labor, no other occupation came close to spinning, and no new female occupation appeared to fill the void that was created by its mechanization. Many women and their families had no choice but to migrate to the new mills. Others sought employment wherever they could find it. Eventually, their search for work matched the merchants' and large farmers' search for workers, and a dramatic change occurred in the Caux. Women began to be hired to do men's jobs.

The watershed year was 1808. In Auffay, three young women (aged twenty-two, twenty-five, and twenty-six) were hired as weavers. (All of them had different occupations in 1807 and earlier in 1808.) By 1818, fifteen women who married in Auffay between 1807 and 1817 were employed in weaving, either by the time they married or shortly thereafter. Seven of them were married to weavers. The other eight were married to day laborers, farm servants, carpenters, tanners, and tailors.[64] Clearly, the appearance of female weavers in the *État civil* was not simply the result of a decision to record women who helped their weaver husbands as weavers. Instead, what had previously been an all-male occupation was becoming an occupation for both men *and* women, and, like eighteenth-century spinners, women from a variety of families, not just from weaving families, were again finding work in the cottage textile industry.[65]

The employment of women in weaving broke a longstanding sexual division of labor in the textile industry. Before 1808, no Auffay woman was ever listed as employed in weaving in any parish or civil record. Auffay was not a peculiar case. Despite the fact that most of the looms used by men were small and could have been operated by women (and probably were unofficially), throughout the eighteenth century, women were never formally employed in and paid for weaving. This was a man's job. A woman might help when her husband, father, or brother was ill or absent for some reason, but she was not considered to be a weaver.

Similarly, men as well as young boys probably helped women with spinning and carding, but they were almost never regarded as spinners. In the 1796 census of the twenty-one communes in the canton of Auffay, no woman is listed as a weaver and very few adult men appear as spinners. The vast majority of male spinners were under the age of sixteen or over sixty. The few who were in their thirties and forties may have been operating fairly large cottage jennies or *mull jennies* in local factories.[66] This may have foreshadowed the change from female to male labor that was to occur later in spinning mills, but it is impossible to tell if this was the case from the mere listing of occupations.

In theory, the textile merchants could have employed women in men's jobs and paid them less than they normally paid men at almost any point. When women worked in sexually segregated occupations, they were always paid less than men. The best female spinners, for instance, were paid less than neophyte male weavers. But the textile merchants abided by the traditional sexual division of labor in the *pays* and did not hire women to weave even during the 1790s, when the interruption of trade and the building of spinning mills were eliminating jobs for cottage spinners, and women, who were desperate for jobs, would have accepted very low wages in weaving. As long as enough men were available to fill jobs regarded as men's work, women had no entrée to those jobs, even if it had occurred to them to apply.

The persistence of sexual divisions of labor like those in the *cauchois* textile industry, in spite of seemingly compelling economic reasons to end them, is a common phenomenon. Valerie Oppenheimer has suggested that one reason for this persistence is the conception that each sex has

Table 5.2. *Ages of male spinners, canton of Auffay,*
an IV (1796)

Ages	Number	Percentage
12–16	61	55.0
17–29	6	5.4
30–39	6	5.4
40–49	4	3.6
50–59	8	7.2
60–69	17	15.3
70–83	9	8.1
Total	111	100.0

Source: ADSM L367.

innate skills that suit it for the jobs it holds. Thus, far from appearing economically irrational, the sexual segregation of occupations appears economically rational, and the traditional system is maintained:

[Employers] desire workers with traits that are considered attributes of one sex or the other. . . . These traits may be innate or acquired – it matters little . . . which they are. Furthermore, they may not even be proven traits of one sex or the other – it is sufficient that employers believe they are, or believe that one sex has an advantage over the other in some important respect.[67]

By 1808, however, the new spinning machines were producing more yarn than male weavers could use. No longer content to let the size of the work force determine production, the merchants began to search for new workers. Production became more important than tradition. Attempts to draw more men into weaving by raising wages had limited success. Even when the wages of weavers were raised, weaving remained one of the most poorly paid male occupations, and artisans, merchants, and men with land to farm would not leave their established occupations for weaving. Older day laborers, the most readily transferable source of male labor, did not have the strength or skills required of weavers. Moreover, now that the quality of cotton yarn had improved, the merchants began to be more concerned with the quality of the fabric produced in the Caux. What they wanted was a young, strong, and easily trained work force. Young women filled the bill, *and* they could be, and would be, paid less than men. Unable to satisfy their demand for male workers, the merchants broke with tradition and offered weaving jobs to young women. Desperately in need of work to support themselves or to contribute to their families' incomes, and unable to find jobs in spinning, young women readily took the offered jobs.

As the spinning machines installed in mills became larger and heavier, a change in the sexual composition of the spinning labor force also occurred. Spinning lost its appellation as a soft occupation, and men became head spinners, employing women and children to work for them at subsidiary tasks.[68] This reversal in the sex typing of spinning, unlike the integration of women into hand weaving, was based on technological changes in the work process. Machine spinning was a new occupation. Male spinners could view themselves not as entering a previously female occupation, but as taking new jobs that only men could adequately fill. Such a change posed less threat to the concept of the sexual division of labor and the notion of male superiority than did the sexual integration of weaving. Moreover, the change in the gender of spinners took place on the periphery of the Caux, whereas the change in weaving took place in the villages.

At the outset, it may appear surprising that there is no evidence of men protesting the entry of women into weaving in the Caux. They were, after all, losing their monopoly on a very old and very large occupation. There was, however, no shortage of jobs for village men in this era, and women were not replacing men as weavers. They were, instead, being hired into a rapidly expanding labor force. If the merchants had attempted to break the male monopoly on weaving in an era of male unemployment, sharp protest undoubtedly would have ensued. (When spinning machines were introduced two decades earlier, they were dismantled and burned precisely because they were viewed as a threat to employment, in this case, female employment.) Now, however, there was a surfeit of job opportunities for men, and there was little, if any, opposition to the hiring of women weavers. Indeed, it was only *because* men had multiple job opportunities and were unable to meet the labor demands of the Rouen merchants that the change in weaving occurred. Thus, by 1818, not only was cottage cotton spinning dead, but also the identification of hand weaving as a male occupation was about to become a thing of the past. A new era was beginning.

6

~·~

The golden age of cottage weaving

In the nineteenth century, what had been a sexual division of labor between spinning (performed by women) and weaving (performed by men)
became a geographical division of labor. Spinning moved from the center
of the Caux to its borders, where it concentrated along the tributaries of
the Seine. By 1823, there were 121 spinning mills in the Seine-Inférieure.
Only ten were on small streams in the interior of the Caux, and most of
these would not survive for long. Ninety-five were in the valleys near
Rouen, nine were near Le Havre (the entry point of raw cotton), and
seven were near Dieppe. The yarn produced in these mills continued to
be put out into the villages of the Caux for weaving, however, and much
of the cloth produced for the Rouen merchants continued to come from
looms set up in the homes of the *cauchois* peasants.[1] Now, however, both
men and women worked at these looms.

The rise of cottage weaving

It is impossible to tell exactly how quickly spinning disappeared as a
cottage occupation in Auffay because the recording of female occupations in the civil registers is almost nonexistent for the quarter century
between 1803 and 1828.[2] After that period, however, female marriage
occupations are recorded more systematically, and it is clear that by the
1830s cottage spinning was dead in Auffay and the other *cauchois* villages. Only three of the 161 Auffay women who married between 1829
and 1850 were spinners,[3] and one suspects that they were working with
flax or hemp rather than with cotton because these fibers continued to be
spun by hand much longer than cotton did.

Although the water-powered *mull-jennies* killed cottage spinning as an
occupation for women, they created a steadily growing demand for cottage weavers. Their ranks rose from roughly 20,000 in the 1780s to
103,000 in 1810, and to 110,000 in 1848 – an increase in the neighbor-
hood of 500 percent over the late eighteenth century.[4] It was the golden
age of hand weaving.

It was also the age of the female weaver. The trickle of women into this work that began in 1808 became a veritable flood in the second quarter of the century. By 1850, women dominated the occupation. In Auffay, there were three times as many female as male weavers in 1851 (fifty-four women versus seventeen men),[5] and it was not an exceptional case. (See Table 6.8.) Throughout the Caux, female weavers outnumbered male weavers by midcentury. In St. Maclou de Folleville, 51 women and only 6 men were weavers; in Totes, 200 women and only 40 men; and in Biville la Baignard, 160 women and 120 men.[6]

The preponderance of female weavers means, of course, that many women wove while their husbands worked in agriculture or artisan crafts, just as their mothers and grandmothers had spun while their husbands had farmed or produced other goods. But in some families, everyone helped with the production of cloth, just as they had earlier when women and children spun and carded and men wove. Now, however, the major division of labor was based on age rather than on sex. Adults of both sexes wove. Young children wound yarn onto bobbins for the weavers' shuttles and ran errands for the family. Older children (age ten or eleven and up) learned to weave.[7] Isidore Mars, a native son of Auffay, remembered these families as being constantly at work:

Adolescents, the father and the mother wove: and one heard only the regular noise of the shuttle which passed and repassed through the threads, and the beat of the loom which regularized the work; . . . and it was often the children of the family who were obliged to take care of all the demands of commercial affairs, or of the agriculture work. They attended to the work, transported the merchandise, and worked their land, planted and harvested the crops.[8]

Despite the impression conveyed by Mars, age was not the only determinant of tasks in weaving families. Men and women did not weave the same type of cloth. Men continued to weave heavy fabrics as they had in the eighteenth century, whereas women produced the new light-weight calicos and kerchiefs. The rationale behind this division of labor was that calicos required less strength to produce (i.e., a less vigorous blow of the beater against the weft threads) than did heavier fabrics.[9] The difference in strength requirements, as well as in the actual strength of men and women, was slight, however, and the assertion of male superiority was far more important in the emergence of this new sexual division of labor than was physical strength.

When women first entered weaving, male dominance could be maintained by establishing an apprenticeship period for women. But weaving was not a highly skilled craft in the Caux, and any notion of women's inferiority at weaving that was based solely on experience must have quickly disappeared. The assignment of women to calico weaving was probably a more effective way of allowing men to retain the sense of superiority they had had when women performed the subsidiary task of spinning. It may also have been one of the devices used by the Rouen merchants to reduce male opposition to the hiring of female weavers in the first place.

Male weavers, in fact, quickly came to see the new division of labor as based on natural differences between the sexes that went far beyond physical strength and, therefore, as proof of their superiority. Charles Noiret, a Rouen weaver, declared in 1836 that although he saw no reason why women should not weave, he certainly did not think they could weave the same kinds of fabric as men. Women, he argued, "make the articles that are the most easily made and consequently are the least lucrative, *because* they are more suited to their (weaker) physical strength and their inferior intelligence." Men, on the other hand, "are *naturally* inclined toward the articles whose construction is more laborious and difficult *because* they procure higher benefits."[10]

Women may not have viewed the new division of labor in textiles as quite as natural as Noiret did, but their need for jobs to replace spinning left them in no position to challenge it or to argue for higher piece rates. Ironically, it was the low wages for which they would work (a situation apparently encouraged by the attitude of male weavers) and their assignment to the production of light fabrics that account for the speed with which women came to dominate weaving. Their lower piece rates made them more attractive employees than men, and they were employed in the sector of the weaving industry in which the demand for fabric and weavers was constantly growing. The decisions and values that gave male weavers a sense of superiority also undermined their dominance of the craft by confining them to the production of the least popular goods. It is important to note again, however, that a shortage of male weavers in relationship to the merchants' needs, *not* wage differentials, was the major force behind women's entry into the weaving labor force.

In its early stages, the mechanization of spinning led to high piece rates for weavers. Early in the century, it was possible for them to earn as much as 5.00 francs a day.[11] But when women entered the field and high piece rates were no longer necessary to attract a work force, weaving once again became one of the most poorly paid of rural occupations. During the second quarter of the century, male weavers earned only 0.75 to 1.25 francs a day in villages like Auffay.[12] Urban weavers earned half a franc a day more than their rural counterparts, but that was to compensate for higher living costs in the city and not to induce rural weavers to move to Rouen.[13]

Even though men's wages fell with the entry of women into weaving, they remained better than women's wages. Women were handicapped because they took up weaving only after they had lost jobs in spinning and were in no position to bargain for high wages or even for wages equal to those of men, and because they lived in a culture that thought it was appropriate to pay them less than men. It is unlikely that the women themselves thought they should be paid the same piece rates as the men. Consequently, they were able to earn only 0.50 to 0.90 francs a day as weavers.[14] Any woman who had no means of support other than weaving was in a very difficult position because the minimum necessary wage for survival, judging by what was paid to able-bodied indigents for public work, was 0.75 francs a day.[15]

For a variety of reasons, the survival of weaving families was often precarious. The growing separation between agriculture and cottage industry was partially responsible. Although some weavers continued to leave their looms during the month of August to help harvest the grain crops, the merchants now discouraged this practice. Unlike hand spinners who had abandoned their wheels to work on the harvest, factory spinners gradually lost their ties to the land and began to produce yarn year-round. With a continuous output of yarn, the merchants were no longer content with part-time weavers. Moreover, serious interruptions in weaving, such as harvest work, made it difficult for weavers to produce cloth of uniform quality. They lost their sense of rhythm when they worked in the fields, and when they returned to their looms, their work was uneven. Even though the Rouen merchants specialized in inexpensive cloth destined for peasants and workers, uniform quality was still desired. Therefore, weavers were urged to stay at their looms and not help with the harvest.[16] The benefit of this to the merchants is clear; for weaving families, however, it meant the loss of a period of intense work and high wages that had been an important supplement to their income from cottage manufacturing.

The putting-out system itself worked against the weavers. They had no contact with the Rouen merchants for whom they worked. Instead, they dealt solely with the porters who transported yarn and warps to them and retrieved their woven cloth. The porter was responsible for paying the weaver out of the wages he received from the *fabricant*.[17] Such a system hurt the weaver during times of crisis or inflation, and these occurred all too frequently in the first half of the nineteenth century. To sustain his own standard of living, the porter reduced the amounts he paid for cloth, thereby increasing his percentage and maintaining his income. Because the weavers were dispersed throughout the countryside and were desperately in need of work during these periods, they were in no position to refuse the reduced piece rates or even to hold out for smaller reductions.[18]

Compounding the weavers' problems were their fixed costs. New looms cost 100 to 150 francs, used looms 15 to 50 francs.[19] Although this encompassed a considerable range, weavers earning between 0.50 and 1.25 francs a day would have found even a used loom to be a substantial investment, and payments on a loom did not cease during bad economic periods. In addition, weavers needed a supply of bobbins and shuttles and had to pay wages for extra help if they made their own warps or did not have children to wind the yarn onto bobbins. Small wonder that men who had many other job options in this region allowed women to take over more and more of the weaving, and that Mars "heard only the regular noise of the shuttle" when he passed by the cottages of weavers. Constant work was necessary for survival.

A variety of circumstances thus combined to keep weavers on the bottom rungs of the *cauchois* economic ladder, despite the increased demand for their labor. In fact, when one examines average daily earnings, the weavers appear to have been worse off than day laborers, whose ranks they still occasionally joined during the harvest. By midcentury, *journaliers* were earning between 1.40 and 1.75 francs a day whereas male weavers earned only 0.75 to 1.25 francs.[20] The same differential existed for female weavers and day laborers. *Journalières* earned between 1.00 and 1.25 francs whereas female weavers earned 0.50 to 0.90 francs per day.[21]

Despite their lower daily earnings and fixed costs, and periodic slumps in the textile industry, there are indications that weaving families in Auffay were better off than day-laboring families. In 1849, for instance, the Municipal Council of Auffay was trying to find winter jobs for thirty able-bodied indigents.[22] The records, unfortunately, do not name the indigents, nor do they tell us what they did during the rest of the year, but it appears that these men and women were suffering from seasonal unemployment. Because agricultural work was still more seasonal than any other work in the Caux, most of these men and women were probably temporarily unemployed day laborers whose earnings between April and November were too low to carry them through the slack winter season

Table 6.1. *Families receiving free tuition for
children, 1833–1851*

Parents' occupations	Number of families
Day laborers	40
Weavers	7[a]
Artisans	6[a]
Other textile work	4
Miscellaneous	2
Total	59

[a] Four of the parents in each of these groups became day laborers
during the period that they had a child in school, raising the number of day-laboring families receiving tuition to 48.
Source: Auffay Municipal Council Records, 1833–1851.

and who could no longer find supplemental work in cottage industry
now that spinning and carding had moved into factories.

Day-laboring families also had much more trouble affording the 4.50
francs annual tuition charged by the Ecole Primaire Elémentaire in Auffay in 1833. The Municipal Council met annually to determine which
boys should be admitted to school without paying tuition. Between 1833
and 1851, eighty-eight children from fifty-nine families received free tuition. The majority of them came from day-laboring families. Weavers, in
contrast, rarely needed charity in order to send their sons to school, and
those weaving families who did need help were often on the verge of
sliding into the ranks of the day laborers.[23] (See Table 6.1.)

The expansion of sewing

Just as the mechanization of spinning produced jobs in weaving, the expansion of cloth production in the nineteenth century produced a rising
demand for dressmakers or seamstresses (*couturières*) in some parts of
the Caux. Sewing was a traditional, but small, employer of women in
this region. In Auffay, for instance, only 19 of the 127 women who married in the spinning era (1751–86) and whose occupations were recorded
in the marriage registers were seamstresses. At the turn of the nineteenth
century, sewing remained a good, but small, occupation for Auffay women.
In 1796, there were twenty-five seamstresses in the village, most of them
the wives and daughters of merchants and artisans, not of poor day laborers and weavers.[24] But 1851, sewing was the single largest employer
of women in Auffay, employing 14.4 percent of all adult women (64 out

of 444 women) and 20 percent of the adult women with a known occupation (321 women). (See Tables 6.7 and 6.8.) Although many of these women were wives or daughters of artisans and merchants, their ranks were now joined by wives and daughters of day laborers, tailors, and employees in a variety of textile-related jobs. Rarely were the wives and daughters of weavers seamstresses, but occasionally it did happen.[25]

The expansion of dressmaking introduced a new, albeit small, hierarchy into female occupations. In 1851, four married women in Auffay had apprentice seamstresses working for them and living in their homes. In the eighteenth century, spinners had worked with each other to help pass the time, but they did not work *for* each other. Now, for the first time outside of agriculture, women became the employers of other women.

The agricultural revolution

In many ways, the changes that occurred in agriculture during the proto-industrial period in the Caux were as dramatic as those that occurred in the cottage textile industry – artificial meadows replaced fallow fields, grain production increased, the labor force expanded, and women were hired to work alongside men in the fields. The latter three developments followed directly from the first. Planting fields with clover or legume crops instead of rotating them into fallow was first tried in the Caux in the mid-eighteenth century. Although some peasants were suspicious of the claims of greater production that were made about the new agriculture, and others could not afford the initial investment in seed, fertilizer, and labor, a steadily increasing number of farmers did move away from fallowing. In the *arrondissement* of Rouen, three-quarters of the arable land that was not planted in grain crops was in artificial meadows by 1836. In the canton of Totes, farther away from the Rouen markets that spurred acceptance of the new agriculture, the situation was almost exactly the same – 72.5 percent of the unplanted arable was planted with clover or some other meadow crop whereas only 27.5 percent lay fallow.[26]

Unlike the traditional grain crops, clover and legumes required weeding and hoeing; the increased numbers of cows and other animals, which the new crop rotations both made possible (by providing more food for them) and demanded (they were the sole source of fertilizer), required care. The combination made the new agriculture much more labor intensive than the old. Thus, as the new crops spread, so did the demand for day laborers and farm domestics. In Auffay, there was a threefold increase in the number of day laborers and farm servants between 1796 and 1851. In 1796, only seventy adults worked year-round as day labor-ers and domestics (10.5 percent of the adult population); by 1851, the number had risen to 201 (22.7 percent of the adult population).[27] (See Tables 6.7 and 6.8.) Auffay was not an exception. In seven other nearby communes that appear in both the 1796 and 1851 censuses, the number of day laborers increased from 195 to 673, again a threefold increase.[28]

As was the case with weaving, men could not meet the increased de-mand for agricultural workers, and women, who were badly in need of new jobs due to the mechanization of spinning, began to be hired. Whether women performed exactly the same tasks as male day laborers and farm domestics cannot be determined from the records, which simply list oc-cupations. New divisions of labor based on gender may have arisen in field work as in weaving. The presence of women in the fields on a year-round basis was new, however, and constituted a second breakdown in the longstanding sexual divisions of labor in the Caux. In the eighteenth century, spinners and other women had participated in cutting and gath-ering the harvest, but they had not worked in the fields at other times. Only women who were married to or were the widows of wealthy farm-ers, or those employed as domestic servants on large farms, worked pri-marily in agriculture, and they worked in the *masure* (farmyard) caring for animals and in the house, *not* in the fields. Even in 1796, when many village men were serving in the army, only one woman was listed as a day laborer in the Auffay census. In contrast, thirty-one women were year-round farm laborers by 1841. By 1851, the number had risen to sixty-three.[29] (See Tables 6.7 and 6.8.)

Auffay was far from unusual when it came to hiring female day labor-ers and farm domestics in the nineteenth century. By midcentury, women comprised between one-quarter and two-fifths of the agricultural labor force in the region.[30] In Auffay, they constituted 41 percent of the day laborers and 30 percent of the farm domestics. In neighboring com-munes, they constituted almost 50 percent of the day laborers (442 out of 892) and 39 percent of the farm domestics (230 out of 590).[31]

For a variety of reasons, women did not come to dominate agriculture the way they did weaving, despite the fact that their employers could and did pay them less than men. In the first place, agriculture did not expand at the same pace as weaving. Whereas there was a threefold increase in farm jobs in areas like Auffay, there was a fivefold increase in weaving jobs. Men were not being replaced with women in either field. Instead, new jobs were going to women, and they came to dominate only the more rapidly expanding occupation. Second, as the wages of weavers fell below those of day laborers and the appearance of mechanical looms harbingered the end of the weaving era,[32] some men may have begun to regard farm work as preferable to weaving and may have made greater efforts to keep women out of agriculture, or at least to limit their numbers, than they did in cottage industry. Conversely, women may have preferred weaving to farm work, even though female day laborers were paid better than female weavers (1.00 to 1.25 versus 0.50 to 0.90 francs), because weaving (and sewing), like spinning in the eighteenth century, could be performed in a woman's home, making it possible for her to integrate at least minimal childcare with paid employment. Mothers who worked in the fields had to find someone else to care for their children or leave them alone.

Women's work and the family economy

The creation of new jobs for women in weaving, sewing, and farming enabled the family economy to continue to function throughout the first half of the nineteenth century. Women's earnings were especially important in families where men were employed in the two most poorly paid of the male occupations – weaving and day laboring. Men in these occupations could marry and make ends meet only if they chose women who had steady jobs. They remained close to the subsistence line just as their eighteenth-century forebearers had, and a period of unemployment or inflation made it impossible for them to survive without going into debt or relying on charity.[33]

Unfortunately for many women and their families, the diversification of female jobs that occurred with the demise of spinning and the enclosing of fields did not result in full female employment. In 1796, 248 Auffay women were employed in cottage work, that is, in spinning and dressmaking (67.9 percent of adult women). In 1851, only 118 women were employed in the cottage trades of weaving and dressmaking (26.5 percent). An additional 77 were now employed as day laborers and farm domestics. But even when these women are added to the cottage workers, still only 195 women are accounted for (43.8 percent).[34] There is a large number of women with unrecorded occupations in 1851, some of whom might have been employed in these occupations, at least as their mothers' assistants. The absence of female occupations from the census does not seem to have been entirely a recording failure, however. Whereas spinning had employed women virtually from the cradle to the grave, the new female jobs did not. Weaving and day laboring required more physical strength than young girls and older women had. Weavers needed strong legs to work the pedals and strong arms to beat the weft threads together, actions they performed between fifteen and twenty thousand times a day.[35] Day laborers had to have the stamina to work all day in the fields, hoeing, digging, planting, weeding, and harvesting. Girls and boys usually began to weave between ages twelve and fifteen and were at their peak between twenty-five and forty.[36] The same is probably true for field workers. Needlework did not require strength, but it did require good eyesight and steady fingers and was dominated by young women. A woman was no longer assured of lifelong employment, nor, perhaps, were all young women able to perform the new jobs. (See Tables 6.7 and 6.8.)

By the middle of the nineteenth century, elderly women were much more likely to end up unemployed and living on charity than was the case at the beginning of the century. In 1796, no Auffay woman was listed as a mendicant on the census, although many of the spinners may have been very poor and in need of aid.[37] In contrast, in 1849, the Municipal Council of Auffay compiled a list of forty-nine people who were either infirm (*invalide*) or the heads of families that were too large for them to support without aid. Twenty-six of them were women – fourteen widows, four wives whose husbands were apparently absent (perhaps in search of work), and eight spinsters. The list contains no information about the ages of these women or the reasons they either could not work or could not earn enough to support themselves and their children.[38] The 1851 census sheds some light on the situation, however. In that year, only eleven women were listed as mendicants by the census taker. The reasons for the difference in the numbers are unclear, but the mendicants on the census are probably those who could find no work at all. Women who needed assistance in addition to their earnings probably appear on the census as employed. What is significant about the census information is the high average age of the female mendicants – sixty-seven.[39] They were simply too old to work in the fields or at a loom. Clearly, unemployment in old age had become a problem for women and for the village (which, in 1849, estimated that it needed 3,550 francs to help the indigent and that it had only 731 francs).[40] For many women, the diversification of jobs that occurred with the mechanization of spinning and enclosure of fields may have created more difficulty in finding and keeping a desirable job than it increased opportunity and variety.

Women were not the only ones who had difficulty supporting themselves in the nineteenth century. In addition to the twenty-six women who needed aid in 1849, twenty-three men were either unable to work or unable to support their families on their earnings. As only three men were listed as mendicants on the 1851 census, it seems likely that most of the twenty-three fell into the latter category, that is, they were employed but unable to support themselves and their families on their earnings. This was not a new problem in the Caux. Throughout the proto-industrial period, piece rates for weavers and wages for day laborers were too low to enable a man to support a family without the contributions of his wife and older children. What was new in the nineteenth century was the inability of many daughters and older women to find jobs. Hence, an increased number of families needed charity even during good harvest years because they depended on only one breadwinner.

Thus, although the opportunity to work as weavers and day laborers and the expansion of sewing enabled many women to continue to contribute to their families' income after the demise of spinning, not all women were able to do this. The heady days of the early nineteenth century, when male weavers earned high wages and women were drawn into the rapidly expanding cottage weaving labor force, were gradually replaced by years of hard work for low pay and a constant struggle by families to make ends meet and to find jobs for their daughters.

Village life in the weaving era

In many ways, life in Auffay remained the same in the weaving era as it had been in the spinning era. It was a village of merchants, artisans, peasants, and cottage textile workers. The noble Thomas family continued to live in the Bosmelet château and to rent land to wealthy tenant farmers. Visiting smiths and merchants arrived periodically, and the weekly markets and triannual fairs brought neighboring villagers into the marketplace to trade their goods and purchase others. By the beginning of the weaving era, the commune had acquired a substantial population for this region of small villages and *hameaux,* and it changed little in size throughout the first half of the nineteenth century, growing by less than a hundred residents between 1800 (population 1,149) and 1851 (population 1,247).[41] (See Table 2.1.)

In some important ways, however, Auffay did change during the proto-industrial era and especially during the weaving era. The general ambiance and living conditions improved. Streets were widened, swampy land was drained, large trees were cut to make the village lighter, and thatched roofs were gradually replaced by wood and tile, a development that both improved conditions inside the houses and decreased the danger of fire.

Figure 6.1. Auffay in 1856 (*Source:* Isidore Mars, *Auffay, ou le vieil Isnelville* [Rouen, 1857].)

The presbytery was improved by the village council, a new cemetery was established, and the central marketplace was enhanced by planting trees on its periphery, renovating the buildings, and turning what had served as a pasture for animals on market days into a village square. In 1846, a school house was purchased by the village, the *mairie* was remodeled, and the Municipal Council began attempts to acquire a fire station, railroad station, bank, and post office for the village. Children grew up on stories of wolves roaming the countryside and invading the village in the winter, but they no longer feared they would encounter one.[42] (See Figure 6.1.)

In the late 1830s, the industrial revolution materialized in Auffay in the form of a small spinning mill that employed young women and men in almost equal numbers. (In 1851, eighteen Auffay men and twenty-two Auffay women worked in the mill.)[43] As the only factory workers in the village, the men and women who worked in the mill stood apart from the other residents. Far more than the cottage weavers, they formed a village proletariat, working with machines they did not own for an employer they did not know.[44] They quickly formed a community of their own, not only working together but also marrying each other,[45] further separating themselves from the rest of the village population.

Other changes were occurring. Auffay and other large villages in the
Caux were becoming more secular and less isolated, and their residents
better educated. The Church never acquired the kind of influence it had
had before the Revolution. Many couples had only civil marriages. There
were twice as many marriages during March (Lent) and almost four times
as many during December (Advent) than there had been before the Revolution when everyone was married in the Church. (See Table 2.12.) And
sixty-five women bore illegitimate children, a marked increase over the
fifteen unmarried women who bore children in the village during the
spinning era (1751–86).[46]

Clearly, the Church's influence and power were on the decline. They
were not totally gone, however. Some couples who had had only civil
weddings were eventually persuaded to solemnize their marriages in the
Church. Most couples avoided marrying during Lent and Advent. Moreover, when it came to their children, people were unwilling to take many
risks. They gave them at least one saint's name and had them baptized,
even when they themselves had had only a civil wedding.[47]

As the century progressed, more and more young men began to leave
the Caux to seek jobs in Rouen or even Paris. (See Chapter 8.) Through
them, information about life in the city made its way back to the villages.
Perhaps even more significantly for some villages, the Rouen – Dieppe
railroad was completed in 1848.[48] Villages that, like Auffay, were stops
on the line suddenly had easy and quick access to the city.

The pull toward the new and the secular, which came with increased
rural – urban contact, is reflected in children's names. By the middle of
the nineteenth century, children were being given more complicated, and
varied names than they were in the mideighteenth century.[49] (See Tables
2.3 and 2.4.) Mary was still the most popular female name, but it was
definitely in decline. Between 1841 and 1850, only 21 percent of the girls
were christened Mary (32 out of 154 girls), in contrast to 83 percent (103
out of 124) of those born between 1751 and 1760. One hundred and
seventeen different names in a variety of combinations were given to girls
in this decade, and, unlike the mideighteenth century, no two girls received exactly the same name. Little girls bore names ranging from the
traditional, like Marie Aimée, to the less traditional, like Marie Olym-
piade, to the new, like Stephanie Zenobie and Arsene Anastasie. Names
ending in *ine* were particularly popular and far from traditional. There
were Alphonsines, Alexandrines, Celestines, Clementines, Josephines, and
Victorines, to mention only a few. Simple, traditional names were given
new endings. There were Julies, Julittes, and Juliennes, and Roses, Rosas,
Rosalies, and Rosines.

Traditionally, no one name had dominated boys' names as Mary had dominated girls' names, but 26.9 percent (32 out of 119) received Jean as their first *prénom* in the 1750s, and there were 13 Jean Baptistes. As was the case with girls, boys had shared a total of only 30 names used in various combinations. In contrast, the 146 boys born between 1841 and 1850 received 103 different names used in combinations, and no two boys received the same combination. Boys' names varied from the traditional, like Jean Baptiste Charles, to the political, like Senateur Theodule and Julien Napoleon, to combinations of the new and the old, like Jules Casimir and Charles Victrix. New male names were also achieved by adding new endings to old names – there were Victors, Victrices, and Victoriens – but most of the variety came from increasing the number of completely different names. Names were no longer something that children shared; instead they denoted individuals. Even if all children were called simply by the first of their *prénoms,* which was unlikely, most would have known who was being addressed.

Judging by the ability of brides and grooms to sign their names, there appears to have been little change in the number of Auffay boys receiving some education throughout the proto-industrial period. The number of grooms who could sign their names fluctuated only slightly from decade to decade and in the weaving era never fell below 65.9 percent. Female literacy, on the other hand, improved markedly during the 1790s and early 1800s compared to the spinning era and then declined again, reflecting far greater variation in the availability of instruction for girls than for boys. (See Table 2.2.)

The improvement in female literacy during the years of the Revolution may simply reflect the success of the Soeurs Grises in teaching girls to write in the last years of the *Ancien Régime,* whereas the decline may reflect their departure during the Revolution. If this is so, then the sisters were more effective educators than Mlle. Benard, who ran a school in Auffay in the early nineteenth century, although she might deserve credit for the fact that female literacy rates were higher throughout the weaving era than they had been before the arrival of the Soeurs Grises. (During the spinning era only 43.2 percent of brides could sign their names versus 57.6 percent in the weaving era.)[50]

As in the eighteenth century, the likelihood that a child would receive an education continued to vary by occupational group throughout the first half of the nineteenth century. Children from the poorest families (those who became day laborers, domestic servants, and weavers) were unable to attend school as long as their families needed their earnings and generally remained illiterate. Almost two-thirds of male day laborers

Table 6.2. *Male literacy by occupation, Auffay,*
1801–1850[a]

Marriage occupation	Total	Illiterate	Percent Illiterate
Factory spinner	14	10	71.4
Domestic (farm)	39	25	64.1
Day laborer	38	24	63.2
Weaver	43	17	39.5
Tailor	10	2	20.0
Merchant or artisan	133	21	15.8
Cultivator	22	0	—
Miscellaneous	28	3	10.7
Unknown	1	0	—
Total	328	102	31.1

[a] For comparative purposes, see Table 4.2.
Source: ADSM Civil Registers, Auffay, 1801–50. First marriages only.

and farm domestics and two-fifths of male weavers were unable to sign their names. The literacy rate was worse for women. Seventy percent of female servants and 74 percent of female weavers were illiterate. On the other hand, men and women who were property owners or substantial farmers were literate, as were the vast majority of merchants, artisans, and seamstresses.[51]

By the 1840s, the least likely of all children to receive an education in Auffay were those who worked in the new spinning mill. This fact may not reflect their families' poverty as much as it does the young age at which people entered the mill. In any case, these young men and women were overwhelmingly illiterate, an ominous indication of what the effects of industrialization could be, even though the Caux would experience industrialization primarily through the loss of jobs and rural exodus, not through the formation of an illiterate rural proletariat. (See Tables 6.2 and 6.3.)

The demise of cottage weaving

During the early nineteenth century, the population of the Caux continued to grow as it had in the spinning era through a combination of favorable birth – death ratios and immigration. However, following the appearance of factories with mechanical looms on the fringe of the *pays*, in 1825, the population increase that had begun in the *pays* in the eigh-

Table 6.3. *Female literacy by occupation, Auffay,*
1801–1850[a]

Marriage occupation	Total	Illiterate	Percent Illiterate
Factory spinner	16	14	87.5
Weaver	47	35	74.5
Unlisted, later weaver	24	14	58.3
Servant	17	12	70.6
Seamstress	53	8	15.1
Merchant	13	1	7.7
Cultivator	6	0	—
Other textile	21	5	23.8
Miscellaneous	12	2	16.7
No occupation	13	0	—
Unknown	107	40	37.4
Total	329	131	39.8

[a] For comparative purposes, see Table 4.1.
Source: ADSM Civil Registers, Auffay, 1801–50. First marriages only.

teenth century came to a halt. The arrondissement of Yvetot in the center of the Caux began to lose population in 1836; the arrondissement of Neufchâtel, in 1841; and the arrondissement of Dieppe, in 1861. The arrondissement of Rouen, on the other hand, was steadily gaining population, as increasing numbers sought work in the spinning and weaving mills.[52] Even communes like Auffay, which maintained steady or slightly growing populations during this period, were experiencing emigration. Between 1801 and 1851, the natural increase of the Auffay population was 238 (there were 1,478 births and 1,240 deaths), but the village grew by only 98 persons.[53] By the 1850s, the handwriting was on the wall as far as the future of cottage weaving was concerned. As the Prefect of the Seine-Inférieure declared in 1854, "Hand weaving is condemned to disappear, even though it fights desperately against the factories."[54]

The weavers did indeed struggle to survive the introduction of the new machines. Throughout the proto-industrial period, they were among the most sedentary of all occupational groups in the Caux. They tended to live where they were born and to marry women from the same village. Of the seventy-nine male weavers who married in Auffay between 1751 and 1850, for instance, fifty-three were Auffay residents as were their brides.[55] Their roots were deep, and moving to Rouen was not attractive. Once there, they congregated in the Boulevard Cauchois area, where they

Table 6.4. *Population changes in the Auffay region, 1800–1891*[a]

Commune	1800	1831	1851	1872	1891
Auffay	1,149	1,137	1,247	1,363	1,413
Biville la Baignard	570	745	761	647	612
Bracquetuit	630	572	528	458	406
Cressy	316	?	408	281	328
Cropus	306	?	304	257	277
Fresnay le Long	312	362	279	220	179
Gonneville	787	832	736	660	558
Heugleville sur Scie	793	848	815	776	721
Montreuil	639	623	528	473	482
Notre Dame du Parc	155	179	187	165	157
St. Denis sur Scie	458	525	527	473	406
St. Hellier	270	?	602	627	479
St. Victor l'Abbbaye	582	637	602	570	526
Ste. Geneviève	486	516	531	426	378
Totes	510	746	933	830	811
Vassonville	305	341	355	331	337
Total	8,268	?	9,343	8,557	8,070

[a] Communes that merged have been omitted from the Table.
Note: For the location of the communes, see Figure 5.1. With the notable exception of Auffay, itself, the communes in this region began to lose population in the 1830s, 1840s, and 1850s.
Source: ADSM L367, 6M1, 6M82bis, 6M229bis, 6M351.

lived and worked among other displaced weavers. Whenever possible, they preferred to walk long distances to work in local mills rather than move to Rouen or the other weaving cities. Agricultural work, the major rural alternative to weaving, was hardly more desirable than moving for these men and women who were accustomed to working indoors, not outdoors, and whose skills were not applicable to farm labor. Eventually, however, virtually all weavers had to make one of two choices – migration and factory work or day laboring. Most chose migration.[56] (See Table 6.4.)

As was the case half a century earlier when spinning mills were built, very few of the new weaving *ateliers* or workshops were built in the interior of the Caux. Instead, they sprang up along the Seine River and the littoral. In those regions, hand weaving disappeared rapidly. In the center of the Caux, it continued to survive fairly well until the 1860s, although the number of weavers as well as their wages were in decline. In 1863, the combination of renewed competition with English fabric and a severe shortage of cotton (a result of the American Civil War)

Table 6.5. *Marriage occupations of women, Auffay, 1751–1850[a]*

	Date of Marriage					
	1751–1786		1787–1817		1818–1850	
Occupation	Number	Percent-age	Number	Percent-age	Number	Percent-age
Agriculture:						
Cultivators	4	2.6	6	3.1	8	3.3
Day laborers	2	1.3	0	—	4	1.6
Total	6	3.9	6	3.1	12	4.9
Nonagriculture:						
Domestics[b]	18	11.7	6	3.1	17	7.0
Spinners	80	52.0	52	27.0	18	7.4
Weavers	0	—	8	4.1	44	18.1
Seamstresses	19	12.3	22	11.4	44	18.1
Textile related	0	—	0	—	12	4.9
Merchants	8	5.2	9	4.7	5	2.1
Artisans	0	—	0	—	2	0.9
Miscellaneous	2	1.3	0	—	3	1.2
Total	127	82.5	97	50.3	145	59.7
No occupation	0	—	0	—	10	4.1
Unknown	21	13.6	90[c]	46.6	76[c]	31.3
Total	154	100.0	193	100.0	243	100.0

[a] Based on first marriages only.
[b] Some of these women probably worked on farms.
[c] The large number of women in the unknown category is due to recording failures and does not necessarily mean these women had no occupations. From 1751 to 1792, marriage occupations of women were usually recorded. From 1793 to 1808, recording was spotty. From 1809 to 1826, occupations were recorded for only 16 out of 128 brides. Beginning in 1827, women's marriage occupations were again recorded systematically. More than half of the women without marriage occupations appear with recorded occupations in later birth and/or death records, some within a year of their marriages.
Source: ADSM Parish and Civil Registers, Auffay, and Family Reconstitution Study.

drove many hand weavers to find other work. Although hand looms still outnumbered mechanical looms by five to one in the early 1870s, hand weavers were producing only coarse *rouenneries* for which the market was steadily declining. All of the finer, lighter-weight calicos were being produced on mechanical looms. The end was at hand. No matter how many hours they worked, and no matter how much they preferred weaving to day laboring or other occupations, by the 1880s, it was virtually impossible for hand weavers to earn a living wage. The Caux became a

Table 6.6. *Marriage occupations of men, Auffay, 1751–1850*[a]

Occupation	Date of Marriage					
	1751–1786		1787–1817		1818–1850	
	Number	Percent-age	Number	Percent-age	Number	Percent-age
Agriculture:						
Cultivators	11	7.2	12	6.2	16	6.6
Day laborers	31	20.1	17	8.8	38	15.6
Domestics[b]	9	5.8	19	9.8	27	11.1
Total	51	33.1	48	24.8	81	33.3
Nonagriculture:						
Spinners (factory)	0	—	0	—	12	4.9
Weavers	20	13.0	37	19.2	22	9.1
Tailors	6	3.9	7	3.6	5	2.1
Textile related	0	—	3	1.6	4	1.6
Merchants	19	12.3	19	9.8	17	7.0
Artisans	41	26.6	65	33.7	73	30.1
Professionals	5	3.3	3	1.6	16	6.6
Miscellaneous	9	5.8	4	2.1	10	4.1
Total	100	64.9	138	71.6	159	65.5
Unknown	3	2.0	7	3.6	3	1.2
Total	154	100.0	193	100.0	243	100.0

[a]Based on first marriages only.
[b]Some of these men may not have worked on farms, but from other records it appears that almost all male domestics were farm workers.
Source: ADSM Parish and Civil Registers, Auffay, and Family Reconstitution Study.

purely agricultural area and, ironically, suffered the problem the farmers had feared cottage industry would create – a severe agricultural labor shortage – as day laborers followed the weavers out of the region to seek higher pay and, they hoped, easier work in the factories.[57] The proto-industrial era was over.

Table 6.7. *Occupational distribution of Auffay in 1796*

Occupation	Men		Women		Total	
	Number	Percent-age	Number	Percent-age	Number	Percent-age
Agriculture:						
Cultivators and proprietors	23	7.6	25	6.9	48	7.2
Day laborers	37	12.2	1	0.3	38	5.7
Farm servants	30	9.9	2	0.5	32	4.8
Total	90	29.7	28	7.7	118	17.7
Nonagriculture:						
Domestics	0	—	14	3.8	14	2.1
Spinners (cottage)	7[a]	2.3	223	61.1	230	34.4
Weavers	32	10.6	1	0.3	33	5.0
Seamstresses/ tailors	6	2.0	25	6.8	31	4.6
Textile related	4	1.3	1	0.3	5	0.7
Merchants	54	17.8	48	13.2	102	15.3
Artisans	93	30.7	19	5.2	112	16.8
Miscellaneous	14	4.6	4	1.1	18	2.7
Total	210	69.3	335	91.8	545	81.6
Mendicants	1	0.3	0	—	1	0.1
Unknown	2	0.7	2	0.5	4	0.6
	3	1.0	2	5	5	0.7
Total adults	303	100.0	365	100.0	668	100.0

[a]These male spinners were all young boys (average age 13.3 years) whose mothers were also spinners.
Source: ADSM L367.

Table 6.8. *Occupational distribution of Auffay in 1851*

Occupation	Men		Women		Total	
	Number	Percent-age	Number	Percent-age	Number	Percent-age
Agriculture:						
Cultivators and proprietors	49	11.1	31	7.0	80	9.0
Day laborers	91	20.6	63	14.2	154	17.4
Farm servants	33	7.5	14	3.1	47	5.3
Total	173	39.2	108	24.3	281	31.7
Nonagriculture:						
Domestics	14	3.2	22	5.0	36	4.1
Spinners (factory)	18	4.1	22	5.0	40	4.5
Weavers	17	3.8	54	12.1	71	8.0
Seamstresses/ tailors	8	1.8	64	14.4	72	8.1
Textile related	10	2.2	11	2.5	21	2.4
Merchants	37	8.4	17	3.8	54	6.1
Artisans	126	28.5	0	—	126	14.2
Miscellaneous	32	7.2	12	2.7	44	5.0
Total	262	59.2	202	45.5	464	52.4
Mendicants	3	0.7	11	2.5	14	1.6
Unknown (adults)	4	0.9	123	27.7	127	14.3
	7	1.6	134	30.2	141	15.9
Total adults	442	100.0	444	100.0	886	100.0

Source: ADSM 6M83.

~~~~~~

Marriage and family in proto-industrial Auffay

On February 10, 1783, Marie Marguerite Varin, a domestic servant, married Jacques Etienne Frichet, a weaver. He was twenty-seven and she was twenty-five. Neither had been married before, and both were residents of Auffay.[1] If the wedding was typical, the couple and the wedding party were conducted to and from the church by a violinist dressed in culottes and a frock coat who, after the ceremony, played while people danced and celebrated the nuptials.

Following the established custom, the fiddler would have returned to Jacques Etienne and Marie Marguerite's home on February 11 to lead them once more to the church for a celebration Mass. When they left the church this time, however, the couple was not led home by the violinist. Instead, they found a group of friends and a donkey waiting for them in front of the cemetery wall. They were mounted on the donkey who, if he was cooperative, heightened the comic mood by braying loudly. The donkey was then led through the streets by a long rope. Two young men were stationed on either side to keep the feted couple from falling or jumping off and escaping. A third lighted the way with an old stable lantern held aloft on the end of a pole, while a fourth encouraged the donkey with a bouquet of hay stuck on the end of a stick. After their public promenade, the couple was led home to a dinner, where they were seated amidst the revelers and subjected to further jokes and puns. When the meal ended and the village interest in the marriage was well established, the couple was finally left alone to begin their life together.[2]

After the wedding, Marie Marguerite became a spinner, an occupation she seems to have pursued consistently for the next forty-four years, although her ability to earn money must have seriously deteriorated after the introduction of spinning machines. Jacques Etienne, like many men, alternated between weaving and day laboring, perhaps with the seasons and perhaps with fluctuations in the availability of warps and weft yarn. The marriage lasted until 1827, when Marie Marquerite died at the age of seventy. Jacques Etienne survived for another twenty-three months, dying in mid-March of 1829.[3]

In many ways, Marie Marguerite Varin and Jacques Etienne Frichet were a typical eighteenth-century couple. They married well into their twenties, presumably following several years of work during which they accumulated some savings and acquired the skills that would enable them to support themselves and a family. Although we do not know when Marie Marguerite became a domestic servant or exactly what kind of work she did in that position, she probably began to work around age fourteen, learning to feed and care for farm animals, to prepare food for a family and large groups of harvest workers, and to spin flax or cotton. We can assume that, like most young women, her major goal in life was to save enough from her meager earnings to purchase the household goods that constituted a dowry. It would have been her responsibility to bring to the marriage the pots and pans, dishes, and linens that rudimentary housekeeping required. She would also have provided some simple furniture, such as, a table and benches, a mattress (and perhaps a bedstead and pillows if she had saved a lot of money), an armoire in which to store her clothes and linens, and because she was a spinner, a spinning wheel. Long years of work were required for a woman to save enough money for a dowry, and Marie Marguerite could consider herself fortunate to have done it by the time she was twenty-five.[4]

Jacques Etienne probably learned to weave from his weaver father when he was between the ages of twelve and fifteen, so that by the time he married at twenty-seven, he had already been working for twelve to fifteen years.[5] His contribution to the marriage would have included a place for the two of them to live, perhaps some furniture, and, because he was a weaver, a loom. Acquiring skills and savings and, in some cases, waiting to inherit either land, a cottage, or the customers for a shop took men at least as long as it did women to acquire a dowry, as Jacques Etienne's marriage age indicates.[6]

As was usually the case in the eighteenth century, marriage was followed almost immediately by pregnancy, and Marie Marguerite bore her first child nine months after the wedding. She then bore children at intervals of two to three years for the next ten years. Unfortunately, as was also common in this era of high mortality, only two of their five children survived to adulthood. Two died in infancy and one in childhood.[7]

Although Jacques Etienne Frichet and Marie Marguerite Varin were a fairly typical eighteenth-century couple, the important question is, Were they a typical *cauchois* couple? The question is important because historians have argued that the improved employment opportunities and income that came with proto-industrialization led to significant changes in demographic behavior. In general, cottage workers appear to have been more likely to marry and to have married at younger ages than their peasant counterparts because their marriages were based not on the inheritance of land or businesses and painstakingly acquired dowries, but on current earnings and optimistic assumptions about future earnings.

The major evidence for this part of the theory of proto-industrialization has been provided by the work of Franklin Mendels, David Levine, and Rudolf Braun. In his pioneering work on Flanders, for instance, Franklin Mendels found that marriage frequency entered an upward spiral during the proto-industrial period, with the number of marriages increasing after good years when the price of linen fabric was high in comparison to that of grain and not declining in bad years.[8] Even more dramatic, Levine found a five-and-a-half-year decline in the mean age at first marriage for both men and women in the late eighteenth and early nineteenth centuries, when framework knitting was at its peak in Shepshed.[9] Although Braun presents no quantitative evidence, he found in his study of the Zurich highlands that marriages were "more numerous and earlier" in areas of cottage industry than in purely agricultural regions.[10] Such unions, often called "beggar marriages" because the young couple had not acquired the dowry, economic skills, and property that were usually regarded as prerequisites for a successful marriage,[11] occurred, to use the language of Hans Medick, because "maximum income opportunities were based on the maximum work capacity of both marriage partners, which reached its optimum at a comparatively early age."[12]

As marriage age fell in Shepshed and the Zurich highlands, the size of families increased, partially because women began childbearing earlier and were at risk to bear children for a longer period of time. In an era when *coitus interruptus* was the major method of controlling conception, lowering the marriage age almost automatically increased the number of children women bore, especially since the additional years added to their childbearing period were the most fertile years of their youth and young adulthood.[13] The increase in family size also appears to have resulted from the availability of proto-industrial work for children, a situation that encouraged couples to begin childbearing early and to have many children.[14]

In the short run, earlier marriage, low celibacy rates, and high fertility rates maximized the income of families at an early point in their life cycle. Families with two relatively young adults and several children working full time could earn more than families in which the parents were past their prime working years or in which there were no working-age children, especially since families without children might have to hire other children to work for them.

In the long run, however, this rural, proletarian demographic behavior set the stage for family and regional crises as the labor supply outstripped the demand for cottage workers. The situation became acute in the nineteenth century, when proto-industries began to lose ground to urban factory production. At first, families attempted to stave off destitution by taking in boarders and extended kin. In proto-industrial Shepshed, for instance, the framework knitting industry was in decline by 1851, and one out of every eight knitting households contained two or more nuclear family units. In contrast, only one out of twenty nonknitting households contained coresident families.[15] This stopgap measure succeeded only briefly, however, because the competition of machine-produced goods, combined with an overabundance of hand workers, drove wages lower and lower. In the end, the only viable solution for most families to the problem presented by the new machines was urban migration, especially since the demographic growth engendered by low marriage ages and high birth rates had produced rural populations that far outstripped the need for agricultural workers.

The data and arguments presented by Mendels, Levine, and Braun dovetailed so nicely that historians began to regard as proved the hypothesis that proto-industrialization caused significant changes in demographic behavior. Pierre Deyon, for instance, asserted that there was "no doubt" that proto-industrialization led to earlier marriages.[16] Hans Medick virtually elevated the theory to the status of economic law in statements like the following: "The new objective conditions of exploiting the family labour of rural cottage industry . . . demanded the formation of a new family economy as early as possible in the life cycle of young men and women."[17] Subsequent analyses of demographic behavior in eighteenth- and nineteenth-century villages have, however, raised questions about the generalizability of the Mendels – Levine – Braun thesis. Myron Gutmann and René Leboutte have published some of the results of their current research on three proto-industrial Belgian villages, results that show the mean female marriage age remaining high and stable throughout the eighteenth and early nineteenth centuries.[18] Similarly, James Lehning has shown that proto-industrialization did not inevitably lead to lower marriage ages and higher marriage frequency in the Department of the Loire.[19] And Rab Houston and K. D. M. Snell have questioned the link between proto-industrialization and falling marriage ages posited by Levine by pointing out that the mean marriage age for women was also falling in some non-proto-industrial, eighteenth-century villages as well as in Shepshed.[20]

Auffay provides an additional challenge to the Mendels – Levine – Braun thesis. In terms of the products produced for the putting-out merchants – yarn and fabric – and the high proportion of the population involved in this production, Auffay was a typical proto-industrial village. In terms of demographic behavior, however, Auffay villagers were far from typical proto-industrial workers. The major question to be addressed is why proto-industrialization led to new, proletarian demographic behavior in some regions and not in others. The major answer to this question lies, I believe, in the sexual composition of the proto-industrial labor force. Despite the universality of sexual divisions of labor (especially in textile production) in Western Europe and England, there has been no analysis of the numbers of women and men employed in cottage industry in the proto-industrial literature. It appears, however, that the industries in Shepshed, Flanders, and the Zurich highlands employed entire families rather than one sex specifically. In Auffay, by contrast, very few families totally depended on the putting-out merchants. Instead, women whose husbands and fathers were employed in a wide range of occupations worked first as spinners and then as weavers for the Rouen *fabricants*. This difference in the labor force led to significantly different marriage and childbearing patterns than those discovered in Shepshed, Flanders, and the Zurich highlands.

Marriage patterns

Celibacy rates

In keeping with the typical proto-industrial pattern, celibacy rates were low in Auffay during the eighteenth century when spinning occupied the majority of women. Between 1750 and 1786, only 3 out of 142 women who died in Auffay at age fifty or older were clearly spinsters. The marital status of an additional eight women who died in this age category is unknown. Even if all of these eight women were spinsters, the celibacy rate for women was not above 7.7 percent, and it may have been as low as 2.1 percent.[21] (Considering that only 2 Auffay women married for the first time after they reached age fifty, the chances of a woman in this age category marrying were very slim.[22] Virtually all of these women would have remained celibate no matter how long they lived.) Even at 7.7 percent, this is a relatively low celibacy rate during this period. In Crulai, another Norman village studied by Etienne Gautier and Louis Henry, the celibacy rate for women in the second half of the eighteenth century ranged between 2.0 and 11.6 percent.[23] For France as a whole, the figure was probably around 12 percent, and in many other western European countries it was much higher.[24]

Male celibacy rates during this period are impossible to determine because death records do not indicate the marital status of men with any regularity. Since there is no evidence of an imbalance in the sex ratio in Auffay during the spinning era, we can assume, however, that the frequency of marriage was equally high for men.

Despite the vascillation in employment and wages in the textile industry and the general decline in female employment during the transition from cottage to factory spinning (1787–1817), the celibacy rate for women (and presumably for men) remained low. Of the 167 women who died at age fifty or older during these years, only six had clearly never married. For an additional eight women, marital status is not recorded. Together, these figures yield a celibacy rate that may have been as low as 3.6 but not higher than 8.4 percent, an insignificant change from the 2.1 to 7.7 percent celibacy rate for the spinning era.[25]

Contrary to what one would normally expect in a proto-industrial village, the celibacy rate for women began to climb during the weaving era (1818–1850). By 1851, it was higher than it had been for at least a century, and many rural women were finding it difficult to find not only a job but also a husband. In that year, almost 16 percent of the 152 Auffay women who were fifty or older were spinsters (twenty-four women).[26] This is double the highest possible celibacy rate for the village in the late eighteenth and early nineteenth centuries. If a woman did not marry in her twenties, it was becoming increasingly unlikely that she would do so at all. By the 1840s, the percentage of brides who were thirty years of age or older fell to 6.9 percent (four out of fifty-eight brides), a considerable decline from the 20.1 percent of brides in this age category during the ninety years before this decade.[27]

The celibacy rate for men remained low, however. In contrast to the twenty-four spinsters over the age of fifty, only 7 of the 120 men in this age group, or 5.8 percent, were not married in 1851. Although some of the difference in celibacy rates might be the result of shorter male life expectancy (there were twenty-six more widows than widowers [forty-four versus eighteen] in the over fifty age bracket), examination of the marital status of men and women in their forties, where mortality clearly is not a factor, reveals similar gender differences regarding celibacy. Out of ninety men, only five were unmarried (5.6 percent); out of eighty-three women, fourteen were celibate (16.9 percent).[28]

The difference in the number of celibate men and women in 1851 was the result *not* of differential mortality rates, but of different male and female migration patterns. As the adoption of the power loom on the fringes of the Caux began to reduce the amount of work available for hand weavers, more and more unmarried men began to leave the plateau to seek jobs as spinners, weavers, and warp winders in urban factories and workshops. Unmarried women were much less likely to leave, even though there were often more mill jobs available for them than for men. In addition, they were more affected than men by the midcentury decline in hand weaving because the early looms were used to produce light-weight calicos, the fabric woven by women.[29] The response of the two sexes to the decline in jobs was thus quite different. Men chose to leave; women, to stay.

In choosing not to emigrate to the city, *cauchois* women were, to a large extent, simply following a well-established cultural pattern. Since the middle of the eighteenth century, the availability of work in the cottage textile industry had made it possible for most women to work and acquire a dowry without leaving home. A few women did, of course, leave their families to work as farm or general household servants. In 1796, for instance, thirteen women were employed by and living with Auffay families other than their own. Of these women, only two had been born and reared in the village. The others had left their families either before or when they found jobs in Auffay.[30] However, domestic service occupied only a small minority of *cauchois* women in the eighteenth century. Many more were spinners and had no need to leave home to earn money. Between 1751 and 1786, when spinning occupied the majority of Auffay brides, only 6.5 percent of them whose parents were living resided away from home[31]

Between 1787 and 1817, when spinning was moving into factories, the tradition of women remaining at home until they married was reinforced in the Caux. Undoubtedly, some women left the region entirely to work in the Rouen factories, but those who stayed in the region stayed in their home villages. To seek work in another village was futile because the loss of spinning jobs was regionwide. Even domestic servant jobs, which in the past had gone to women willing to leave home, could easily be filled with local women, whose reputations were well known by the families who hired them. There was no need for employers to hire unknown young

Table 7.1. *Premarital geographical mobility, 1751–1850*

	Men			Women		
Marriage cohort	Non-orphans[a]	Separate residence[b]	Percent-age	Non-orphans[a]	Separate residence[b]	Percent-age
(1751–1786)	111	10	9.0	124	8	6.5
(1787–1817)	157	27	17.2	165	3	1.8
(1818–1850)	215	66	30.7	214	29	13.6
Total	483	103	21.3	503	40	8.0

[a] Individuals with at least one living parent at the time of their marriage.
[b] Living in a different village from parent(s).
Source: Family Reconstitution Study.

women. All in all, it was wiser to remain at home and look for work than to join the wandering jobless. It is hardly surprising that fewer than 2 percent of Auffay brides in this period were living away from home.[32] (See Table 7.1.)

During the weaving era, female premarital mobility in the Caux began to increase because the new jobs in weaving, sewing, and day laboring were not spread as uniformly across the plateau as jobs in cottage spinning had been. Villages near major roads had more weaving jobs than did isolated villages. Villages that were enclosing fields had more day-laboring jobs than those that continued to practice fallow farming. Auffay, perhaps because of its size, had many more jobs in dressmaking than neighboring villages did.[33] As a result, more young women began to leave home to work before they were married. Even so, only 13.6 percent of the women who married in Auffay were not living at home[34] Although this is twice the mobility rate for women in the late eighteenth century, it is not a very high rate of geographical mobility. To send or allow a daughter to move to a city and work in a mill would have been a sharp break with the custom of keeping daughters at home. It is hardly surprising that women and their families resisted taking this step as long as they could.

For men, the decision to move to Rouen or Le Havre in search of work was not as much of a break with tradition. Throughout the proto-industrial period, men were more mobile before marriage than were women; by the weaving era, almost one out of three men left home before marriage.[35] Many left as young as age thirteen to take jobs as apprentice artisans and farm servants, jobs that simply were not open to women. In 1796, for instance, there were twenty-one farm domestics and fourteen apprentice artisans living with their employers in Auffay. Only five of these young men were from Auffay families (two domestics and three apprentices). The others had left not only their parental homes but also their villages to seek work.[36] To be sure, moving to a city to work in a factory was very different from moving to another rural village to work on a farm or in an artisan craft, but the men who did it did not have to make the same kind of break with tradition that women did.

In addition to habit or cultural tradition, the dangers faced by young women alone in the city may also have affected their migration rate. Parents may have had some sense of what historians have demonstrated to be true – that it was not young women who remained at home, but young women who lived and worked away from home, who were the most likely to be abandoned if they became pregnant.[37] Moreover, most peasants regarded factories and cities alike as dens of immorality. Noiret, himself a weaver who thought it was all right for women to weave at home or in small workshops of two to six employees, was firmly opposed to their working in factories unless they were accompanied by a male relative whose presence would prevent "familiarities."[38] Unless it was absolutely necessary, most *cauchois* families would not have sent or permitted a daughter to work in a mill and live alone in a city.[39]

For a variety of reasons, then, young men were geographically more mobile than young women, and, through the mechanism of male migration, female marriage frequency in the Caux generally remained symmetrical with employment conditions. When jobs in cottage industry were readily available, marriage frequency was high; when they declined, so did the probability of marriage for women. The Flemish pattern of a rising marriage frequency following good economic years with no subsequent decline in bad years is not an inevitable response to fluctuations in a proto-industry.

Moreover, change in the textile industry was not the only factor affecting marriage frequency in the Caux during this period. The mass conscription law of August 1793, which placed young men between the ages of eighteen and twenty-five, unmarried men, and widowers without children in the first draft group,[40] was followed by a marked increased in the number of marriages (and births) in Auffay. Some couples undoubtedly married and had children right away in the hope that the man might not be drafted into the army. Others may have married earlier than they otherwise would have, precisely because the man was leaving for the army. Sixteen marriages took place in 1793 and fifteen in 1794, a sharp increase over the 4 marriages that occurred in 1792. Conversely, during the war, when large numbers of young men were in the army and absent from the village, the number of marriages plummeted to its lowest point in the entire proto-industrial period. (In 1800, seventy-four men were absent from Auffay alone and 348 soldiers were absent from the twenty-one villages in the canton of Auffay.)[41]

Marriage ages

Unlike typical proto-industrial areas, marriage ages in Auffay were very high. During the spinning era, the mean age at first marriage was 28.9 years for men and 26.0 for women. For spinners and weavers, the women and men employed by the textile merchants, the mean age at marriage was almost exactly the same as the general mean – 26.3 years for spinners and 28.7 for weavers.[42] This was a high marriage age, especially for the men. In Vraiville, a textile village in Lower Normandy studied by Martine Segalen, the average male marriage age between 1753 and 1802 was only 26.9.[43] In Crulai, the mean marriage age for men was 27.[44] Women, on the other hand, married at approximately the same age in Auffay and Vraiville (26.0 and 26.3, respectively) but much younger in Crulai where, on the average, they were only 24.[45] Although this study of Auffay begins in the proto-industrial period, it is unlikely that the average ages at which women and men married could have been much, if at all, higher before the intensification of cottage industry because they are on the high side not only for Normandy but also for men and women throughout Western Europe in the eighteenth century.[46]

The combination of low celibacy rates and high marriage ages during the spinning era indicates that the cottage textile industry made it possible for almost all women to acquire a dowry and almost all men to pay the rent on a cottage. However, it did not increase the inclination of either sex to marry without the traditional economic underpinnings of a marriage. The women who married at the youngest ages during the spinning era were the daughters of *laboureurs* and *fermiers* whose dowries were provided by their families rather than earned by the women themselves. All other women married at ages that allowed them to have acquired at least a minimal dowry and skills with which to contribute to the family's income. Jacques Etienne Frichet and Marie Marguerite Varin, who married at ages twenty-seven and twenty-five, respectively, thus were fairly typical of Auffay brides and grooms during the spinning era. In fact, whereas they were old by proto-industrial standards, they were younger than most Auffay brides and grooms. (See Table 7.2.)

Table 7.2. *Mean age at first marriage for female occupational groups, Auffay, 1751–1786*

Occupation	Number	Age
Cultivators	4	21.3
Seamstresses	18	24.6
Merchants	8	24.8
Spinners	80	26.3
Domestics	17	27.8
All women[a]	154	26.0

[a]Brides whose occupations at the time of marriage are unknown or who worked at a variety of miscellaneous jobs are not included in the Table. As a result, the number of women does not add to the total number of women in the marriage cohort.
Source: ADSM Parish Registers, Auffay.

Marriage ages generally continued to be high during the transition period in cottage industry. For women, the mean marriage age stayed almost constant, declining merely from 26.0 to 25.8 years. For men, the decline was only slightly larger, from 28.9 to 28.3 years (roughly six months).

When we examine the mean marriage age of weavers, we see a different picture, however. During the spinning era, these men married at an average age of 28.7 years. During the transition period as a whole, their average marriage age fell by three years to 25.6, and, during the latter part of the transition (1805–17) when the new spinning machines were steadily increasing the demand for weavers, the average marriage age of male weavers fell to 23.7 years, a decline of five years over the spinning era. No one foresaw that the hiring of women to help meet the demand for weavers and the introduction of mechanical looms would soon reduce the wages of male handloom weavers. They married with confidence in the future of their jobs and wages, and they married at young ages. Jacques Etienne Frichet and Marie Marguerite Varin's son, Pierre Servin, was a member of this generation of weavers. Unlike his father, who did not marry until he was twenty-seven, Pierre Servin married Marie Catherine Dupré in 1813, when he was only nineteen.[47]

At twenty-nine, Marie Catherine was ten years older than Pierre Servin. The age difference between the two of them was greater than for any other weavers who married during this period, but the fact that she was older than Pierre was not unusual. Nine of the seventeen male weavers who married between 1805 and 1817 married older women. (For the proto-industrial period as a whole, only 30 percent of the brides were older than their grooms.)[48] As a result, the mean marriage age of the wives of weavers was slightly higher than that of the weavers themselves (they were 24.4 years of age). Perhaps doubly to ensure their future income, a majority of the male weavers married women who not only were older than themselves, but who either were or would become weavers. (Nine married female weavers; three married nonweavers; and five married women for whom neither a marriage occupation nor a subsequent occupation is listed in the Auffay records, although some, if not all, of them may have been weavers.)

The decline in the mean age at first marriage for Auffay weavers between 1805 and 1817 parallels the decline in marriage age found by David Levine in proto-industrial Shepshed, where men generally married at twenty-eight or twenty-nine in the mid-eighteenth century and around twenty-four in the early nineteenth century.[49] It also suggests that the demographic consequences of proto-industrialization in the Caux might have been the same as those found elsewhere if the industry had centered on men or entire families rather than on women. Except for this brief period, however, more women than men worked for the textile merchants, and marriage age remained relatively unaffected by the spread of the cotton industry.

The period of high wages and low marriage ages for male weavers was shortlived in Auffay. As women entered the craft in increasingly large numbers, the wages of male weavers fell, and their marriage ages climbed back to their previously high level. The twenty-two male weavers who married in Auffay between 1818 and 1850 had a mean marriage age of 28.3 years, nine and a half months higher than that of the average Auffay man who married at age 27.5. Like their male counterparts, female weavers married at approximately the same (but slightly higher) age as all Auffay women during the weaving era. Their average age was 25.5, whereas women in general were 25.3 years of age at first marriage. (See Tables 7.3 and 7.4.)

During the final phase of proto-industrialization (1818–50), marriage ages in Auffay continued their very gradual decline. The mean marriage age of men was 27.5, a year and a half lower than it was in the first phase (1751–86), that of women was 25.3 years, a drop of about eight months. When marriage ages are examined by decades rather than by the phases of the textile industry, however, the pattern of gradual decline disappears, and one of vascillation around the mean marriage age for each sex

Table 7.3. *Women's ages at marriage, Auffay, 1751–1850*
(first marriages)

Marriage age	Cohort 1 (1751–1786)		Cohort 2 (1787–1817)		Cohort 3 (1818–1850)	
	Number	Percentage	Number	Percentage	Number	Percentage
Under 20	7	4.5	16	8.3	27	11.1
20–24	64	41.6	70	36.3	119	49.0
25–29	53	34.4	72	37.3	51	21.0
30–39	25	16.2	32	16.6	37	15.2
40 and over	4	2.6	3	1.5	9	3.7
Unknown	1	0.7	0	—	0	—
Total	154	100.0	193	100.0	243	100.0
Mean age	26.0		25.8		25.3	
Median age	24.9		25.1		23.7	

Source: ADSM Parish and Civil Registers, Auffay.

Table 7.4. *Men's ages at marriage, Auffay, 1751–1850*
(first marriages)

Marriage age	Cohort 1 (1751–1786)		Cohort 2 (1787–1817)		Cohort 3 (1818–1850)	
	Number	Percentage	Number	Percentage	Number	Percentage
Under 20	1	0.6	7	3.6	7	2.9
20–24	34	22.1	57	29.5	82	33.7
25–29	62	40.3	62	32.2	54	22.3
30–39	44	28.6	52	26.9	84	34.6
40 and over	11	7.1	15	7.8	13	5.3
Unknown	2	1.3	0	—	3	1.2
Total	154	100.0	193	100.0	243	100.0
Mean age	28.9		28.3		27.5	
Median age	27.8		26.9		26.2	

Source: ADSM Parish and Civil Registers, Auffay.

(25.6 for women, 28.1 for men) appears until the 1840s, when there are declines of 2.3 years in the mean marriage age of men and 3.3 years in that of women. (See Table 7.5.)

The drop in mean marriage ages for both sexes in the 1840s is due

Table 7.5. *Mean marriage ages by decade, Auffay*
1751–1850

Dates	Number	Men	Women
1751–1760	42	27.6	25.8
1761–1770	34	29.4	25.9
1771–1780	44	28.25	26.0
1781–1790	60	30.1	27.1
1791–1800	73	29.25	25.5
1801–1810	41	27.4	24.7
1811–1820	82	28.0	26.2
1821–1830	70	26.6	25.5
1831–1840	81	28.3	26.6
1841–1850	56	26.0	23.25
1751–1850	583[a]	28.1	25.6

[a]Seven marriages in which the age of one or both spouses is miss-
ing were eliminated from the calculations.
Source: ADSM Parish and Civil Registers, Auffay, 1751–1850.

almost entirely to the building of a small spinning mill in Auffay and the
creation of a new occupation group – factory spinners. There are no wage
figures for the Auffay mill, but if they were comparable to wages paid at
other mills (and there is no reason to assume otherwise), they were better
than what men and women could earn in any other occupation. Women
were paid between 1.10 and 1.40 francs a day in the mills. In sewing and
day laboring, their maximum earnings were 1.25 francs a day and they
might be as low as 0.90 francs. In hand weaving, they were lucky if they
made the latter figure. Male spinners earned 2.35 to 2.75 francs a day,
higher wages than those earned by any other workers including artisans.[50] In the face of such earnings, savings and dowries seemed unnecessary prerequisites for marriage. A cottage could be rented; furniture
and cooking utensils could be purchased on credit. Couples did not have
to postpone marriage until their late twenties. Instead, female spinners
married at an average age of only 21.2 years; male spinners, at 24.2
years. (See Table 7.6.)

The contrast between the nuptial behavior of most men and women in
the Caux, on the one hand, and that of the mid-nineteenth-century mill
workers and the early nineteenth-century weavers, on the other, suggests
that wages were a key factor in determining marriage age. Until the 1840s,
female spinners and weavers were paid well enough and had secure enough
jobs to enable most of them to marry, but their wages were not high

Table 7.6. *Mean age at first marriage for female occupational groups, Auffay, 1818–1850*

Occupation	Number	Mean age
Factory spinner	18	21.4
Seamstress	44	24.5
Day laborer	4	25.0
Hand weaver	44	25.5
Merchant	9	26.9
Cultivator	5	27.4
Servant	17	29.0
All women[a]	243	25.3

[a]Brides whose occupations at the time of marriage are unknown or who worked at a variety of miscellaneous jobs are not included in the Table. As a result, the number of women does not add to the total number of women in the marriage cohort.
Source: ADSM Civil Registers, Auffay.

enough to enable them to marry without acquiring a dowry. Male weavers were consistently paid more than female spinners and weavers, but, except for a brief period in the early nineteenth century, they remained among the most poorly paid male workers in the Caux. They married, but not before they had acquired skills and some savings with which to pay the rent on a cottage and perhaps a small plot of land. Had the textile industry paid higher wages, marriage ages in the Caux might have fallen as they did in other proto-industrial regions. As it was, however, only rarely did cottage or factory work appear to offer the ongoing high wages and economic security that encouraged men and women in other regions to take the risk of marrying at young ages.

Wages were not the only factor affecting nuptial behavior in the Caux during the proto-industrial period, and, in some ways, they were simply a reflection of the major factor – the sexual composition of the textile labor force. Unlike Flanders, Shepshed, and Switzerland, where proto-industries significantly altered either the frequency or the age of marriage, and where entire families appear to have been employed by the putting-out merchants, *cauchois* women worked for the merchants, whereas the men farmed, ran shops, or worked in artisan crafts. Consequently, fluctuations in employment opportunities and wages in the textile industry affected the marriage decisions and marriageability of women much more directly than they did those of men. Any tendency for full employment in cottage industry to lower female marriage ages could be and was offset by conditions and wages in the male occupations, which experienced few changes during the proto-industrial period. Throughout the period, men worked as artisans, merchants, day laborers, weavers, farmers, and farm domestics. With few exceptions, wages, job constraints, and employment opportunities remained fairly constant and functioned in a way that kept marriage ages high. Artisans and domestics could not marry young unless they were willing and able to find other jobs. Weavers and day laborers earned subsistence wages and could not afford to marry young.

The persistence of a high male marriage age may indirectly have kept the female marriage age relatively high and constant, because the tradition in this region was for brides and grooms to be close to each other in age. A declining female marriage age in conjunction with a steady male marriage age would have increased the age gap, and that increase may not have been considered desirable by the community. Change, in fact, occurred in the opposite direction. Brides and grooms grew closer, not farther apart, in age as the proto-industrial period progressed.

The marriage patterns in Auffay make the village significantly different from other proto-industrial villages and regions that have been studied and indicate that the sexual division of labor and wage levels are crucial variables in the analysis of economic and demographic change. Beggar weddings clearly were not an inevitable result of the presence of a large-scale cottage industry. At least in the Caux, where such an industry employed primarily women rather than men or entire families and where wages remained low, celibacy rates were low but symmetrical with employment and wages, and marriage ages were stable and high. Without an analysis of the sexual composition of the labor force, such a divergence from the commonly accepted thesis that proto-industrialization produced low celibacy rates and low marriage ages would be inexplicable.

Endogamy and family relationships

The changes in women's occupations that occurred during the proto-industrial period in Auffay had a much more profound effect on family work patterns than on demographic behavior. In the eighteenth century, men and women generally worked in different places at different tasks, regardless of the man's occupation. With the entry of women into weaving and day laboring in the early nineteenth century and into factory spinning in the late 1830s, the spatial and occupational division between women's and men's work broke down in many families, and husbands and wives found themselves working side by side at the same or very similar work, albeit for different wages.

In the eighteenth century, the vast majority of women worked in homes from which the men were absent during the day. They spun or, in some cases, made garments, whereas the men worked in the barns and fields, plowing, planting, and threshing, in *ateliers* or smithies making everything from bricks to furniture to shoes, or in small shops selling clothes, food, candles, and so forth. In some cases, there were family businesses or farms where husbands, wives, and children pooled their labor, but even then, men's and women's work often took place in separate spheres. On large farms, men worked in the fields and barns whereas women labored in the house and barnyard. Only among textile, tanning, and service-oriented merchants did husbands and wives work together in the same place. In the textile-producing families, of course, this work was sexually divided. The same may have been true in tanning and merchant businesses, although no division is indicated in the Auffay records.[51]

Families in which husbands and wives worked at complementary tasks (e.g., weaving and spinning, farming) or possibly at the same tasks (e.g., tanning, innkeeping, café-keeping) were the exception in Auffay. In most families, women's work for the putting-out merchants bore no relationship to their husband's work. A woman's ability to earn money was usually more important than whether her economic skills complemented those of her husband.

The changes in women's occupations that occurred with the mechanization of spinning and the enclosure of land had little effect on the families in which men worked in artisan crafts, merchant businesses, and large-scale farming. As in the eighteenth century, when most women in these families earned money by spinning, a clear segregation of jobs and work place continued in the nineteenth century as women switched to weaving and dressmaking. (Women in these families did not work as day laborers.) Women's work changed, but the relationship between their work and that of their husbands did not.

These families constituted the economic elite of the village. The range of their wealth is well illustrated in the tax roles. The *laboureurs* and *fermiers* (called *cultivateurs* on the eighteenth-century tax roles) were clearly the wealthiest group in the village. In 1771, there were nine *laboureur* and *fermier* families in Auffay. They employed a total of twenty-six domestic servants and owned forty horses, thirty cows, and seven flocks of sheep. The average salt tax assessment for them was almost 100 *livres*, and this was only one form of the taxes they paid.[52] Charles Jullien was the wealthiest of the farmers. He rented a 150-acre farm and was required to purchase 150 *livres* of salt (54 *pots*). Much poorer, but still wealthy by village standards, was Nicholas Gibert who rented only 20 acres and was charged 44 *livres* for salt (16 *pots*). Although no merchant or artisan was as wealthy as Charles Jullien, several of them had substantial incomes and capital assets. Pierre Nicolle, the miller, employed six domestics to work at the mill and two *chassemouttes* to transport grain and flour between the mill and the villagers. He was assessed 111 *livres* (40 *pots*), the fourth largest assessment in the village. Pierre Saunier, a master tanner, paid 44 *livres* for 16 *pots* of salt, placing him well below Jullien and Nicolle on the economic ladder but on the same rung with Gibert. (See Table 7.7.)

Although there are no records that provide this kind of economic information for the Caux during the first half of the nineteenth century, there is no reason to believe that there was a significant change in the composition or wealth of the families at the top of the economic ladder. If anything, they grew wealthier. The demand for and price of grain remained high, and the income of farmers stable; merchant and artisan crafts and businesses continued to thrive in the absence of any challenge from machines; and the city council of Auffay invested time and money to improve the shops, inns, and public buildings and successfully attracted a bank, post office, railroad station, and new businesses to the village.[53]

Even though women's and men's occupations in this group tended to be unrelated, there was a high degree of endogamy for each of the occupations throughout the proto-industrial period. Between 1751 and 1850, 60.8 percent of the women whose fathers are known to have been artisans, farmers, and merchants married men with one of these three occupations. (See Table 7.7.) The artisan crafts were by far the most endogamous. Over forty-three percent of the known daughters of artisans married artisans. In many cases, they married men in exactly the same craft as their fathers, even though tanning was the only village craft in which women assisted their husbands. For example, Marie Aimée and Marie Adelaide Baudard, the daughters of a nailmaker, both married nailmakers in the 1790s, although neither woman assisted her father or her husband. What was important in these marriages was *not* the specific occupational skills of the bride (although an ability to keep the books, and hence, a literate bride may have been important considerations when ar-

Table 7.7. *Salt taxes paid by occupation groups, Auffay, 1771*

Occupation	Number in group	Highest assessment (*pots*)	Average assessment (*pots*)	Lowest assessment (*pots*)
Cultivators	9	54[a]	35.6	16
Merchants	18	40	9.4	4
Artisans	48	18	6.6	2
Weavers	17	8	4.3	2
Day laborers	32	8	4.3	2
Tailors	7	6	2.9	1
Domestics	2[b]	8	5.0	2

[a] 36 *pots* of salt cost 100 *livres*.
[b] Most domestics lived with the families for whom they worked and were not assessed separately. The average assessment of 5 *pots* of salt for these two domestics obviously does not represent the economic position of this occupational group as a whole.
Source: ADSM 219BP364.

tisans chose wives) *but rather* social contacts and a familiarity with and tolerance for the work rhythms and problems of particular crafts.

Among artisans, the endogamy was not strict, however. As many daughters of artisans married men whose crafts were different from those of their fathers as married men in the same craft. Social contacts and the forging of alliances among the wealthier families in the community were important factors in such unions. The same was true when artisan, merchant, and *fermier* families intermarried. In 1776, for instance, Marie Magdeleine Jullien (the daughter of Charles Jullien, the wealthiest farmer in Auffay) married Pierre Saunier, a member of one of the old tanning families. In 1807, their son, Pierre Louis Saunier, married Marie Anne Justine Nicolle, a member of the wealthy miller family. As a result, by 1807, three of the wealthiest farming, tanning, and merchant families were linked by marriage. (See Table 7.8.)

At the other end of the economic spectrum were the families in which the men worked as weavers, domestic servants, and agricultural day laborers. Their economic situations were tenuous throughout the proto-industrial period as the smallness of their tax assessments (still, perhaps, too high for their means) in the eighteenth century indicates.[54] In the eighteenth century, most of the husbands and wives in these families, as in the wealthier Auffay families, worked at unrelated tasks, except during the harvest, when everyone worked in the fields for the *fermiers* and la-

Table 7.8. *Occupational endogamy, Auffay, 1751–1850*

Bride's father's occupation	Groom's occupation								
	Domestic	Day Laborer	Textiles	Cultivator	Artisan	Merchant	Other	Unknown	Total
Domestic	3	2	3	0	1	0	1	0	10
Day laborer	12	17	13	2	17	5	8	0	74
Textiles	7	8	13	2	8	4	1	1	44
Cultivator	2	5	2	11	14	3	3	0	40
Artisan	7	7	15	2	46	12	16	1	106
Merchant	3	0	7	1	21	2	8	1	43
Other	1	2	3	4	10	1	10	1	32
Unknown	20	39	42	23	62	26	20	9	241
Total	55	80	98	45	179	53	67	13	590

Source: Family Reconstitution Study.

boureurs. The major exception to this pattern were families in which both men and women worked for the textile merchants. Even in these families, however, men's and women's work was not always performed in the same place. (Women and girls frequently gathered together to spin with their wheels and distaffs and to gossip and talk, leaving their husbands at home working at stationary looms or other tasks.)[55] In families in which the men did not weave and consequently worked outside the house during the day, husbands and wives may have had little sustained contact. Nevertheless, a high rate of endogamy also existed in these families. Sixty-one percent of the daughters of men known to be domestic servants, day laborers, or weavers married men with these occupations.

Although the entry of women into weaving and day laboring and the building of a small spinning mill in Auffay in the 1830s had little effect on the wealthier families, they created new *joint* wife–husband occupations in many of the poorer families. Between 1818 and 1850, both spouses in fourteen couples who married in Auffay formed family economies based entirely on weaving. In eight marriages both spouses were day laborers. And twelve male factory spinners married female factory spinners. Altogether, these marriages account for 43 percent of the marriages in which the man was a hand weaver, factory spinner, or day laborer. Sometimes men and women already had the same occupation when they married. Other times, one or the other of the spouses changed jobs and took up weaving, spinning, or day laboring alongside the other.[56]

The social and psychological effects of the changes in female occupations on families at the lower end of the economic ladder are difficult to determine. Both sexes lost some of the autonomy and camaraderie with same-sex groups that they had had when they worked at separate tasks in separate places. Women no longer made trips together to the textile markets to sell their yarn, as they did when they were spinners, and they no longer were able to congregate while they worked.[57] Mothers who left their cottages to work in the fields as day laborers or in factories as spinners faced a new problem because they could no longer integrate childcare with their work. Now they were forced to leave their children unattended or to find someone to care for them.

The entry of women into weaving and day laboring was undoubtedly facilitated by the need of families for women's earnings and by the fact that employment in these fields was expanding. Women were not taking jobs from men. But whether these changes were experienced primarily as invasions of privacy and freedom, or as opportunities for families to work and share together, is impossible to tell. Some families may have experienced the change in one way, others in another.

Male weavers, on the one hand, probably experienced little change in autonomy because they had always done much of their work in the presence of women and children, who spun yarn and wound and replaced shuttle bobbins for them. On the other hand, the presence of women at the loom rather than at a spinning wheel may have posed a serious threat to their authority. The perception of this threat may lie behind the relegation of women to the weaving of light-weight calicos. Although much of the notion of innate sex-linked skills that had supported the old sexual division of labor could hardly be applied to this new division, the claim to greater strength did give men some continued claim to authority.[58]

Unlike male weavers, male day laborers saw not only the notion of innate skills come under challenge, but also the hitherto male province of the fields (except during the harvest) invaded by women. Whether they found ways to maintain a division of labor and sense of superiority is unclear.

Beyond the questions of autonomy, freedom, and same-sex community lie the questions of the effects of proto-industrialization, in general, and of the entry of women into male jobs, in particular, on personal or affectional relationships and on women's position in the family. The current proto-industrial literature does little more than touch on this subject, but in so doing it conveys the impression that proto-industrialization increased the familiarity between young women and men before marriage, heightened sexual consciousness, and allowed young adults more choice in the selection of marriage partners. After marriage, it further suggests, the breakdown of the sexual division of labor in some rural industries led to greater equality of status between husbands and wives, and, in regions in which there was more employment for women than men, household tasks previously considered women's work were assumed by the men as the family strove to maximize income.[59]

There is no evidence that the presence of cottage industry in the Caux increased the familiarity between young men and women before marriage. Rudolf Braun, who has argued that increased intimacy and sexual exploration before marriage was a consequence of proto-industrialization in the Zurich highlands, based his analysis on the assumption that unrelated young men and women were working together during the daytime. This increased social contact led, he suggests, to increased premarital sexual contact.[60] This simply was not the case in the Caux. Most daughters remained at home and worked for their parents until they married.

There were neither male boarders nor male day employees in these cottages, and contact between the sexes remained based in the family rather than in nonfamilial occupational groups. Only the young women and men who worked in the Auffay spinning mill in the late 1830s and 1840s had sustained contact with the opposite sex on the job, and their low marriage ages and high rate of endogamy parallel Braun's findings for Switzerland. But this was really more of an industrial than a proto-industrial labor force. Among cottage-industry and day-laboring families, daily contact and sexual intimacy between husbands and wives may have increased with the entry of women into weaving and day laboring, but contact and presumably sexual intimacy between unmarried men and women did not.

In his study of proto-industrialization, Hans Medick has argued that cottage industry could "erase the traditional division of labour between the sexes and age groups" and could lead to "a more flexible allocation of the role responsibilities of family members than was the case for the peasant family."[61] The argument is based on a handful of reports from eighteenth- and nineteenth-century observers of cottage-industry families in Switzerland and the German states, where men assumed household tasks when more work was available for their daughters and wives than for them. Again, there is no evidence of such a breakdown in the sexual division of labor in the Caux. In the eighteenth century, when women were more consistently employed in spinning than men were in most of their occupations, men may have helped with carding and spinning, tasks many of them had learned as children. In the absence of any comments about any other changes in the division of household labor, this seems to be more likely a sharing of work than men assuming responsibility for cooking and childcare, because this women's work was at least paid work. In the nineteenth century, when weavers and day laborers were employed year-round in their tasks, economic logic would again have assigned non-paid work to women rather than to men. Men's wages were higher, and it was important for them not to lose any more time from work than necessary. The invasion of male occupations by women was probably bad enough without the men facing the possibility of taking up women's (unpaid) work. The family's best economic strategy in this region, in light of the lower wages women earned (both as spinners in the eighteenth century and as weavers and day laborers in the nineteenth), would have been for women to remain responsible for childcare and housework, unless men were totally unemployed or unable to help them with their paid work.

Medick has also suggested that the improving status of women in cottage industry families can be seen in the participation of women in high-status public consumption.[62] In the Caux, status consumption in public was done in the cafés and taverns, and these remained male-dominated spheres. In fact, not only did public gathering places remain male dominated, but women also lost their opportunities for private gatherings when they began to work at stationary looms rather than at portable wheels.

As is true for most places, the evidence about family relationships, the sharing or division of tasks within the family, and the status of women in the family is very slight for the Caux. But what evidence exists does not point toward increased egalitarianism or the sharing of nonproductive tasks or public recreation areas by men and women. If anything, women's low wages, their increased difficulty in finding work after the mechanization of spinning, and the loss of opportunities to congregate with other women over their work and to market their yarn indicate that women's economic independence and emotional support declined. Hence, their status in the family and the community declined as proto-industrialization proceeded and the old sexual divisions of labor broke down. Ironically, this deterioration in women's freedom and community occurred when they entered the more highly paid male occupations, a development that, on the surface, looks as if it should have improved their economic and social status; but did not because they continued to work for lower wages and to receive lower piece rates.

Male–female relationships are an area of the past for which we probably will always have more questions than answers, and answers will be tentative, at best. But the case of the Caux raises questions about the picture of family life that has begun to emerge in the proto-industrial literature and again points to the need to consider proto-industrialization as a process with varied, rather than uniform, consequences. The current picture is drawn from very little evidence, and it seems to be far from a universal portrait of proto-industrial regions.

Childbearing

Throughout the entire period from 1750 to 1850, marriage and the beginning of childbearing were closely linked events. Twenty-four percent of the women who married and subsequently bore a child in the village were pregnant when they followed the fiddler to the church and took their wedding vows. Those who had not already conceived a child, did so soon after. Sixty-two percent of the brides who bore a child in the village had their first baby before they reached their first wedding anniversary, and 87 percent had their first child before their second anniversary.[63] Male weavers and their brides, that is, those families who depended most on the putting-out merchants, were no different from other couples. Twenty-five percent of the weavers' brides were pregnant when they married, and 60 percent of them (including those who were pregnant when they walked down the aisle) had a child within the first year of their marriages.[64]

When we examine the childbearing patterns of completed families, however, we see important changes in the number of children women bore and in the practice of contraception as the proto-industrial period progressed. Completed families are those in which the wife was thirty or younger when she married and forty-five or older when the marriage ended. In these families, childbearing was not truncated either by beginning very far into the wife's childbearing years or by ending while she was still likely to bear children. (Only one woman in the completed family study bore a child after reaching age forty-five, and her last confinement was at age forty-six.) Because fecundity varies with age for both men and women, unlike other demographers, I have included only those couples in which the man was also under thirty at the time of marriage in the analysis of completed families.[65] Thirty-nine couples who married between 1751 and 1786 and forty-four who married between 1787 and 1817 meet the completed-family criteria, and these two groups – one marrying during the spinning era and the other during the transition era – followed different childbearing patterns.[66]

In the first group, twenty-four women bore five or more children. Only one couple had no children at all. Like Marie Marguerite Varin and Jacques Etienne Frichet, who were part of this cohort, the average couple had five children. And like them, most couples experienced the death of at least one infant or child. Marie Marguerite and Jacques Etienne were less fortunate than many of their contemporaries, however, because they lost three of their five children (one after two days, one after seven months, and one after three and a half years), giving them a completed family of only two children. For the average couple, 3.6 out of 4.8 children survived to adulthood. An average of eleven years passed between the time a woman conceived her first child and bore her last. Because childbearing began almost immediately after marriage, the average woman spent the first twelve years of her marriage bearing children and the first seventeen years with children under the age of five in the household.

Most of the women in the completed family group were employed by the putting-out merchants. Thirty-two of them were spinners during all or part of their married years (82.1 percent). That they and the few seamstresses and merchants who formed completed families bore an average of almost five children each, and that 3.6 of them survived childhood is a sign of the relative well-being the cotton industry brought to the Auffay region and of the compatibility of spinning, childbearing, and childrearing. Women probably lost only minimal amounts of time from work when they were pregnant and caring for children because children were far from smothered with attention during this period and there was no tradition of women resting during pregnancy.[67] Nevertheless, they lost some time (only the mother could nurse a baby), and they might have been in danger of losing their jobs in a tight job market. The demand for spinners was so high, however, that women did not have to worry about this. They only had to worry about reduced income if they lost time from work. And, far from discouraging women from bearing children, the availability of work in spinning probably encouraged them to have children who could learn to wash, comb, and spin cotton at early ages.

Although most couples watched one or more of their children die during infancy or childhood, the money women earned from spinning made it possible for couples to support young children, kept the infant mortality rate fairly low (between 1751 and 1786, it was 170 for every 1000 live births in Auffay),[68] and encouraged large families by offering the incentive of increased family income in a few years' time. Although the interval between births increased with the birth of each child for couples who had four or more children, there was no marked increase in the size of the last birth interval and, hence, no evidence that couples in this marriage cohort were attempting to limit the size of their families.[69]

Couples who married during the transition from cottage to factory spinning (1787–1817) followed a different demographic pattern. Despite the fact that their childbearing began as soon after marriage as it did for the first cohort, they had smaller families than their predecessors. Only 34 percent of the couples in the completed family group for this marriage period, in contrast to 61 percent of the first cohort, had five or more children (fifteen couples versus twenty-four couples in the earlier cohort), and the average number of children born per marriage was four rather than five. (See Table 7.9.)

Some couples, of course, continued to bear larger numbers of children, and, in fact, two women who married in 1794 when they were both twenty years old bore more children than any of the women in the completed family group of the first marriage cohort. Marie Magdeleine Recher,

Table 7.9. *Fertility patterns of completed families, Auffay*

Fertility pattern	Cohort 1 (1751–1786)	Cohort 2 (1787–1827)
Number of completed families	39	44
Marriages with no children	1	4
Marriages with 5 or more children	24	15
Children born per marriage	4.8	3.9
Couples experiencing death of an infant or child	25	22
Actual completed family size	3.6	2.8
Mean age of wife at marriage	24.1	25.7
Mean age of wife at last birth (if children ≥ 1)	36.3	35.2
Average childbearing period (years)	11.0	9.5

Source: Family Reconstitution Study.

a spinner, bore fourteen children (none of them twins) during her marriage to Pierre Louis Restencourt, a carpenter. The average interval between confinements for her was only seventeen months. Such a rapid succession of births indicates that she probably bore a child, nursed it for eight to ten months, and then immediately conceived again. Like Marie Marguerite Varin and Jacques Etienne Frichet, Recher and Restencourt watched several of their children die – one after only thirteen days and four during childhood. Considering the frequent pregnancies of Marie Magdeleine, however, and the number of children that she bore, the survival of nine to adulthood seems fairly remarkable.

Another Marie Magdeleine (Marie Magdeleine Delaunay) and Antoine Grege, a dressmaker and coppersmith, were the parents of another large family. Over an eighteen-year period, Marie Magdeleine bore twelve children, the last two being twin boys. Delaunay and Grege were not as lucky as Recher and Restencourt. Only five of their children survived to adulthood. Three, including the twins, died in infancy, three others died during their childhood years, and one died at age fifteen.

These were unusual families, however. The trend was clearly toward smaller families. A variety of circumstances might account for this change. The absence of one spouse or the other (such as the departure of husbands to serve in the army) might have disrupted childbearing for some couples. The advancing age of one or both partners, ill health, poor nutrition, or difficult pregnancies and confinements might account for the cessation of childbearing for others. Furthermore, some couples might have made conscious decisions to limit the size of their families and practiced contraception.

The drafting of men to serve in the Revolutionary and Napoleonic armies certainly disrupted the lives of many men and women in Auffay. Some married and began childbearing earlier than they otherwise would have. Others undoubtedly had to postpone or even forego marriage, whereas still others found their marriages interrupted. Conscription appears to have had little or no effect on the couples whose marriages meet the criteria for completed families, however. Marriage ages for women rose only slightly between the first and second cohort, despite the fact that many of the marriages in the second cohort occurred during the Revolutionary and Napoleonic periods, and most of the gaps in childbearing for the second cohort occurred late in the couples' marriages, not when the men were of draftable age.

Advancing age also does not seem to account for the cessation of childbearing and, hence, the smaller family size for the second marriage cohort, because the mean age of women at their last confinement was a year lower in this cohort. Nor is there any reason to believe that ill health or difficult pregnancies and confinements were any more prevalent for couples married between 1787 and 1827 than they were for those married between 1751 and 1786. These problems were undoubtedly confronted by many Auffay women, and they may have caused some to seek ways to limit childbearing whereas they left others sterile. They are unlikely, however, to account for the general changes in family size that occurred.

Since part of the period from 1787 to 1827 was one of poor harvests, intermittent employment, and low wages in cottage industry, the possibility that poor nutrition led to reduced fecundity could explain the reduced family size for the second marriage cohort.[70] Mortality figures for the village indicate, however, that with the exception of a few very bad years in Auffay (e.g., 1793, 1796, and 1803) when there were many more deaths than births,[71] the period was not markedly worse than the later years of the *Ancien Régime,* and reduced fecundity was not the cause of the reduction in family size. The infant mortality rate, for instance, declined from 170 for every 1,000 births during the spinning era to 138 during the transition era. (During the weaving era, it rose again to 189.)[72] Such a reduction during the late eighteenth and early nineteenth centuries would hardly have been possible if nutrition levels were seriously reduced. In keeping with this decrease in infant mortality during the first two phases of proto-industrialization, the percentage of completed families that experienced the death of an infant decreased slightly between the two marriage cohorts. In the first cohort, seventeen out of thirty-eight couples who bore a child (44.7 percent) watched one or more of their children die before their first birthday. In the second cohort, only sixteen out of forty-four couples (40 percent) had to bury such a young child.

Couples in the second marriage cohort also lost fewer of their children between the ages of one and twelve. Close to half of the couples in the first cohort (seventeen out of thirty eight) lost a child in this age bracket, compared with less than one-third of the couples in the second cohort (twelve out of forty). If anything, these reductions in infant and child deaths may mean that family size declined in Auffay because couples did not need to bear as many children in order to have some survive to adulthood. That is, family size declined as a result of family limitation, *not* because couples were unable to conceive children.

It seems unlikely, however, that the downward trend in the infant mortality rate during the transition period was perceived at the time. Between 1750 and 1850, not a year passed without the death of least one infant in Auffay. Years with nine or ten infant deaths must have seemed worse than others, but they were frequently followed by years of only one or two deaths, making short-term swings more noticeable than long-term trends. Moreover, even if their own children were relatively healthy, every couple was surrounded by families in which infants and children died. Diseases, accidents, and famines could strike at any time, and even relatively healthy and prosperous families might be forced helplessly to watch their children die. Marie Magdeleine Delaunay and Antoine Grege, for instance, watched three of their four living children die during the winter of 1803, one at age ten months, one at age three, and one at age eight. Such an experience might have affected the childbearing decisions both of Delaunay and Grege and of their friends more than trends in mortality rates or the economy. (See Table 7.10.)

There is, however, evidence that couples who married during the transition from cottage to machine spinning practiced contraception more often (or more successfully) than their predecessors. The major evidence for this lies in the fact that the average length of the last birth interval for couples in the completed family study, who bore four children or more, increased from 40.5 months for the first cohort to 53.1 months for the second cohort. An increase in the interval between the penultimate and ultimate birth in large families is a prime indicator that a population is increasing its practice of family limitation. The assumption is that married couples do not begin to try to limit births until they have produced

Table 7.10. *Completed families experiencing the loss of an infant or child, Auffay*

	Families			
	Cohort 1 (1751–1786)		Cohort 2 (1787–1817)	
Loss	Number	Percentage	Number	Percentage
One or more infants	8	20.5	10	22.8
One or more children	8	20.5	6	13.6
Infant and child	9	23.1	6	13.6
Total	25	64.1	22	50.0
Do not lose either	13	33.3	18	40.9
Do not have a child	1	2.6	4	9.1
Total marriages	39	100.0	44	100.0

Source: Family Reconstitution Study.

the number of children they want. They then attempt to stop conceiving children. A rise in the last birth interval occurs for a variety of reasons. Some couples who have begun to practice contraception reverse their decision. (A couple might decide, for instance, to replace a child who has died.) Other couples might forget to take precautions against conception (after a festive evening, perhaps) or might conceive a child despite their preventive attempts (i.e., the contraceptive system might fail).[73] (See Table 7.11.)

Although couples who married during the transition phase in cottage industry as a group limited conceptions more than their predecessors did, the practice of contraception, of course, varied from couple to couple. Some couples clearly did not practice any (successful) form of contraception; others apparently tried and, for reasons that are not clear, failed at various points; still others successfully limited the size of their families.[74] The couples who produced the five largest families (eight, nine, ten, twelve, and fourteen children) had children at an almost constant pace from the time they married until the birth of the last child. They appear to have made no attempts to limit the size of their families, although one wonders if the women in these families might not have preferred some respite from the cycle of pregnancy, birth, nursing, and pregnancy.

Couples who had three, four, five, and six children usually conceived children at regular intervals during the early years of their marriages and

Table 7.11. *Birth intervals in completed families*
with four or more children

Interval	Cohort 1 (1751–1786)	Cohort 2 (1787–1817)
0–1	9.4[a]	11.7
1–2	24.0	26.0
2–3	29.7	32.1
3–4	36.9	32.8
Last	40.5	53.1
No. of families	28	20

[a] All birth intervals given in months.
Source: Family Reconstitution Study.

then, either because of advancing age and reduced fecundity, the onset of menopause, or the successful practice of contraception, ceased to bear children. For older couples, the reasons for the cessation of childbearing are unclear. Marie Aimée Drouet and Antoine Dubus, for instance, who married in 1790 when she was twenty-nine and he was thirty, had five children at regularly spaced intervals between 1791 and 1799. Marie Aimée was thirty-eight and Antoine was thirty-nine when she bore their last child. Since many women continued to bear children into their forties, it is impossible to tell whether advancing age or the practice of contraception accounts for the cessation of births in this family. Either is possible.

For younger couples, however, the cessation of childbearing frequently appears to be the result of contraception. This is particularly true for couples who bore only three or four children. Marie Rose Maillet, for instance, married Nicolas Joseph Petit in 1800, when she was twenty-two and he was only seventeen. She bore her first child nine months after the wedding and subsequent children in 1802, 1805, and 1808. Then, at the age of thirty, she ceased to bear children. Because they stopped bearing children at an age at which many couples began their families, it appears that four children, all of whom survived to adulthood, were all that Maillet and Petit desired, and they began to practice some form of effective contraception.

Other couples were less successful than Maillet and Petit when it came to practicing contraception. After the passage of considerable amounts of time during which they bore no children, another was conceived. Because there is no discernable reason for most of these couples to have changed their minds about the desirability of another child, it appears that their previously effective contraceptive system ceased either to function or to be used by them, for some unexplainable reason. Marie Anne Saunier and Jacques Etienne Havel, for instance, were married in 1787 when she was twenty-one and he was twenty-nine. Eleven months later, Marie bore her first child. By 1799, she had had five children, two of whom had died in infancy. For seven years, she bore no more children; she and Jacques raised their three children and worked for the textile merchants, he as a weaver and she as a flax spinner. Then, in 1807, when she was forty-one and Jacques was forty-nine, Marie bore a sixth child. The conception of this child did not follow the death of any other child in the family, and her birth appears, at least to modern eyes, to have been an accident rather than the result of a decision to have another child.

Still other couples appear to have altered contraceptive practices after the death of a child. Marie Magdeleine Blondel and Joseph Augustin Mallet married in 1805. Between 1806 and 1817, they had four children at fairly wide intervals. (There were fifty-nine, forty-eight, and thirty-one months between the births of their children.) The last of these children and the only son, Joseph, died in January 1819, when he was only seventeen months old. Eight and a half months later, Marie Magdeleine bore a fifth child and second son, once again named Joseph. Although we cannot be sure, it seems quite likely that this conception was a deliberate decision to replace the ailing or dead son.

While individual couples made individual decisions about childbearing, the change in the demographic patterns in Auffay clearly indicates that couples who married during the transition phase in cottage industry practiced some form of birth control, as it became apparent that the overall decline in female and child employment was permanent. This does not appear to have been an unusual response to the loss of employment in cottage industry in proto-industrial regions. David Levine found an increased practice of birth control in Shepshed betwen 1825 and 1851, when the village was in a state of industrial involution, and has argued that the latter caused the former. Similarly, he has argued, the increase in the size of the last birth interval (which Wrigley found in the village of Colyton in the second half of the seventeenth century) was a response to the loss of employment in the woolen industry.[75]

The practice of birth control in proto-industrial Auffay once again illustrates the importance of women's earnings to the family economy and to decisions about childbearing, because only women (and children), not men, were experiencing a major, long-term decline in employment. More important, however, than the decrease in the size of completed families or the rise in female celibacy as the cottage textile industry began to contract is the narrow range of change in the demographic patterns in Auffay, compared with what historians have found in other proto-industrial regions. This difference between the Caux and the other regions stems to a large degree, I argue, from the fact that at all stages in the proto-industrial process, cottage industry in the Caux provided employment primarily for women rather than for entire families. In Auffay, very few families depended totally on the putting-out merchants for employment. Instead, women whose husbands and fathers were employed in a wide range of occupations worked first as spinners and then as weavers. Consequently, fluctuations in labor demand were felt throughout the entire community and, for most families, were muted by the general stability of male occupations. In Auffay, at least, men and women were not cut free from the traditional economic constraints on marriage age and childbearing. In fact, both marital and childbearing decisions were more responsive to the contraction of women's employment in the nineteenth century than they had been to its expansion in the eighteenth.

8

Widowhood, remarriage, and the sexual division of labor

In 1783, Jacques Etienne Quevillon married Marie Anne Moisson. He was a twenty-seven-year-old weaver and she was a twenty-eight-year-old spinner, occupations that they appear to have held consistently throughout their marriage. Nineteen months after the wedding, Marie Anne bore a daughter, Marie Anne Felicité. Four and a half years later, she bore a second child, a son named Charles Tranquille. In 1794, the five-year-old Charles Tranquille and his mother died within two weeks of each other, perhaps of a contagious disease, although the parish and civil registers for Auffay never report the cause of death. Less than four months after the death of his wife and son, and with a ten-year-old daughter to care for, Jacques Etienne married again. He was thirty-eight. His new wife, Marie Magdeleine Saunier, was four years his junior and, like Marie Anne Moisson, was a spinner.[1]

Nineteenth-century middle-class observers of peasant life were shocked by the rapidity with which men like Jacques Etienne Quevillon remarried after the death of a spouse. In their eyes, this was proof that peasant marriages were merely economic arrangements, and that no emotional bond existed between husband and wife.[2] Some historians have subscribed to this view and believe that peasant marriage was based purely on financial considerations. Others have taken a different view of the haste with which many peasants and artisans remarried and have argued, either implicitly or explicitly, that although a rapid second marriage might have been motivated primarily by economic considerations, it is not necessary to assume that economic need was the only reason for a couple to marry or for a widow or widower to remarry. The existence of the family economy and a desire to reestablish it after the death of a spouse did not, they suggest, necessarily preclude physical attraction, affection, and love.

The positions scholars have taken in this debate depend largely on their views of the sexual division of labor and of men's attitudes toward women's work. In general, male historians have viewed the division of labor and roles within the family as having been much more rigid and the position of women as much more inferior than female historians have. Writing in 1972, for instance, Micheline Baulant suggested that the rapidity with which many men and some women remarried could largely be explained by "solid economic reasons." Expanding the point, she went on to describe the division of labor and mutual dependence that existed between the sexes in the vine-growing region near Paris:

. . . in a household of small peasants – the vine-growers and hired men typical of the region – not only did the wife cook, keep house, mend, and raise her own children and those of previous marriages, but she also spun and cared for the livestock, both poultry and cows. Without a wife, there was no cow and therefore no milk and no cheese, nor were there hens, chicks, and eggs. In addition, inventories made after death for bachelors or men who had been widowers for a number of years are always characterized by an almost total lack of linens – shirts, sheets, tablecloths, napkins. On the other hand, although the wife, always as busy as a bee, could care for the vineyard or "saw" the grain almost as well as a man, the male was irreplaceable for certain types of heavy work, especially for the vintage. . . . In addition, only the man was capable of bringing a sufficient amount of money into the household. Not only was the woman less well paid for a similar amount of work – about half as much as a man – but many fewer oportunities for work were available to women.[3]

Baulant's account leaves little doubt that in this region where a sexual division of labor existed both inside and outside the family and where women were paid less and had fewer job opportunities than men, marriage (and remarriage) improved the economic well-being of both sexes. The man needed the housekeeping/childrearing and animal husbandry skills of the woman; the woman needed the greater earning capacity and physical strength of the man. For economic reasons alone, most widows and widowers with young children had no choice but to remarry quickly, regardless of how deeply they mourned their lost spouse. Although Baulant did not explore the point, she also suggested, however, that "the climate of insecurity that made solitude difficult to bear" might have been a factor in the speed with which men and women remarried,[4] thus leaving us with a picture in which men and women sought each other out not only for economic reasons, but also for companionship.

In contrast to Baulant, and basing his judgment on the reports of physicians and government officials that male peasants were more likely to call a veterinarian to attend a sick cow than a doctor to attend a sick wife (" 'The first may only be recuperated with money; the second is repaired with another woman, who will bring with her some money and furniture and who, instead of impoverishing the household, will increase its wealth.' "),[5] Edward Shorter argued in 1975 that "the prospect of death seemed to arouse no deep sentiments between spouses."[6] Indeed, he ventured, "On the farm, man and wife got along in quiet hostility and withdrawal," a state of affairs that was both created and perpetuated by a "strict demarcation of work assignments and sex roles."[7]

The difference between Baulant's and Shorter's views of peasant marriages is largely a result of their differing views of the sexual division of labor. Baulant's description of it conveys a sense of complementarity and mutual dependence between spouses (albeit within a larger society that paid women less than men for similar work). Shorter, on the other hand, sees the division between men's work and women's work as "sanctifying the wife's subordination to her husband."[8]

In addition to Shorter, François Lebrun, whose work on family life in the *Ancien Régime* also appeared in 1975, described a strict boundary between men's work and women's work in language clearly indicating that he viewed women's contributions to the family as subsidiary to and less valuable than men's:

. . . to the husband, professional tasks; to the wife, manager of existing goods more than producer of new goods, the domestic tasks, that is to say raising the children after bringing them into the world, preparing meals, washing the laundry, keeping the house proper, while the husband keeps a careful hand on the external affairs of the household. Yet the woman of the popular classes *is forced* to participate also in professional work, but always in a well-defined arena, and *at tasks which are fitting for her.* Thus among urban merchants and artisans, she keeps the shop. In textiles, she spins, leaving to her husband the heavy loom of the weaver. In the countryside, the man is occupied with the horse, she, with the courtyard and the milking shed; he reaps, she gathers; he threshes, she winnows; he hunts, she cooks.[9]

Following Baulant rather than Shorter and Lebrun, Joan Scott and Louise Tilly, writing in 1978, emphasized not the strictness and hierarchy of the division of labor, but the complementarity of male and female tasks in the family and the mutual dependence of husbands and wives. "Although the jobs they performed may have differed," they argued, "the work of husband and wife were equally necessary to the household."[10] Focusing on women, they concluded that remarriage was the best solution for a widow, because the low wages paid in female occupations meant that she was unlikely to be able to support herself. Widows who failed to find new spouses, as charity roles illustrate, ended up in poverty.[11]

The themes of interdependence and complementarity that appeared in the work of Baulant and Tilly and Scott were repeated and expanded in the 1980 works of Martine Segalen and Françoise Zonabend.[12] Rejecting completely the picture of rigidly maintained divisions of labor drawn by

Shorter and Lebrun, Segalen and Zonabend argued, in separate works, that the sexual division of labor was highly fluid and that women's work was complementary rather than subordinate to men's work. In Zonabend's view, "marriage was a symmetrical association in which the husband and wife performed different but complementary activities, without one being subordinated to the other or considered as accomplishing less valuable tasks."[13] As evidence, she cites the fact that husbands and wives called each other by their first names, referred to "my husband" and "my wife," and were called "le patron et la patronne" by outsiders.[14] In fact, she thinks, the division of labor was more apparent than real, more maintained in public than in private.[15]

Although she cites different evidence, Segalen clearly agrees with Zonabend. As evidence of the fluidity of the sexual division of labor, she notes that it varied from place to place and season to season, depending on the family's need for workers at a particular task.[16] To be sure, there were communal norms that governed male and female work and behavior, but the norms were not, she thinks rigidly enforced, and each sex was well aware that "the future of the household depended on the complementary and interdependent labor of the spouses."[17] In short, Segalen and Zonabend both acknowledge the existence of a general male–female hierarchy but argue that it was less pronounced within the family than in the labor market and legal codes. By implication, Baulant, Scott, Tilly, Segalen, and Zonabend would not regard rapid remarriage as proof of affectionless marriages. Instead, it was a reestablishment of the essential economic unit, not out of callousness but out of necessity. This was not a necessity that precluded all choice, however, as Shorter and Lebrun appear to imply. When men and women looked for new spouses, they were looking for more than a worker.

There is no evidence that women were as subordinated in marriage or that the sexual division of labor was as strict in Auffay as Shorter and Lebrun have argued was the case elsewhere in France. To the contrary, there is evidence that the sexual division of labor was fluid long before it broke down in the nineteenth century. Childcare and housekeeping may have been exclusively female tasks (there is no evidence to the contrary), but men who had learned to comb and spin as children probably helped their wives with these tasks when they had finished their own work, and wives and daughters probably took turns at the loom. Such labor exchanges probably lie behind the ease and speed with which the sexual division of labor in textiles and agriculture broke down in the nineteenth century. It seems likely that much more social upheaval would have occurred if the sexual division of labor had been rigidly observed before the introduction of spinning machines.

The persistence of wage differentials between men and women and the reappearance of a sexual division of labor in weaving as the nineteenth century wore on indicate, however, that complementary and relatively fluid sexual divisions of labor should not be confused with sexual equality. A general male–female hierarchy did exist in Auffay. Men were paid more than women, and it was undoubtedly easier for women to enter men's occupations than it would have been for men to enter women's. It was also easier for men to find a new spouse. In fact, the need to reestablish an economic partnership after the death of a husband and the ability to do so were inversely related for women, and the poorest widows, as Scott and Tilly pointed out, ended up on the charity roles.

Widowhood and remarriage in Auffay

The Auffay peasants and artisans were no exception to the general European pattern of rapid remarriage after the death of a spouse, although men generally remarried more rapidly and more frequently than women.

Like Jacques Etienne Quevillon, seventeen of the forty Auffay widowers who found second wives remarried within a year of their first wives' deaths. An additional nine remarried during the second year of their widowhood (making a total of 65.0 percent who remarried before two years had passed). In contrast, only four of the eighteen Auffay widows who remarried in the village did so within a year of their first husbands' deaths, and only three remarried during the second year (a total of 38.9 percent). If a woman did not remarry within a few years of the loss of her husband, it was unlikely that she would ever do so, although there were some exceptions.[18]

The Family Reconstitution Study of Auffay brides and grooms shows that the chances of a widower remarrying were much greater than those of a widow. Of the 590 single women and men who married in Auffay between 1751 and 1850, 96 women and 83 men survived their spouses and continued to live in the village until they either remarried or died. Less than 20 percent of the women but almost 50 percent of the men married again.[19]

The parish and civil records of Auffay marriages show the same pattern – more frequent remarriage for men than for women. In addition, they show a marked decline in the ratio of remarriages to marriages as the proto-industrial period progressed. During the spinning era in Auffay

Table 8.1. *Frequency of remarriage and length of widowhood,*
Auffay widows and widowers, 1751–1850

	Women		Men	
	Number	Percentage	Number	Percentage
Remarry:				
Yes	18	18.8	40	48.2
No	78	81.2	43	51.8
Total	96	100.0	83	100.0
Widowhood length (Years):				
If remarry		4.2		1.7
If do not remarry		14.0		8.5

Source: Family Reconstitution Study.

(1751–86), 28 percent of the marriages in Auffay were a remarriage for
at least one person. During the transition from cottage to factory spinning (1787–1817), the percentage of marriages involving a widow or
widower declined by more than 10 percentage points. The decline continued during the weaving era so that between 1818 and 1850 only 13.2
percent of the marriages in the village involved a widow or widower. The
decline affected both women and men, but it was much greater for women.
Whereas three widows remarried for every four widowers in the spinning
era, only one widow remarried for every two widowers in the weaving
era.[20]

The difference in the speed and frequency with which Auffay women
and men remarried is typical of eighteenth- and nineteenth-century peasants and artisans, although it is not clear whether the same factors were
at work in all communities. In Auffay, the possibility that the difference
was the result of a shorter life expectancy for widows than for widowers
can be easily eliminated from consideration. The average widowhood
length for women who did not remarry was 14.0 years, whereas it was
only 8.5 years for men.[21] Similarly, the overall decline in the remarriage
rate during the proto-industrial period cannot be attributed to the dis-
appearance of widows and widowers from the community – in 1851,
there were twenty-eight widowers and fifty-two widows in Auffay.[22]

Instead, the continuously lower female remarriage rate and the general
decline in the number of remarriages reflect a variety of cultural values
and economic realities, such as, the age of widowhood, the preference of
men for younger rather than older women, the sexual division of labor

Table 8.2. *Types of marriages, Auffay, 1751–1850*

Type of marriage	Cohort 1 (1751–1786)		Cohort 2 (1787–1817)		Cohort 3 (1818–1850)	
	Number	Percent-age	Number	Percent-age	Number	Percent-age
First marriage for both spouses	154	72.0	193	82.8	243	86.8
Remarriage for one or both Spouses	60	28.0	40	17.2	37	13.2
Total	214	100.0	233	100.0	280	100.0
Remarriage for women	30	14.0	18	7.7	17	6.1
Remarriage for men	40	18.7	31	13.3	29	10.4

Source: ADSM Parish and Civil Registers, Auffay.

within the family, the relative earning capacity of men and women, and changes in the female labor market. Together, these factors determined the fate of many widows and, once again, tell us how important the cottage textile industry was to the women in this region.

The age at which widowhood occurred was a major factor in determining whether a man or a woman would remarry. The majority of both men and women who were widowed in their twenties and thirties (74 percent of the women and 86 percent of the men) did remarry.[23] It was, however, more common for men than for women to be widowed before they reached age forty. Of the 107 Auffay brides who watched their husbands die, only ten were still in their twenties and thirteen were in their thirties (21.5 percent). Of the 106 Auffay grooms who lost their wives, 15 were in their twenties and 26 were in their thirties when they were widowed (38.7 percent).[24]

The greater likelihood of young widowhood for men than for women was largely a result of the health risks women encountered in pregnancy and childbirth. Sometimes marriages were tragically short. In September 1768, for instance, Marie Marguerite Asselin, a spinner, married Guillaume Louvard, a furniture maker. He was only twenty-seven and she was thirty-three. Eight months after the wedding, Marie gave birth to a son, Guillaume. The child lived for only four days; Marie Marguerite, for nine. At twenty-eight, Guillaume was a widower. Even women who had given birth to several healthy children might not survive pregnancy and childbirth. Marie Anne Dubuc, for instance, who married Charles Berquier in 1764, bore four healthy children in seven years. The fifth child, born when Marie Anne was only twenty-nine, was sickly and died three days after birth. Marie Anne survived another five weeks and then she too died, leaving behind three small children (her fourth child had died at age ten months) and a thirty-two-year-old husband. Altogether, between 1751 and 1850, seventeen Auffay brides died following childbirth. Fourteen of them left husbands who were in their twenties and thirties.[25]

There was no comparable killer of men in the early years of marriage, although women, too, could be widowed at young ages. In 1768, for instance, Louise Grillère watched her seven-month-old daughter, ten-year-old son, and forty-year-old husband die. Suddenly, she was a thirty-four-year-old widow with three small children (aged eight, four, and three) to support.[26] It was rarer, however, for women to be widowed in their twenties and thirties than it was for men. This fact partially accounts for the higher percentage of Auffay widowers, as compared with widows, who remarried, because the younger the widow(er), the greater the chances of remarriage.

The younger average age of men at widowhood does not sufficiently explain their higher remarriage rate, however, because men were more likely to remarry at every age, and men widowed in their forties and fifties were six times more likely to remarry than were women who were widowed at these ages (53.6 percent of the men versus 8.7 percent of the women remarried).[27] Other interrelated factors were also at work.

All men, but especially widowers, tended to marry women who were younger than themselves. Sixty-two percent of the single men who married in Auffay married younger women. Among widowers, the rate was even higher. Seventy-one percent married younger women, and 56 percent married women who were more than five years their junior.[28] Since the mean marriage age for men was 28.1 at first marriage and 42.8 at remarriage,[29] it is hardly surprising that only four of the seventy-five women who were widowed in their forties, fifties, and sixties were able to find new husbands. (see Table 8.3.). Widows, in fact, were more likely to marry younger men than were women who were marrying for the first time. Forty-five percent of them, compared with 30 percent of first brides, married younger men.[30] Their willingness to marry younger men could not offset, however, the preference of single and widowed men for younger

Table 8.3. *Remarriage of men and women according to age at which widowed, Auffay, 1751–1850*

Age at end of marriage	Widow remarries			Widower remarries		
	Yes	No	Total	Yes	No	Total
20–29	6	1	7	8	0	8
30–39	8	4	12	10	3	13
40–49	3	14	17	8	3	11
50–59	1	28	29	7	10	17
60–69	0	21	21	6	11	17
70–79	0	8	8	1	11	12
Total	18	76	94	40	38	78

Note: Thirteen widows and twenty-eight widowers who cannot be followed to another marriage or their own death are not included in the table.
Source: Family Reconstitution Study.

women, which, combined with the relatively high age at which most women were widowed, automatically reduced their chances of remarrying.

Given the economic nature of the marriage partnership in the proto-industrial world, the male preference for younger women probably reflects the effects of age on a woman's earning ability. Earnings in cottage industry depended on output, and younger women could produce more than older women, especially in the nineteenth century when weaving replaced spinning as the employer of female labor. The same was true of sewing and agricultural day laboring. Young women could produce more than older women and hence earn more. An older man (whose earning capacity was also reduced in certain occupations) who was searching for an additional breadwinner would have been wise to marry a relatively young, able-bodied woman rather than a woman in his own age group. In addition, widowers, many of whom had children of their own, may have preferred unmarried (hence younger) women to widows because they did not have children. This was not inevitably the case, however, because the Auffay widows who remarried in their twenties and thirties frequently had children.

Although widows were always less likely to remarry than were widowers, the difference between the two gender groups increased after the introduction of spinning machines. Again, women's earning ability is the key to this change. After the mechanization of spinning, it became much

Table 8.4. *Age differences between widows and*
widowers and their new spouses, Auffay,
1751–1850

Age difference	Widow remarries		Widower remarries	
	Number	Percentage	Number	Percentage
Woman older	29	44.6	27	27.0
Same age	3	4.6	2	2.0
Man older	33	50.8	71	71.0
Total	65	100.0	100	100.0
Mean age		39.4		42.8

Source: ADSM Marriage Registers, Auffay.

more difficult for village women to find employment. Those who lacked
a job could not find a first or a second husband. It was as if the men in
Auffay had read the eighteenth-century English advice manual that said,
"None but a fool will take a wife whose bread must be earned solely by
his labour and who will contribute nothing towards it herself."[31] Unfortunately for many widows, this meant that their ability to find a second
husband declined at the same time that their economic need to find one
increased.

Just as the sexual divisions of labor in the paid labor force affected a
widow's ability to find a husband, the sexual division of labor within the
family affected a widower's need to remarry and was an additional factor
in the higher remarriage rate for men than for women. Leaving aside
companionship, sex, and other intangible reasons for remarrying, the major
advantage of remarriage for a woman was the addition of another breadwinner to the household. For a man, remarriage provided not only another breadwinner, but also a person who would cook and care for the
house, garden, animals, and children – all essential aspects of everyday
life. Even widowers who had helped their wives with these activities possessed no expertise in them and would have violated communal norms if
they had begun to perform tasks that were regarded as women's work.
A widower who did not remarry quickly needed the help of a mother,
sister, older female child, or servant to carry on everyday life. For many
men, such wife surrogates must have been difficult to find, and the only
viable solution to the problems created by a wife's death was rapid remarriage.

Although most women had few if any resources to fall back on after the death of their husbands, a few widows of land or business owners were left relatively well off. In the eighteenth century, the *pays'* inheritance laws automatically awarded women the dowry they had brought to the marriage, one-third of the moveable goods owned by the husband before or acquired by the couple after the wedding, and a lifetime right to the income from one-third of the landed property. When a widow's children were young, she had the use of, and responsibility for, all the moveable and immoveable property.[32]

With the introduction of the Napoleonic Civil Code in 1804, women lost their usufructory rights but became equal inheritors with their brothers in their parents' property, and their inheritance rights vis-à-vis their husbands were spelled out in marriage contracts. In the first half of the nineteenth century, as in the second half of the eighteenth, several widows in Auffay controlled considerable property, and the wives of artisans and merchants inherited and carried on several of the major businesses in the village.

Paradoxically, these widows, who were the least in need of remarriage from an economic standpoint, were precisely the ones who were the most attractive marriage partners. Eleven of the eighteen women who married, lost their husbands, and remarried in Auffay were the widows of artisans, merchants, and cultivators – the three most lucrative village occupations. For them, remarriage was less of a financial benefit than it was for poor spinners, weavers, and day laborers. Instead, it was a way of reestablishing a sharing of burdens. It freed them from the burden of having to run both a home and a tannery, mill, large farm, or smithy. Seraphie Fouquet's marital history clearly illustrates the possibilities open to economically secure widows.[33]

In 1808, seventeen-year-old Seraphie, the daughter of a merchant, married Charles Fouché, a thirty-two-year-old tanner and currier of leather. Although the marriage register listed Seraphie as a merchant, it was not an occupation she pursued after her marriage. Instead, she worked as a seamstress and spinner until 1812, when she began to help her husband with the tannery, a job she continued to hold throughout the rest of their marriage. Pregnant when she married (which probably accounts for her unusually young marriage age), Seraphie bore eight children to Charles and was seven months pregnant when he died in 1823.

Eleven months after Charles' death, Seraphie, now the mother of six living children and again pregnant, married David Gabriel Allain, another tanner. Like her first husband, he was many years her senior (he was forty-five; she was thirty-three). David and Seraphie had only one child, Aline Alexandrine, born six and a half months after the wedding. Pregnancy may have hastened this marriage, as it did her first, but Seraphie was clearly a good match for David Allain. All of her children were young, and she was the undisputed operator of the tannery, which she clearly was experienced in running. During their fourteen-year marriage, Seraphie and David acquired a café, which Seraphie ran while David operated the tannery. When David died in 1838, Seraphie again found another husband within the year. Now aged forty-eight, she married Charles Jullien, a *fermier* who was two years her senior and previously unmarried. By 1851, Seraphie had ceased to operate either the café or the tannery (which had been sold or leased) and was helping to run the farm.

Although pregnancy may have hastened two of Seraphie's marriages, all of them resulted, at least in part, from her good financial situation and not from her need for economic support. And whereas each marriage took her another rung up the economic ladder, none created a life of leisure for her. When she appears in the civil registers and censuses, she is always listed as employed, even in eras when it was common not to record female occupations. By marrying Allain and Jullien, she gained someone to share the work of running a tannery or farm, additional income, a legitimate lover, a father for her children, and, perhaps, a companion, but *not* someone who would "take care of" her.

Widows like Seraphie, with good opportunities to remarry if they wished, were the exception in Auffay. Most inherited little or nothing and had only their earnings in cottage industry or agriculture to offer a prospective husband. As a result, life alone for a widow (as for a spinster) was more likely to have been imposed by economic hardship rather than chosen out of a desire for independence.

Women who did not remarry

When necessary, it was possible for women to support themselves on their earnings in cottage industry, although it was far from easy. In this sense, Auffay was notably different from many other villages in which a widow could not survive alone and had to move in with other members of her family, take in boarders, or herself become a boarder.[34] In Auffay, it was possible for a widow to survive alone. In 1771, for instance, eighteen out of the 170 households were headed by widows (10.6 percent).[35]

The circumstances in which widows lived varied considerably. The widows of landowning peasants were better off than any of the others. In 1771, one widow lived in a house surrounded by a *masure,* farmed three acres of land, and owned two cows. Another held a two-acre farm, and two had houses and *masures* but no arable land. At the other end of the spectrum were eleven widows who possessed only a *couvert* (a very poor cottage with no land). No occupation is listed for any of these women, but, given the prevalence of spinning as a female occupation, most of them were probably supporting themselves by working for the putting-out merchants. The poorest among them lived close to the subsistence line, and the addition of another adult wage earner to their households (particularly a male wage earner because men were paid better than women) surely would have been desirable. They were, however, able to survive without taking in boarders and without becoming boarders themselves. Moreover, only two of the women had sons over the age of twelve living with them and contributing to their income.

In 1796, sixty-one of the 256 households in Auffay were headed by women (23.8 percent).[36] Two-thirds of these women were spinners. Even though cottage spinning was already in jeopardy by this time, no women in the village were listed as *mendicantes,* and many were able to support themselves and their children on what they earned from the putting-out merchants. Eighteen of the twenty-four women who lived alone (or only with children under the age of twelve who were not listed in the census) were spinners and must have had few resources other than their wages.

Women who depended on their own and sometimes their children's earnings from spinning did not live well, but they did survive. Only ten out of fifty widows in Auffay were living in the households of relatives in 1796. Forty were able to support themselves and to remain in their own homes.[37] Men, on the other hand, appear to have been much less able to survive without the contributions of a woman. In contrast to the fifty-two households in Auffay that contained no adult men (over the age of twenty) in 1796, there were only seven households without an adult woman. This difference is to be expected, given the higher remarriage rate for widowers than for widows, but that rate itself probably reflects the men's need for women.

As the employment opportunities for women declined in the nineteenth century, so did their ability to support themselves without the contributions of an adult man. By 1851, the percentage of households headed by women had declined to 19.2 percent, the percentage of widows who were living with their children rather than heading their own households had risen from 20.0 to 26.9 percent, and eleven women were

Table 8.5. *Living arrangements of widows, Auffay,*
1796 and 1851

Living arrangement	1796 Number	1796 Percentage	1851 Number	1851 Percentage
Head of household:				
Living alone	12	24.0	22	42.3[a]
Supporting children	28	56.0	15	28.9
Total	40	80.0	37	71.2
Living with kin	10	20.0	14	26.9
Boarding	0	—	0	—
Servant	0	—	1	1.9
Total	10	20.0	15	28.8
Total	50	100.0	52	100.0

[a]The increase in the percentage of widows living alone probably reflects
the increased migration of unmarried adult men, i.e., sons who in an
earlier era might have lived with their mothers, out of the region in the
mid-nineteenth century.
Source: ADSM L367, 6M83.

dependent on charity. Of the thirty-five women who lived entirely alone,
five were *mendicantes,* four were trying to earn money by spinning (which
was almost impossible by 1851), and nine were day laborers – work that
must have been very difficult for women who ranged in age from fifty to
seventy-nine.[38] As Scott and Tilly observed, "Remarriage was clearly the
happiest solution for a widow, since an economic partnership was the
best means of survival."[39] Unfortunately, it was not always possible.

Widows and widowers who did not remarry and who managed to
maintain their own households were the lucky ones. Those who could
not survive on their own because of poverty or frail health were forced
to reside with a child or other relative or to seek charity. The decision to
live with a child was not taken lightly by either party. Before the move
took place, the elderly parent and child often drew up a legal contract
stating what goods the parent possessed, who was to retain possession of
these goods if the parent were to leave the child's household, what the
parent was to contribute to his or her own support, and what the child
owed the parent in exchange for the use of certain goods or money.

Typical of the contracts drawn up in the Caux was one signed by Florence Bimont and her son, David Houdeville, in 1800. Florence Bimont

Table 8.6. *Sex and marital status of heads of households, Auffay, 1796 and 1851*

Head of household	1796		1851	
	Number	Percentage	Number	Percentage
Single man	1	0.4	25	6.9
Married man	165	64.5	243	67.5
Widower	9	3.5	23	6.4
Adult man[a]	20	7.8	0	—
Total	195	76.2	291	80.8
Single woman	4	1.6	21	5.8
Married woman	1	0.4	11	3.1
Widow	40	15.6	37	10.3
Adult woman[a]	16	6.2	0	—
Total	61	23.8	69	19.2
Total households	256	100.0	360	100.0

[a]The 1796 census does not list marital status for several men and women. It is likely, however, that many of these individuals were unmarried. Hence, there probably was no significant increase in the number of households headed by single men and single women between 1796 and 1851.
Source: ADSM L367, 6M83.

had been widowed twice and was seventy-seven years old. She declared that, because of her advanced age and infirmities, she was no longer able to live alone or to work and that she was going to live with her son by her second marriage. He agreed that he would "receive her, provide her with food, and a place to sleep, heat, light, clean clothes, and [would] care for her until the end of her days."

Florence listed the goods that she was taking to her son's home. They included a spinning wheel (the one item that virtually every woman owned in the eighteenth century), dishes, a poor wooden bed, a mattress, and some clothes. There was to be no communal ownership of her furniture and clothes. They were to remain her property, and "in case of incompatibility of temperament or otherwise," she would leave her son and would take either her possessions or a money payment for them.[40]

It is remarkable that there were not more Auffay women in the position of Florence Bimont – forced by age and poverty to seek help from a relative. But even though the number of impoverished widows and spinsters in the Caux increased as women lost jobs first in spinning and then in weaving, as late as 1851 most widows were able to support themselves in their own households. Earnings from spinning, weaving, sewing, and dressmaking were too low to make it easy for women to survive alone, but they did make it possible. Life alone was far from comfortable for most widows and spinsters, but it was more attractive than the loss of freedom and pride that accompanied residence with a child or financial dependence on the church or the government. In short, even the long hours and low pay that cottage workers faced were preferable to the poverty and hopelessness endured by jobless women in this or other regions.

~.~

9

Unwed mothers and their children

When Marguerite Saunier walked down the aisle of the Auffay church in 1777, she was four months pregnant. When her daughter, Marie Marguerite Baudouin, made the same journey thirty years later, she was seven months pregnant. And when her granddaughter, Marguerite Josephine Maillard, married Evariste Sylvain Hallebout in 1833, she was still recovering from the birth of her first child, born five weeks earlier and probably fathered by Hallebout, although we cannot be certain because the child died at birth and there was no need for him to declare his parenthood at the wedding.[1]

At first glance, this may appear to be the story of the moral decline of a family. But although individual experiences and decisions lie behind the pregnancy of every woman, Marie Marguerite Saunier, Marie Marguerite Baudouin, and Marguerite Josephine Maillard were typical of their generations. In the mid-eighteenth century, one-fifth of the women who married in Auffay were pregnant. In the last decade of the century and on into the nineteenth, this number increased to well over one-quarter; while the number of women who bore children out of wedlock increased sixfold from midcentury to midcentury. The reasons for these changes are complex, as were their effects on the Auffay community. Taken together, they illustrate the extent to which fluctuations in the textile industry and the French Revolution disrupted traditional behavior patterns and undermined the authority structure in Auffay, as well as the remarkable degree to which the community was eventually able to adapt to social and economic change.

The demographic evidence

In the spinning era, sexual relations preceded marriage for many couples, and pregnancy was almost always followed by marriage. Between 1751 and 1786, one-fifth of the women who married in Auffay were pregnant when they walked down the aisle. Although some time elapsed between the time a woman became pregnant and the time she married (see Table

9.2.), very few failed to marry the father of the child before it was born. In all, only sixteen women bore illegitimate children during these years.[2]

During the transition from spinning to weaving as the dominant form of employment in the cottage textile industry (1787–1817), the percentage of pregnant brides increased from one-fifth to over one-quarter, and the interval between conception and marriage began to lengthen. Even more strikingly, the number of women who bore illegitimate children increased to fifty-two, a threefold increase over the spinning era. It remained difficult for single mothers to marry, however, and only three women who married during this era are known to have borne a child out of wedlock.[3]

During the weaving era (1818–50), the percentage of brides who were pregnant fell back to one out of five, but the interval between conception and marriage continued to lengthen (eleven brides, compared to only one during the spinning era, were into the final two months of their pregnancies before they took their wedding vows), and the number of women who bore illegitimate children rose to sixty-five. Even more significant in terms of social connotations was the dramatic increase in the number of brides who were already mothers. Whereas only five women who can be identified as having borne a child out of wedlock married in Auffay during the spinning and transition eras combined, twenty-two brides (14.0 percent of all Auffay brides who bore a child in the village either before or after marriage) were the mothers of illegitimate children during the weaving era. Illegitimacy was becoming much more common, and it was becoming much easier for the mothers of illegitimate children to marry than it had been earlier in the proto-industrial period.[4] (See Tables 9.1 and 9.2.)

When the figures on illegitimate births are broken down by decade, it becomes clear that although there was a slow increase in the incidence of illegitimacy in the second half of the eighteenth century, the major increase began at the turn of the nineteenth century. In the 1801 to 1810 decade, 10.5 percent of all the births in Auffay were to women who were not married, more than double the percentage in the previous decade. From then until the middle of the century, one out of every eleven children was born out of wedlock.[5] (See Table 9.3.)

As illegitimate births increased, the number of pregnant brides decreased. Between 1791 and 1800, fifteen Auffay brides were pregnant and fifteen children were born out of wedlock. Between 1801 and 1810, the number of pregnant brides fell to six, whereas the number of illegitimate births climbed to twenty-eight.[6] The number of women conceiving

Table 9.1. *First conceptions of Auffay brides, 1751–1850[a]*

Type of conception and birth	Cohort 1 (1751–1786)		Cohort 2 (1787–1817)		Cohort 3 (1818–1850)	
	Number	Percentage	Number	Percentage	Number	Percentage
Illegitimate birth	2	1.8	3	2.4	22	14.0
Prenuptial conception[b]	22	19.6	36	28.1	31	19.8
Legitimate conception	88	78.6	89	69.5	104	66.2
Total	112	100.0	128	100.0	157	100.0

[a] Based on first marriages in which the wife bore a child in Auffay. Women who bore illegitimate children but did not marry are not included in the table.
[b] Child born within seven months of the marriage.
Note: One woman in Cohort 2 and one in Cohort 3 bore an illegitimate child and was pregnant with another when she married. These women are counted in both the prenuptial and illegitimate categories.
Source: Family Reconstitution Study.

Table 9.2. *Interval between conception and marriage, Auffay, 1751–1850[a]*

Interval	Cohort 1 (1751–1786)		Cohort 2 (1787–1817)		Cohort 3 (1818–1850)	
	Number	Percentage	Number	Percentage	Number	Percentage
60–90 days	3	13.6	4	11.1	3	9.7
90–120 days	5	22.7	8	22.2	7	22.6
120–150 days	1	4.6	9	25.0	2	6.4
150–180 days	5	22.7	4	11.1	2	6.4
180–210 days	7	31.8	4	11.1	6	19.4
210–240 days	0	—	4	11.1	5	16.1
240–270 days	1	4.6	3	8.4	6	19.4
Total	22	100.0	36	100.0	31	100.0

[a] Based on first marriages.
Source: Family Reconstitution Study.

Table 9.3. *Legitimate and illegitimate births in Auffay,*
1751–1850[a]

Date	Total births[b]		Illegitimate births	
	Number		Number	Percentage of all births
1751–1760	249		5	2.0
1761–1770	265		4	1.5
1771–1780	262		8	3.1
1781–1790	285		10	3.5
1791–1800	324		15	4.6
1801–1810	266		28	10.5
1811–1820	278		25	9.0
1821–1830	317		26	8.2
1831–1840	333		26	7.8
1841–1850	332		31	9.3

[a] Only includes children born to residents of Auffay.
[b] Includes stillbirths and children who died without being named.
Source: Parish and Civil Registers, Auffay.

a child out of wedlock was not changing much, but their fate was. For reasons that are explored later in this chapter, it was becoming increasingly difficult for a woman to convert pregnancy into marriage. Over the period of a half century, the change in the number of illegitimate children and unwed mothers in Auffay was considerable. Between 1751 and 1800, there were forty-two illegitimate births in Auffay. Between 1801 and 1850, there were 136 illegitimate births.[7] Until the community adjusted its attitudes toward illegitimacy, the vast majority of the mothers of these children would remain unmarried. Then, late in the proto-industrial period, both the mothers of illegitimate children and the grown children themselves would begin to marry in hitherto undreamed of numbers.

Auffay was not the only village in France in which illegitimacy was increasing in the late eighteenth century. What was happening here was part of a European-wide development, the causes of which have been hotly debated by demographic and social historians. Edward Shorter has ascribed the rise in illegitimacy to an increase in premarital sexual activity that, in a society whose major means of preventing conception was *coitus interruptus,* frequently resulted in the conception of a child.[8] He views this increase in sexual activity as a result of a change in the attitudes of young adults who "deliberately decided to remove their intimate lives from subjection to communal supervision"[9] when they "awakened to the fact that life involves more than just doing your duty in the eyes of the local social authorities and doing your work in the same way that your father had done it, and his father before him."[10] Despite the male orientation of his language, Shorter ascribes most of this awakening to the participation of young, unmarried women in the free-market labor force where they became economically independent and learned to pursue their own self-interest, a lesson they soon applied to their personal relationships where the search for self-fulfillment became a search for sexual fulfillment.[11] Shorter's argument is primarily designed to explain the rise of urban illegitimacy rates, but he does suggest that employment in what he calls "the cottage-industrial system", that is, market-oriented putting-out systems, had the same effect on values and behavior as industrialization proper.[12] The increase in illegitimacy is, for him, the end link in a causal chain that began with the rise of market capitalism, led to a change in values, and ended with a change in sexual behavior.

In direct contradiction to Shorter, Louise Tilly, Joan Scott, and Miriam Cohen have argued that market capitalism, far from liberating women economically and sexually, made them lonely, economically insecure, anxious to establish a family economy with a man, and, therefore, increasingly vulnerable to marriage promises and abandonment.[13] Sex outside of marriage was not new in their eyes, and women, they suggest, engaged in it as a part of courtship, not as an end in itself. Women's persistence in this behavior, combined with the increased geographical and occupational mobility that came with industrialization, made it easier for men to abandon lovers than it had been in the past. In their view, the nineteenth-century increase in illegitimacy was the result not of a change in attitudes and beliefs, but of "men and women engag[ing] in intercourse with established expectations, but in changed or changing contexts."[14] Like Shorter, they focus on the urban world, but their analysis can also be applied to rural communities where geographical, if not occupational, mobility came with proto-industrialization and industrialization.

David Levine and Keith Wrightson have argued along the same lines as Tilly, Scott, and Cohen in attempting to explain the sixteenth-century increase in illegitimacy in England.[15] They also regard sexual relations as a common feature of courtship in the preindustrial rural world and argue that the persistence of betrothed couples in this behavior, in periods where "fundamental demographic, economic, social, administrative and ideological changes" made marriage more difficult, resulted in increases in illegitimacy.[16] Cissie Fairchilds, focusing specifically on the urban area of

Aix-en-Provence in the late eighteenth century, has seconded and emphasized the vulnerability part of the Tilly, Scott, and Cohen thesis, arguing that a variety of developments, including worsening economic conditions that disrupted courtships and the naïveté and physical vulnerability of young women who worked and lived away from their parents, not the search for sexual fulfillment, lay behind most illegitimate births.[17]

The demographic patterns and economic conditions in Auffay between 1750 and 1850 lend much more support to the positions of Tilly, Scott, Cohen, Levine, Wrightson, and Fairchilds than they do to the Shorter thesis. By the mid-eighteenth century, sexual relations were a common part of courtship in this region, and marriage quickly followed the discovery of pregnancy. By the beginning of the nineteenth century, however, the number of women who were conceiving a child out of wedlock was increasing, and the majority of them were not marrying before the child was born.

A variety of circumstances – a decrease in contraceptive practice or an increase in contraceptive failures for unmarried couples, an increase in sexual activity outside of marriage, or an increase in unstable and long betrothals – might account for such a change. The first two explanations seem improbable. The increase in bridal pregnancy and illegitimacy occurred at the same time that married couples were limiting the size of their families. (See Chapter 7.) That contraceptive information, practice, or success would have declined in the unmarried sector of society while it increased in the married sector seems unlikely because the decline in female employment opportunities, which preceded the decline in marital fertility, affected the economic situation of unmarried women at least as much as it did that of married women. Declining employment opportunities and the low wages paid to women in this region made it extremely difficult for a woman to support herself and a child without the assistance of an adult male wage earner. Only a perception that pregnancy would precipitate marriage could have made it desirable to most unmarried women, and, in the nineteenth century, a woman had only to look around her to see that her chances of marrying after she became pregnant were deteriorating, not improving.

The increase in conception outside of marriage could also have resulted from an increase in the sexual activity of unmarried women. Such a development would lend some support to Shorter's claim that the cottage-industrial system made women economically independent and led them to seek self-fulfillment through sexual fulfillment. But given the very low wages paid to women in cottage spinning and weaving in this region and the decline in female employment that followed the mechanization of spinning, this also seems an unlikely explanation of the increase in the number of illegitimate births and pregnant brides and the lengthening intervals between conception and marriage.

A more plausible explanation is that courtship was lengthening, and the likelihood of its leading to marriage was declining. Because sexual relations were a common part of courtship, a lengthening of the time between betrothal amd marriage would increase not so much the number of women who engaged in premarital sexual intercourse, but the period during which they were at risk to become pregnant outside of marriage. In an era of largely ineffective contraception, any lengthening of the period of sexual activity would lead to an increase in the number of conceptions. The pattern of change in Auffay – first an increase in the number of pregnant brides, followed by an increase in the interval between conception and marriage, followed by an increase in the number of illegitimate births – indicates that the demise of cottage spinning was making it increasingly difficult for young couples to acquire the economic resources necessary for marriage, and that courtship was becoming increasingly long and unstable, not that women were becoming increasingly free and sexually active. In short, I think, sexual behavior remained the same, but the consequences of that behavior changed, as Tilly, Scott, Cohen, Levine, and Wrightson have suggested.

The testimony of pregnant and unmarried women supports this interpretation of the demographic data. It also, however, makes it clear that not all sex outside of marriage occurred within the context of betrothal.

Unwed mothers in Auffay

On December 27, 1799, twenty-six-year-old Marie Heron, a domestic servant in the household of the shoemaker, Louis Blanchemin, presented herself to the justice of the Peace in Auffay, as she was required to do by law, and declared that she was seven months pregnant. She had, she said, been "seduced in anticipation of marriage" by Henry Maillon, an Auffay weaver who was also a soldier in the Army of the Republic. Two months later, she would join the ranks of the unwed mothers in Auffay.[18]

Marie's explanation of her pregnancy was a common one. Women reported over and over again that the father of the child had "seduced her with promises of marriage," "promised to marry her and never to abandon her," or that she had succumbed only after "the most lively solicitations and under repeated promises to marry her."[19] Sometimes the promise was fulfilled, lending credence to the claims in general. Nineteen-year-old Madelaine Binet, for instance, accompanied by her parents, reported her pregnancy on October 26, 1793, and named Pierre Desert, a weaver, as the child's father. Three weeks later, Binet and Desert were married, well before the birth of their child on March 27, 1794.[20] Madelaine Binet's experience was the one women hoped to have if they became pregnant. Second best was marriage after the birth of the child. This rarely happened in the eighteenth century, however, and even in the nineteenth, when illegitimate births became more common, many more unwed mothers raised their children alone than ever managed to marry. (Between 1751 and 1817, only five of the sixty-eight women who bore illegitimate children in Auffay are known to have married the father of the child. In contrast, between 1818 and 1850, twenty-two mothers of illegitimate children married in Auffay, whereas sixty-five bore children out of wedlock in the village.)[21]

Some of the women who made depositions to the notary or the Justice of the Peace in Auffay reported that their pregnancies were the product of long-term relationships. Rose Lecomble of Cressy, for instance, reported that she and Jacques Luas had been living together for a year when she discovered she was pregnant. Similarly, Thèrèse Elie of Bracquetuit reported that Denis Archay, the father of her unborn child, had "promised to marry her for two years, until two months previously when he ceased to speak to her."[22] In these cases, it is easy to see why the women thought they either had or were going to establish permanent relationships with the men who fathered their children. In other cases, the women apparently believed promises they should not have, because the men were in no position to carry them out. One was involved with a married man, one with a member of a religious order, and one with her cousin, whom she may or may not have been able to marry because dispensations were possible.[23]

In still other cases, women appear to have been unlucky in short-term affairs. Thèrèse Fabulet, for instance, who lived with her parents in Cropus, reported in 1796 that she had had intercourse with Michel Delamare exactly twice – once on March 20 and again on March 25. Now she was six months pregnant.[24] In the 1790s, several young women had affairs with soldiers who were camped in the area or home on leave, only to discover that they were pregnant after the men had rejoined their regiments or the regiment itself had moved on to another camp.[25]

Sometimes the women clearly were full participants in secret affairs;

other times they were the victims of rape. Marie Magdeleine Angot's deposition in 1793 chronicles an affair that sounds as if it required stealth and nerve and certainly required her cooperation. She reported that she and François Baudouin had had intercourse several times: once in the bake house (*four*), once in the house, once in the bed where he slept at his employer's, and several times "of which she does not recall the circumstances." The danger of being caught may have heightened the attraction of this pair to each other, but, like most women, Marie Magdeleine also reported that François had promised to marry her, a promise that was broken when she became pregnant.[26]

Marie Lepetre of Bracquetuit, on the other hand, reported in 1796 that her pregnancy was "the work of an unknown whom she had encountered in the woods . . . and who had seduced her by force with violence, being armed with a shotgun."[27] When the man was known and the woman was a minor, he could be forced to pay damages. On May 19, 1776, sixteen-year-old Marie Dieutre of Heugleville-sur-Scie gave birth to a child. She and her guardian charged that this was "the work" of François Olivier, a journeyman shoemaker living in Auffay, who had overpowered her despite her resistance. Olivier was required to pay ninety-six francs to Marie, a rather small sum in light of the fact that Jean Baptiste Maromme was fined 200 francs in 1775, and Jean Crevon was forced to pay 250 francs in 1776, after similar accusations by other women.[28]

In several cases, the extent to which the woman was forced or consented to sexual relations is unclear. Several were domestic servants who succumbed to the advances of fellow servants, employers, or employers' sons.[29] In all of these cases, the woman might have hoped for marriage, but that does not mean she chose to sleep with the man in question. As Olwen Hufton and Cissie Fairchilds have pointed out, employers and their sons could easily threaten a reluctant young woman with the loss of her job, and male servants had numerous opportunities to take advantage of young female servants who were away from their families.[30]

In many ways, the most interesting illegitimate relationship that appears in the Auffay records existed between Marie Anne Mascarel Chanterine and Ignace François Jacquinet, although technically their children were not illegitimate and she was not an unwed mother. Marie Anne moved to Auffay in 1776 with two daughters and without her husband, Melchior Godfroy Chanterine. She was a tenant farmer and merchant and far from impoverished, paying 4 *livres* and 10 *sous* in *taille* and 11 *livres* in salt taxes in 1781.[31] Between 1779 and 1785, Marie Anne bore four children, all of whom bore the surname Chanterine, although the priest was more than a little suspicious of Marie Anne's marital status, not to mention the paternity of her children. At each baptism, he recorded that Marie Anne, the mother of the child, claimed to be married to Melchior Godfroy Chanterine, although he was unknown in the parish and she had no proof of the marriage.[32]

By 1781, Marie Anne was listed in the tax roles with the merchant Jacquinet.[33] Exactly when he arrived in the village is unclear. There can be very little doubt, however, that he was the father of her last two children (born in 1782 and 1785), and he may have fathered all four of the children born in Auffay.

Whereas the priest's suspicion of the identity of the father of Marie Anne's children was well founded, his suspicion of her marital status was not. It was unlikely that she would make up the name Melchior Godfroy Chanterine for a fictional husband. Moreover, on December 26, 1792, Marie Anne received the only divorce granted in Auffay during the revolutionary period. Twelve days later she married Jacquinet. Because she had been legally married to Chanterine when she bore Jacquinet's children, they were not legitimized at the wedding and continued to bear the name Chanterine.[34]

Although it is easy to imagine why pregnant women might have lied about the circumstances leading to their pregnancies, and especially why they might have tried to conceal their own complicity in these relationships by claiming they had been physically overpowered or seduced with promises of marriage, their testimony reveals a wide range of sexual experiences and relationships outside of marriage. Just as important as the variety in the testimony, however, is the claim of most women that they engaged in sex with the expectation of marriage, in short, that sexual relations were a normal part of courtship. Whether as many men promised marriage as these unwed mothers-to-be claimed is, of course, an open question. The frequency with which the claim is offered to explain the pregnancy indicates, however, that sexual relations in the context of courtship were socially acceptable behavior in this section of the Caux.

In the eighteenth century, women had good reason to believe that sexual relations were a prelude to marriage. They were in their prime marriageable years, and the promises were often fulfilled.[35] But in the 1790s, the traditional progression from pregnancy to marriage was interrupted, and more and more women found themselves confronting the problems of raising a child without the emotional or economic support of a man. Why did this happen? The answers are war, revolution, and economic depression.

The changing context of sexual relations

The 1790s and early 1800s were a period of economic depression in the proto-industrial Caux. Whenever shipments of cotton arrived, work was plentiful and wages were good. When cotton was unavailable, so was work. To add to the woes of the region, periodic harvest failures created high grain prices just when cottage workers could least afford them. David Levine has argued that it was just such a situation in proto-industrial Shepshed that led to an increase in illegitimacy in that village:

Ambiguity breeds instability, and this uncertainty was critical because it meant that courtship took place against a backdrop of quickly changing fortunes. In these circumstances decisions would perforce become reversible. In this one proto-industrial village the reverberations of international diplomacy and its natural extension, war, were felt at the most personal level. . . . the level of illegitimacy rose.[36]

In Auffay, as young women found themselves unable to get work in spinning, they also found their suitors unwilling to marry them. Instead of precipitating marriage, pregnancy made young women even less desirable as mates, and the illegitimacy rates rose.

In the 1790s, young men also began to be drafted into the French armies to fight against the Austrians, Prussians, Russians, and British. By 1800, seventy-four men from the commune of Auffay alone (and 348 men from the canton) were serving in the army and absent from their villages.[37] In some cases, the imminence of conscription precipitated marriages as men sought to avoid the draft.[38] In others, it resulted in broken courtships and the birth of illegitimate children. Although the absence of some soldier fiancés (and, conversely, the presence of soldiers *en congé* in the region at various points) is not solely responsible for the increase in illegitimate births, it is undoubtedly a factor.

In addition to creating economic instability and removing young men from *cauchois* villages, the Revolution undermined the traditional authority structure in Auffay and created open antagonisms. The worst period was between 1792 and 1803, when the curé Hauchecorne was in exile. Those who supported Hauchecorne and the Church sneaked their children into the woods to be baptized by refractory priests. Those who supported the Revolution viewed them as traitors and expended great efforts to stop them.[39] In 1797, Jacques Pierre Truffier was removed from public office because he had sounded the clock on the Auffay church to announce the hour of the religious offices, an act that branded him as a "fanatic and opposed to the principles of government."[40]

Although Hauchecorne returned from exile in 1803, the damage to the Church's authority was permanent. It was not able to impose religious marriage on couples who had their children baptized (many couples continued to be married only in the civil ceremonies that had been established by the government, although they continued to have their children baptized and sometimes, after the passage of years, succumbed to the pressure of the priests and married in the Church),[41] much less to impose civil or religious marriage on couples whose sexual activity had resulted in the conception of a child.

In Auffay, the undermining of local authority had the same effect that migration had in other communities.[42] When men were not forced by social or moral pressure to marry their pregnant lovers, they often broke their promises of marriage and left the women to rear the children alone or, if they were lucky, with the help of families. If a young woman's parents were still living and in the same village, they might still be able to impose marriage on the young couple. But they alone did not have the kind of clout that they and a strong priest had had in the eighteenth century.

In the 1820s and 1830s, economic, social, and political stability returned to the Caux. Men returned from the army. New jobs for women opened up in weaving, dressmaking, and day laboring. The number of poor roaming the region declined. Antagonisms no longer had the potential for violence they had had during the Revolution. Religious services were again held regularly, and the Auffay market thrived. By the 1840s, living conditions in the village were improving, the railroad was on its way, and local businesses were prospering. But the illegitimacy ratio remained high. One out of every eleven births occurred to an unmarried woman.

Part of the explanation for the continuing high illegitimacy rates in Auffay lies in the Church's continuing inability to reestablish its authority throughout the entire community. Parents were unwilling to take risks with their children's salvation, and all infants were baptized. But several couples continued to resist the priests' attempts to draw them back into the fold. It was not unusual for such rebellious couples to bear an illegitimate child before their civil wedding ceremonies. Veterance Victorine Aveterance Raillot and Pierre Jean Baptiste Delauné, for instance, had two children before their civil marriage in 1838, and, despite repeated pressure from the Church to consecrate their marriage when each of their next six children was born, they refused to have a religious ceremony until 1846.[43] Couples like Raillot and Delauné certainly did not produce a majority of the illegitimate children of the village. Their importance lies, rather, in the apparent ease of their rebellion against the old norms. It was no longer possible for the community or the Church to impose the old standards.

Perhaps even more important than the Church's lost authority, was the worsening employment picture for women. After the mechanization of spinning, women never were fully employed again, despite their entry into weaving and agricultural day laboring. To make matters worse, by the 1840s power looms were threatening employment in cottage weaving. Again, the first jobs to be affected by the introduction of machines, that is, those of calico weavers, were held by women. As their employment options decreased, so did young women's chances of marrying, whereas their chances of bearing an illegitimate child increased. Young men began to migrate to the cities, leaving behind not only their homes and families, but also broken engagements and pregnant women. Indeed, for some men, part of the incentive for migration may have been the pregnancy of a precariously employed or unemployed lover.

The women most likely to find themselves pregnant and unmarried were domestic servants and employees in the new Auffay spinning mill. Unlike young women who worked at home, these women worked with their peers and were removed from parental control either completely or for many hours every day. Their opportunities for sexual encounters were thereby increased, whereas their contact with older adults who might have urged or enforced caution and virtue was reduced. They were more likely to believe promises of marriage and, perhaps, more likely to take chances than were the women who lived and worked with their families. Moreover, they were in a less protected environment, making them more vulnerable to demands and force. In the 1840s, their pregnancies account for 58 percent of the illegitimate children born in the village. See Table 9.4.)

It was women, of course, who bore the burden of illegitimacy in Auffay. The lucky ones married; the majority, however, did not, at least not in the village and probably not at all. Many left, but whether to marry the fathers of their children who lived in other villages or to seek work (and perhaps a husband) elsewhere is unknown. Because women commonly married in their home village rather than in the village of the groom, it seems unlikely that most of the unwed mothers who left the village were actually going to join the fathers of their children.[44]

For most women, having a child without a husband made a tenuous economic situation worse, especially since the increase in illegitimacy co-

Table 9.4. *Occupations of unwed mothers, Auffay,*
1801–1850

Occupation of mother	Date of birth of child				
	1801–10	1811–20	1821–30	1831–40	1841–50
Spinner (cottage)	15	13	8	0	0
Spinner (factory)	0	0	3	1	8
Weaver	2	8	4	12	3
Domestic	5	2	3	7	10
Dressmaker	0	0	1	3	4
Loom threader	0	0	0	1	0
Bleacher	0	0	0	0	1
Day laborer	0	0	0	1	3
Merchant	1	0	0	0	0
Farmer	0	0	0	1	0
No occupation	0	0	0	0	2
Unknown	5	1	7	0	0
Total	28	24	26	26	31

Note: Women who bore twins in 1813 and 1832 are counted only once.
Source: Civil Registers, Auffay.

incided with the mechanization of spinning and the decline in female employment. These women were in worse positions than widows with children because they had not acquired dowries or inherited a cottage, land, money, or a business from a husband. Very few unwed mothers were able to live alone with their children at any point in the proto-industrial period. Instead, they lived with their parents or with siblings.[45]

A few women bore more than one illegitimate child in Auffay and can be identified as forming what Peter Laslett has called a "bastardy-prone sub-society." Although Laslett has argued that increases in illegitimacy rates were "disproportionately due to those prone to such a form of childbearing having a greater number of confinements," this was not the case in Auffay. However, the number of women who bore more than one child out of wedlock did increase as the illegitimacy rate increased.[46]

Between 1751 and 1786, when very few illegitimate children were born in Auffay, only four women bore more than one illegitimate child, and one of them (Marie Anne Mascarel Chanterine) bore children who were not technically illegitimate because she was legally married. Between 1787 and 1818, seven unmarried women bore two children, two bore three, and one bore five (including one set of twins). Between 1818 and 1850, seventeen Auffay women bore more than one child out of wedlock. Between 1751 and 1850, these thirty-one women produced seventy-six illegitimate children, a sizeable number. Even so, they bore less than half of the illegitimate children born in the village and constituted only 23 percent of the women who bore illegitimate children.[47] (See Table 9.5.)

Jacques Depauw has suggested that families, as well as individuals, can be regarded as bastardy-prone and should be examined in the search to explain increases in illegitimacy.[48] Such families are clearly visible in the Auffay Reconstitution Study. Sometimes sisters bore illegitimate children. Marie Felicité Dubois (b. 1774) had five illegitimate children between 1797 and 1813; her sister, Marie Anne (b. 1775) had one. Sometimes daughters followed in their mothers' footsteps. Marie Anne Duval (b. 1761) bore a daughter in 1786, four years before her marriage to Jean Poyer, who was not the father of the child. After her marriage to Poyer, she had three more children, all daughters. In 1811, her illegitimate daughter, Marie Rose Duval, bore an illegitimate daughter, and Seraphie Poyer, one of her legitimate daughters, bore illegitimate sons in 1826 and 1830.

In an even more striking case, Marie Dorothée Hébert (b. 1790) had four illegitimate children after the death of her husband, Pierre Louis Recher, in 1822. These children were born in 1826, 1830, and 1832 (twins). In 1843, her youngest legitimate child, Leonore Clementine (b. 1822) gave birth to an illegitimate son, and, in 1847, the first of her illegitimate children, Merie Dorothée, bore an illegitimate son.[49]

In these 3 families alone, 8 women bore 16 illegitimate children. Five of them, however, bore only one child out of wedlock and appear to fit a pattern of repeated illegitimacy only when viewed in the context of their families. Although the number of illegitimacy-prone women and families thus increased, this group does not account for all of the increase in the illegitimacy ratio at the end of the eighteenth century. On the contrary, after several decades with the ratio near 10 percent, illegitimacy was far from being confined to a subgroup. It was diffused throughout the community, and the number and percentage of families with a link to illegitimacy were steadily rising. Only eleven out of the 214 couples in the first marriage cohort (5.1 percent) had a primary link to illegitimacy that can be traced. In these families, one of the spouses was born out of wedlock, the wife bore an illegitimate child before she was married or after she was widowed, or the couple had an illegitimate grandchild. Twenty-two out of the 234 couples in the second marriage cohort had a traceable link to illegitimacy (9.4 percent), however, and by the weaving era, 50 out of the 280 couples (17.9 percent) had such a link. If the third

Table 9.5. *Illegitimate children borne per woman, Auffay,*
1751–1850

Number of illegitimate children	1751–1786		1787–1817		1818–1850	
	Mothers	Children	Mothers	Children	Mothers	Children
1	12	12	42	42	48	48
2	2	4	7	14	13	26
3	0	0	2	6	3	9
4	2[a]	8	0	0	1	4
5	0	0	1	5	0	0
Total	16	24	52	67	65	87

[a]Includes Marie Anne Mascarel Chanterine whose children were technically not illegitimate.
Note: Women are listed in the time period in which they bore their first illegitimate child.
Source: Family Reconstitution Study.

cohort were traced beyond the 1851 cutoff date for the Family Reconstitution Study, the number of families with a link to illegitimacy would undoubtedly increase.[50] (See Table 9.6.)

As the number of illegitimate children increased, so did confusion over what to call them. In 1799, Dominique Feret, who was not married, gave birth to a son, François. When he married Marie Rose Frémont in 1821, he was listed as François Feret (with the last name of his mother). Between 1822 and 1833, when his six children were born, he appears variously in the village records as simply "François" and as "François le François". When his eldest son, Joseph Amand, was married in 1844, his father's given name became his surname and he was listed as Joseph Amand François.[51] It appears that neither François himself, his children, or the civil and religious officials knew what to call him or his children.

As illegitimacy became more common and diffused throughout the community, it became increasingly acceptable. What had earlier been a tolerance for prenupital pregnancy became a tolerance for illegitimate children and their mothers. Between 1818 and 1850, nineteen brides and six grooms were the children of unwed mothers, and twenty-seven brides had borne children out of wedlock. The grooms in these couples were peasants, artisans, weavers, factory spinners, and merchants.[52]

The textile industry was partially responsible for the increase in illegitimacy and the tolerance with which the Auffay community accepted this deviant behavior, not because it brought economic individualism but be-

Table 9.6. *Links to illegitimacy, Auffay, 1751–1850*

Link	Cohort 1 (1751–1786) Number	Cohort 2 (1787–1817) Number	Cohort 3 (1818–1850) Number
Wife illegitimate	2	3	19
Husband illegitimate	1	2	6
Wife bears illegitimate child before marriage	2	4	27
Daughter bears illegitimate child before 1851	5	10	2
Son fathers illegitimate child before 1851	0	1	0
Widow bears illegitimate child before 1851	1	3	0
Total	11	23[a]	54[b]

[a] One couple has two links.
[b] Four couples have two links.
Source: Family Reconstitution Study.

cause it brought economic insecurity and contact with the outside world through its traveling merchants and porters. By the 1840s, the village had witnessed and adapted to enormous social and economic changes as the cotton industry expanded and contracted, the sexual divisions of labor in textiles and agriculture broke down, and the out-migration of young men increased. In addition, it had participated in the power struggles of the Revolution and had watched the authority and power of the Church decline. Now, a new economic disaster was in the offing – the mechanization of weaving. The villagers had survived the turmoil of the past by adapting, that is, by allowing women to take traditionally male jobs, by enclosing their fields and adopting the new agriculture, and by controlling the size of their families. They had, in a sense, learned to tolerate and accept what they could not change. In the 1840s, they faced renewed economic instability and the departure of young men for Rouen. Once again, they adapted to the circumstances they could not change. They accepted the pregnant women and illegitimate children left behind by the men who moved to Rouen. Far from being a stagnant and rigid community, proto-industrial Auffay was resilient and flexible, traits for which the unwed mothers of the 1840s must have been grateful.

IO

~.

Conclusions: the causes and consequences
of proto-industrialization

By 1850, the cottage textile industry, hence, the proto-industrial period in the pays de Caux, was about to collapse. Every slump in the cotton industry drove more hand-loom weavers out of the craft and produced more power-loom operators until finally, in the 1870s, the bottom dropped completely out of the hand-weaving industry, and the rural exodus that had begun in the 1840s became a mass migration. The changes wrought by the spread of the cotton industry paled beside those created by its demise. The Caux bcame more purely agrarian and much more sparsely populated than it had been in at least a century and a half. Farmers found it more and more difficult to hire laborers as virtually everyone who did not own property pulled up stakes and moved to the city. Weaving families who did not move found themselves forced into agricultural day laboring.

Because of its drama, factory building and urbanization have a much more extensive history than does the eighteenth-century expansion of cottage industry. But no study that assumes that the process of industrialization was a purely urban phenomenon paints an accurate picture of the transition from cottage to factory production. The current research on proto-industrialization thus provides an important corrective to what has often been an oversimplified and inaccurate view of the industrialization process. However, it also has its problems, and it is time to reassess part of the picture that has emerged from recent studies.

As is often the case in a new field, the study of proto-industrialization has proceeded through a series of case studies. This presentation is, of course, one of these. What makes this study particularly valuable is that the pays de Caux differed in several ways from the other proto-industrial regions that have been studied. Its differentness broadens our understanding of the variety and complexity of proto-industrial regions and of the proto-industrial process, highlights the problems in current proto-industrial theory, and points the way, I believe, toward a more nuanced and accurate view of the causes and consequences of the expansion of textile manufacturing prior to the factory era. Above all, it illustrates the misperceptions of the past that arise when only the experiences of men and not those of women are examined and analyzed.

Redefining the causes of proto-industrialization: the complementarity of needs

The standard picture of a proto-industrial region projected by earlier studies is that of an increasingly poor, subsistence, or pastoral farming region being forced out of cereal production by a process of regional specialization. This region, as a result of demographic growth and either the practice of partible inheritance or the subdivision of leaseholds, had fragmented landholdings and a large impoverished peasantry. The Caux diverges from this model. It was not a subsistence farming or pastoral region. Nor was it a region where rising population and partible inheritance or tenant farming led to land fragmentation. It was, instead, one of the most fertile regions in France, a *bons pays,* specializing in the production of cereal crops, many of which were shipped to urban markets.

By the eighteenth century, the majority of the population was land poor, not because of partible inheritance or the division of leaseholds, but because of the needs of agriculture. Most of the land was rented in large plots to farmers, who worked them with a heavy plow and plow team and hired local men, women, and children to work for them, especially during the harvest. Most families held either very small plots or no land at all and depended heavily on the wealthy *fermiers* and *laboureurs* for employment and income. Farm work was highly seasonal in this, as in virtually all, commercial and subsistence farming regions in the eighteenth century. During the harvest, men, women, and children easily found work. During the rest of the year, farm work employed only a handful of men. Families could not survive on harvest wages alone, and, like their counterparts in subsistence and pastoral regions, people desperately needed off-season jobs and readily responded to the advances of the Rouen merchants when they began to expand the putting-out system.

Clearly, then, neither subsistence agriculture nor general land fragmentation was a necessary prerequisite for the spread of proto-industries, and the conclusions that have been drawn about the relationship between agriculture and cottage industry need to be revised. Not subsistence or pastoral agriculture, but the seasonal nature of all traditional agriculture work (with the exception of viticulture) created a need for cottage industry as a supplementary source of income in all regions that relied on an indigenous labor force to harvest crops. This need was especially acute in areas with a large landless population. Such landlessness could be caused by a variety of developments, for example, population growth, partible inheritance, the subdivision of leaseholds, or the concentration of land in a few hands to facilitate production. The important factors are seasonal unemployment and landlessness, not their causes.

Given this widespread need for cottage industry, what ultimately determined the location of proto-industries were such nonagricultural factors as the closeness of urban markets, the size of the urban labor force, the ease of transportation between the region and its markets, and the labor demands of urban merchants. The Caux was proto-industrialized because it was close to the port of Rouen, because the city itself could not supply the number of workers desired by the merchants, and because transportation on the plateau was relatively easy, making it economically feasible to put work out into the countryside. The merchants' search for workers complemented perfectly the need of the landless *cauchois* peasants, especially the female peasants, for nonharvest employment and the desire of the *laboureurs* and *fermiers* to keep their harvest labor force in the region.

If cereal agriculture had demanded year-round attention, as viticulture did, the need for off-season cottage work, as well as the supply of cottage workers, would have been considerably reduced. If the region had relied on migrants to harvest the crops, the need for off-season work would have existed where the migrants lived, not in the Caux. If land had been more evenly divided, more families would have been able to live off their holdings, and the need for nonfarm work would have been less. (However, the production of cereals would have been considerably reduced in this land of heavy clay soil because the tenants or owners of small plots would not have had the resources to maintain or possibly even to rent the essential plow and plow team.) And, if the Rouen merchants had not wanted to increase production beyond what was possible within the city itself, many landless peasants would have been forced to leave the region, and the *fermiers* and *laboureurs* would have had to rely on migrant workers to bring in the harvest.

The major key, then, to the location of proto-industries is the complementarity of urban and rural needs. Such complementarity was most likely to exist in regions in which agricultural work was highly seasonal, land was highly fragmented or concentrated in a few hands, population was fairly dense, and small merchant cities were seeking to expand production in a nonmechanized industry. Both subsistence agricultural regions and commercial grain-producing regions with these characteristics were likely candidates for rural- or proto-industrialization in the eighteenth and early nineteenth centuries.

The sexual division of labor

Earlier studies of proto-industrialization have paid little attention to the sexual division of labor. It was often, however, a crucial factor in determining the compatibility of labor force needs in agriculture and cottage industry and the social, economic, and demographic consequences of proto-industrialization. The failure to analyze the sexual composition of the labor force has led to a variety of misconceptions about the prerequisites for proto-industrialization, the importance of women's earnings in the economic well-being of families and regions as a whole, and the relationship between economic and demographic change. Analyzing the work of both sexes provides a much fuller and more accurate picture of the proto-industrial process and of women's roles and activities in peasant communities.

In Rouen and the Caux, the established sexual divisions of labor in agriculture and textiles complemented each other perfectly. Virtually all of the nonharvest agricultural work was performed by men, leaving most women unemployed during the winter. Fortunately for the women and for the region as a whole, the Rouen merchants were looking primarily for female employees, because they needed ten times as many spinners (and carders) as weavers, and spinning was defined as women's work. If both the large farmers and the merchants had wanted to hire the same sex, their labor demands would have conflicted, and either farming, the manufacture of cloth, or both would have suffered. As it was, there was very little conflict between the two production systems, as long as the merchants were willing to reduce production during the harvest and agriculture remained highly seasonal in its labor demands.

The failure to analyze the sexual composition of the work force may lie behind the argument of historians that commercial cereal agriculture and cottage industry were incompatible. The proto-industrialization of the Caux certainly illustrates that this was not necessarily the case. When agriculture employed primarily or exclusively men in the nonharvest season, as was traditionally the case in both subsistence and commercial farming regions, *and* when cottage industries employed many more women than men, which was generally the case in textiles (the quintessential proto-industry) before the mechanization of spinning, the two production systems were far from incompatible. Complementary sexual divisions of labor were far more of a factor than was subsistence farming in the expansion of rural manufacturing.

In the Caux, an analysis of the sexual division of labor, or, more precisely, of women's employment, is the key to understanding both the economic importance of the textile industry and the impact of its expansion, transformation, and contraction on village life and culture. In Auffay, as throughout the Caux, many more women than men were employed in the cottage textile industry in the eighteenth century. Their earnings, although lower on an individual level than those of men and hardly enough to support an individual, were essential to the family economy of a majority of peasant, artisan, and merchant families. Women's earnings were largely responsible for the relatively high standard of living in the region (this should not be exaggerated) and its ability to sustain a large population.

Women were not only important breadwinners in this region but also were the first group of workers to experience the technological unemployment that could come with mechanization and industrialization. Fifty years before the power loom began to displace male weavers, female spinners watched spinning jennies and mules eliminate their major source of employment. Shortly thereafter, however, the demand for hand weavers increased, and the traditional and longstanding sexual division of labor in the cottage textile industry broke down. More and more women began to find jobs in weaving, until they came to dominate this branch of textile manufacturing almost as much as they had dominated cottage spinning. An exclusive focus on male occupations would miss both the size of the textile industry and this major change in the sexual division of labor, because the number of men and the kinds of work they did in the textile industry remained unchanged throughout the proto-industrial period.

Such a focus would also miss a parallel change in the agricultural labor force. In the late eighteenth century, the planting of root crops began to replace fallow farming, and the demand for year-round agricultural workers increased. As was the case in the weaving industry, men were unable to meet this increased demand for labor, and the sexual division of labor in agriculture broke down. Women, as well as men, were hired to work in the fields throughout the year.

The sexual integration of these two formerly male occupations, plus the building of a small spinning mill in Auffay that hired both women and men, had a profound effect on many families. During the spinning phase of proto-industrialization, the vast majority of husbands and wives worked at completely unrelated tasks. Regardless of what their husbands did, most women spun cotton or flax for the putting-out merchants. Only in a handful of families where both spouses ran a shop, an inn, or a large farm, or where both worked in textile production, were the occupations of men and women related; and in virtually all of these jobs, male and female tasks were differentiated by sex. In contrast, during the first half of the nineteenth century, close to 50 percent of the brides and grooms in the lower socioeconomic group (day laborers, textile workers, domestic servants) shared a common primary occupation. They worked side by side in the fields, in the spinning mill, and in their cottages at hand-powered looms.

The effects of this change on family relationships is far from clear. There is no evidence that other tasks like childcare and housework lost their sex-specific identification, but in some families that might have happened. In many cases, the entry of women into male jobs must have undermined the notion of male superiority, because they entered low-skilled occupations and quickly became proficient at them. Whether men experienced this as a threat or an opportunity is impossible to tell. Some probably experienced it one way; others, another.

On the whole, women's entry into formerly male occupations did not represent an improvement in their social or economic positions. They were entering the most poorly paid of the male occupations and, because they had lost jobs in spinning before entering these jobs, they were in no position to bargain for wages. As a result, they continued to work for much lower wages than men. At the same time, they began to face new problems: the integration of childcare with work outside the home (a problem for agricultural workers and mill workers); increasingly insecure employment in old age (a problem in virtually all the "new" female occupations, including mill work, day laboring, weaving, and sewing, a traditionally female but now expanding occupation); and isolation from other women (a problem especially for female weavers who worked at home). Men retained control of the local taverns and cafés where they gathered during their leisure hours; women lost the common bond of spinning and the opportunity to gather together for evening work and for the journey to the textile markets. In addition, new sexual divisions of labor began to appear in weaving (women wove calicos; men wove heavier fabric) and probably in day laboring, which facilitated the payment of unequal piece rates and reestablished the male sense of superiority.

The breakdown of sexual divisions of labor in textiles and agriculture was facilitated by the need of *cauchois* families to replace the income formerly provided by women's work in spinning and by the existence of virtually full male employment. Nevertheless, it was a major cultural change and indicates the degree to which economic considerations were taking precedence over tradition and custom. Production goals were no longer adapted to the size of the labor force, as they had been during the spinning era. Instead, employers changed their hiring practices and, in turn, the character of the work force in order to meet constantly rising production goals.

Ironically, the major developments of the industrial and agricultural revolutions – the mechanization of spinning and the end of fallow farming – and their major cultural consequence – the breaking of the traditional sexual divisions of labor – delayed the full effects of industrialization on the Caux. The employment of women in agriculture and rural industry allowed most families to resist the lure of urban factory jobs and to maintain the traditional family economy until well into the second half of the nineteenth century. What was, in many ways, a radical change actually had more conservative than radical consequences.

Proto-industrialization and demographic change

Much of the recent work on proto-industrialization has focused on the changes in demographic behavior that occurred in these regions. The general picture that has emerged is one of significant, often dramatic change. In the short run, the improvements in employment opportunities and income that came with proto-industrialization, it is argued, made it possible for cottage workers to marry at younger ages and with greater frequency than their peasant counterparts. A man no longer had to wait to inherit a small piece of land, or a woman to acquire a dowry, before they could take their wedding vows. The availability of industrial work for children encouraged couples to begin childbearing early and to have many children, and family size increased. In the long run, this rural, proletarian demographic behavior set the stage for family and regional crises as the labor supply outstripped the demand for cottage workers. Such crises became particularly acute when proto-industries began to lose ground to urban factory production in the nineteenth century. Attempting to stave off destitution, families increased the number of breadwinners by taking in boarders and extended kin. This stop gap measure was only partially successful, however, and the competition of machine-produced goods eventually forced most cottage workers to migrate to the cities.

Although the sexual composition of the labor force has not been clearly analyzed in other proto-industrial studies, they appear to be studies of industries that employed entire families and were dominated by men. In the Caux, this was not the case. The cottage textile industry employed many more women than men, and it employed women from a broad spectrum of rural families. As a result, fluctuations in employment levels and wages were felt not by an identifiable group of families, but by the entire community, and were muted by the general stability of employment and wages in male occupations.

Demographic behavior changed only slightly in the Caux and was generally symmetric with employment levels and wages. In the eighteenth century, high female employment in cottage spinning, combined with virtually full male employment in a variety of jobs, led to high marriage frequency. The low wages paid to spinners and other women kept marriage ages high, however. Childbearing began with marriage, and families were large in this era, partially perhaps because of the availability of employment for children in carding and spinning. (Children as young as six could begin to contribute to the family's income.) When the mechanization of spinning created serious unemployment problems for women, their attractiveness as marriage partners declined. Young men began to migrate out of the region, leaving unmarried, and frequently pregnant, women behind. Those people who did marry began to limit the size of their families. Nuclear families continued to be the standard family unit, even when employment levels declined and couples postponed marriage rather than live with one of their parents after marriage. Unemployed young women remained in their parental homes, working whenever possible. Young men who had difficulty finding work left for Rouen where they hoped to find work (and probably working wives).

The differences in the effects of proto-industrialization on demographic behavior between the Caux and other regions can be understood only in light of the fact that cottage industry in the Caux provided work primarily for women in both its spinning and weaving phases. The implications of this for other studies of proto-industrialization are clear. Only if the sexual division of labor, along with female wage and employment levels for various age groups, is fully analyzed can we begin to draw an accurate picture of the effects of cottage industry on rural communities.

There is a more general historical lesson to be drawn from this as well. Developments in the Caux illustrate that some rural areas in Europe felt the effects of technological development and the fluctuations in supply and demand, which are characteristic of developing capitalist economies, primarily through their impact on the female labor force. Attention to the sexual division of labor and to the economic roles of women is, therefore, essential to understanding one of the central developments of modern European history – the transition from small-scale merchant capitalism to large-scale industrial capitalism.

Appendix

~~~~~~

Vital statistics for Auffay

Date	Births	Deaths	Stillbirths[a]	Marriages
1751	17	24	0	9
1752	24	18	0	8
1753	22	24	0	6
1754	25	41	2	5
1755	21	9	0	10
1756	28	11	0	4
1757	31	15	0	6
1758	23	23	0	4
1759	25	48	0	3
1760	31	38	0	4
1761	29	19	1	4
1762	19	16	1	9
1763	25	23	0	4
1764	31	20	0	11
1765	28	22	0	7
1766	30	21	0	4
1767	23	23	0	2
1768	26	33	0	7
1769	30	27	0	7
1770	26	19	0	3
1771	21	21	2	5
1772	24	16	2	6
1773	20	34	1	9
1774	28	7	0	6
1775	25	23	0	8
1776	28	15	1	5
1777	26	31	0	5
1778	22	26	0	2
1779	33	20	0	9
1780	29	38	0	3
1781	21	17	1	4
1782	32	23	1	5
1783	23	27	1	10
1784	26	12	3	12
1785	32	34	0	2
1786	29	14	1	6
1787	31	14	0	8
1788	27	21	0	7

Date	Births	Deaths	Stillbirths[a]	Marriages
1789	29	19	0	5
1790	28	20	0	8
1791	33	27	3	8
1792	29	18	0	4
1793	27	30	1	16
1794	29	27	1	15
1795	27	28	5	6
1796	30	53	2	2
1797	36	25	2	13
1798	31	24	2	15
1799	32	17	1	9
1800	32	18	1	9
1801	23	22	1	3
1802	29	13	1	2
1803	18	30	2	3
1804	34	27	1	5
1805	24	18	0	5
1806	26	21	2	2
1807	25	15	2	13
1808	28	29	1	4
1809	16	14	1	5
1810	30	21	2	6
1811	28	21	0	8
1812	20	16	1	5
1813	24	16	2	16
1814	32	27	1	8
1815	31	30	2	10
1816	26	17	1	9
1817	25	27	0	5
1818	21	20	0	11
1819	33	21	1	15
1820	30	32	0	9
1821	34	26	0	8
1822	31	29	1	5
1823	38	15	0	8
1824	31	30	0	11
1825	39	20	0	2
1826	29	30	1	6
1827	33	21	0	15
1828	23	27	0	10
1829	28	20	1	8
1830	28	25	0	8
1831	47	30	0	8
1832	24	39	0	6
1833	33	22	5	7
1834	32	25	0	12
1835	36	19	0	12
1836	25	21	1	14
1837	38	32	1	15

Date	Births	Deaths	Stillbirths[a]	Marriages
1838	33	30	0	5
1839	23	27	2	9
1840	32	31	1	5
1841	37	19	1	9
1842	27	38	0	4
1843	29	22	3	5
1844	30	33	3	7
1845	31	23	1	9
1846	25	31	0	3
1847	39	21	1	8
1848	34	19	3	10
1849	34	47	1	12
1850	32	31	1	4
	2832	2413	83	727

[a]Stillbirths include children who were born dead or died within a few moments of birth without being named.

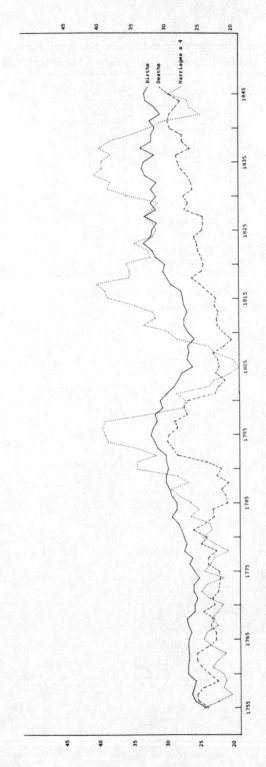

Nine-year moving average of births, deaths, and marriages (x4), Auffay

Notes

~~~~~~

Introduction

1. Franklin F. Mendels, "Proto-Industrialization: The First Phase of the Industrialization Process," *Journal of Economic History*, XXXII (1972): 241–61.
2. See Joan Thirsk, "Industries in the Countryside," in *Essays in the Economic and Social History of Tudor and Stuart England*, edited by F. J. Fisher (Cambridge: The University Press, 1961), pp. 70–88; Jan de Vries, *The Dutch Rural Economy in the Golden Age, 1500–1700* (New Haven: Yale University Press, 1974), pp. 2–3; Mendels, "Proto-Industrialization," p. 248. In England, between the fifteenth and seventeenth centuries, cottage woolen industries that produced fabric for national rather than local markets developed in regions of pastoral agriculture and large land-poor populations. In the sixteenth and seventeenth centuries, a new production pattern based on regional agricultural specialization developed in northern and western Europe. Grain from the Baltic region; cattle from Russia, Poland, Hungary, and Jutland; wine from France and Germany; and dairy products from the North Sea coast flowed through the markets of the Netherlands and southeastern England, destined for areas with less favorable growing conditions for each product. At the same time, areas like Saxony, Lusatia, and Northern Bohemia expanded rural handicraft production for export to Austria, Poland and Hungary. Such regional specialization and trade were hallmarks of proto-industrialization.
3. Mendels, "Proto-Industrialization;" Franklin F. Mendels, "Agriculture and Peasant Industry in Eighteenth-Century Flanders," in *European Peasants and Their Markets*, edited by William N. Parker and Eric L. Jones (Princeton: Princeton University Press, 1975), pp. 179–204; Franklin F. Mendels, "Seasons and Regions in Agriculture and Industry During the Process of Industrialization," in *Region und Industrialisierung*, edited by Sidney Pollard (Göttingen: Vandenhoeck & Ruprecht, 1980); Franklin F. Mendels, *Industrialization and Population Pressure in Eighteenth-Century Flanders* (New York: Arno Press, 1981); Rudolf Braun, *Industrialisierung und Volksleben* (Erlenbach-Zurich und Stuttgard: Rentsch, 1960); Rudolf Braun, "The Impact of Cottage Industry on an Agricultural Population," in *The Rise of Capitalism*, edited by David Landes (New York: Macmillan, 1966), pp. 53–64; Rudolf Braun, "Early Industrialization and Demographic Change in the Canton of Zurich," in *Historical Studies of Changing Fertility*, edited by Charles Tilly (Princeton: Princeton University Press, 1978), pp. 289–334; David Levine, *Family Formation in an Age of Nascent Capitalism* (New York: Academic Press, 1977); David Levine, "The Demographic Implications of Rural Industrialization: A Family Reconstitution Study of Shepshed, Leicestershire, 1600–1851," *Social History*, no. 2 (1976): 177–96.
4. Olwen H. Hufton, "Women and the Family Economy in Eighteenth-Century France," *French Historical Studies*, IX (Spring 1975): 1–22; Joan W. Scott, and Louise A. Tilly, "Women's Work and the Family in Nineteenth-Century Europe," *Comparative Studies in Society and History*, 17 (January 1975): 36–64; Louise A. Tilly and Joan W. Scott, *Women, Work, and Family* (New York: Holt, Rinehart and Winston, 1978). Also see Madeleine Guilbert, *Les Functions des femmes dans l'industrie* (Paris: 1966); Theresa

Abbreviations used in the notes: ADSM – Archives Départementales de la Seine-Maritime; AN – Archives Nationales.

McBride, "The Long Road Home: Women's Work and Industrialization," in *Becoming Visible*, edited by Renate Bridenthal and Claudia Koonz (Boston: Houghton Mifflin, 1977); Martine Segalen, *Mari et femme dans la société paysanne* (Paris: Flammarion, 1980); and, Françoise Zonabend, *La mémoire longue: Temps et histoires au village* (Paris: Presses Universitaires de France, 1980).

5. M. Fleury and L. Henry, *Des registres paroissiaux à l'histoire de la population: Manuel de dépouillement et d'exploitation de l'état civil ancien* (Paris: Institut National d'Études Démographiques, 1956). See also M. Fleury and L. Henry, *Noveau manuel de dépouillement et d'exploitation de l'état civil ancien* (Paris: Institut National d'Études Démographiques, 1965); E. Gautier and L. Henry, *La population de Crulai, paroisse normande* (Paris: Presses Universitaires de France, 1958); E. A. Wrigley, *Population and History* (New York: McGraw-Hill, 1969).

6. This double record keeping makes it possible to determine the time lag between civil and religious marriages, and the number of couples who had children baptized but who were not married within the church. See Chapters 7 and 9.

The pays and the village

1. For a description of the problems involved in determining the population of Rouen before the nineteenth-century, see Michel Mollat, ed., *Histoire de Rouen* (Toulouse: Edouard Privat, 1979), pp. 218–25. Before the middle of the nineteenth century the only provincial cities larger than Rouen were Marseilles, Lyons, and Bordeaux.

2. Jules Sion, *Les paysans de la Normandie Orientale: Pays de Caux, Bray, Vexin Normand, Vallée de la Seine. Etude géographique* (Paris: Armand Colin, 1909), p. 2.

3. Ibid., pp. 4–5.

4. Armand Frémont, *L'élevage en Normandie: Etude géographique* (Caen: Association des Publications de la Faculté des Lettres et Sciences Humaines de l'Université de Caen, 1967), pp. 431–32.

5. Sion, *Paysans*, pp. 6, 109.

6. Ibid., pp. 67–76; Frémont, *L'élevage en Normandie*, pp. 423–7.

7. Marc Bloch, *French Rural History: An Essay on its Basic Characteristics*, translated by J. Sondheimer (Berkeley: University of California Press, 1966), p. 48; ADSM C537; Service du Cadastre, Dieppe (Maps of Auffay, First Empire).

8. Sion, *Paysans*, p. 20.

9. Sion, *Paysans*, p. 470; ADSM C537. The *masures* connected to large farms were often quite large. Most, however, were small. The sixty-three *masures* in Auffay in 1770 ranged in size from one with 6 acres (coupled with 66 acres of arable land) to thirty-eight with less than 1 acre.

10. *Description topographique et statistique de la France: Département de la Seine-Inférieure*, 1810, p. 11; René Musset, "A propos de la maison normande: du pays de Caux au Bocage normand," *Problèmes et Annales de Normandie*, V (1955): 271–287; Sion, *Paysans*, pp. 472–6; Isidore Mars, *Derniers souvenirs du bon vieux temps d'Auffay depuis 1793 jusqu'à 1840 environ* (Dieppe: Paul Leprêtre & Cie., 1876), pp. 31–2.

11. G. Lecarpentier, *Le pays de Caux (Etude géographique)* (Rouen, 1906), p. 6.

12. Marguerite Bruneau, "Le costume normand," *Connaître Rouen*, Tome III (Rouen: Les Amis des Monuments Rouennais, 1976), p. 121.

13. Ibid., pp. 10–11, 20–2.

14. Ibid., p. 10, 15–17.

15. Emmanuel Le Roy Ladurie, "A System of Customary Law: Family Structures and Inheritance Customs in Sixteenth-Century France," in *Family and Society*, edited by Robert Forster and Orest Ranum, translated by Elborg Forster and Patricia M. Ranum (Bal-

timore: The Johns Hopkins University Press, 1967), pp. 88–9; David Houard, *Dictionnaire analytique, historique, étymologique, critique et interpretatif de la coutume de Normandie* (Rouen, 1780–82).

16. Sion, *Paysans*, pp. 264–5.

17. AN F^{12}560, M. Latapie, "Réflexions préliminaires sur un mémoire intitulé Voyage de Rouen ou observations sur l'état actuel des arts et manufactures de Rouen, Elbeuf, Louviers, Evreux et Andely faites dans le mois de mai, juin et juillet 1773; ADSM 6MP5110; Sion, *Paysans*, pp. 12, 168–86; Pierre Dardel, *Histoire de Bolbec des origines à la Révolution: Le commerce et l'industrie à Bolbec avant 1789* (Rouen: Lestringant, 1939), pp. 52, 77–80.

18. Mars, *Derniers souvenirs*, p. 6; ADSM C2391, L1771.

19. ADSM C1730, 219BP364; E. LeParquier, *Cahiers de doléances du bailliage d'Arques (secondaire de Caudebec) pour les états généraux de 1789* (Lille: Camille Robbe, 1922), p. 51. Dumoulin's figures are included in LeParquier for each commune in the bailliage of Arques. For Auffay, see page 51. In the Caux, two separate tax roles were compiled annually – one for the *taille* and one for the *gabelle* (the salt tax). (The pays de Caux was in a *grandes gabelles* region where peasants were required to purchase a certain quantity of salt from the government based on the number of people and animals in their households.) Of the two sets of records, the *taille rôles* are the less accurate guide to village population because they separate married sons and fathers even if they lived in the same household, include the owners or leaseholders of land even if they lived in a different commune, and list as "fugitives" residents of the commune whom the tax collector regarded as temporarily absent even though such absences might be permanent.

The *sel rôles* provide a better count of the households in a commune because they list married sons and fathers who lived together as members of the same household and do not record landowners who lived in other communes. They also have the virtue of noting the number of residents over the age of eight in each taxable household. Neither the *taille* nor the *sel rôles* were very concerned with households whose income was too low to be taxable, however, and in some communes that could be a considerable number. If nothing else, it was easier for the tax collector to consider families and individuals who were poor and had been in the commune only a short time as residents of somewhere else than it was to try to extract taxes from them. For more information, see Marc Bouloiseau, "La fiscalité du sel dans la France du XVIIIe siècle," in *Le rôle du sel dans l'histoire*, edited by Michel Mollat (Paris: Presses Universitaires de France, 1968), pp. 249–50.

20. ADSM 219BP364.

21. ADSM L367.

22. The 1831, 1841, and 1851 censuses divided the population of communes into the central village and the surrounding *hameaux*. For Auffay in these years, between 71 and 76 percent of the households and of the total population of the commune were in the central village. See ADSM 6M1, 6M23, 6M83. In contrast to Auffay, in some communes the population of the central village was less than the population in the *hameaux*, and, in a few cases, the population of the central village was dwarfed by that of a particular *hameau*, a situation in which the historical and legal leadership of the commune was no longer in keeping with the actual demographic or economic structure of the commune.

23. Isidore Mars, *Auffay, ou le vieil Isnelville* (Rouen: Lecointe Frères, 1857), pp. 8–10, 107–115; J. Daoust, *Auffay et sa collégiale* (Auffay: Philippe Vicaire, 1969), p. 3; LeParquier, *Cahiers*, p. 51.

24. Mars, *Auffay*, pp. 76–82.

25. Ibid., pp. 92–7; Sion, *Paysans*, pp. 285–7.

26. Mars, *Auffay*, pp. 98–106.
27. Sion, *Paysans*, p. 286.
28. Charles de Robillard de Beaurepaire, "Recherches sur la population de la généralité du diocèse de Rouen avant 1789," *Mémoires de la Société des Antiquaires de Normandie*, 3ᵉ série (Paris, 1870), p. 376; Sion, *Paysans*, pp. 286–7.
29. Mars, *Derniers souvenirs*, p. 3.
30. Ibid., p. 3.
31. Ibid., pp. 6–9.
32. ADSM 219BP.
33. Mars, *Derniers souvenirs*, pp. 4–5, 42–3.
34. Ibid., pp. 45–6.
35. Eugene Noel, *Rouen, Rouennais, Rouenneries* (Rouen: Schneider Frères, 1894), p. 164.
36. Mars, *Derniers souvenirs*, pp. 17–18.
37. Ibid., pp. 9, 41.
38. Ibid., pp. 22–4.
39. ADSM Parish Registers, Auffay, 1751–60. The ability to sign one's name is, of course, not a perfect indicator of literacy – some people who could not read may have been able to print their names, others may have been able to read but not write – but it is the only indicator that we have. For a discussion of the problems involved in determining literacy, see Daniel P. Resnick and Lauren B. Resnick, "The Nature of Literacy: An Historical Exploration," *Harvard Educational Review*, 47 (1977); 370–85: François Furet and Jacques Ozouf, *Lire et Ecrire: l'alphabetisation des français de Calvin à Jules Ferry* (Paris, 1977).
40. Mars, *Auffay*, pp. 155–6.
41. ADSM Parish and Civil Registers, Auffay, 1751–1850.
42. Mars, *Derniers souvenirs*, pp. 93–5, 108–9. Mars gives no date for the arrival or departure of Mlle. Bernard but it is clear from the text that she had left Auffay by 1828.
43. Ibid., p. 158; LeParquier, *Cahiers*, p. 51; Daoust, *Auffay*, pp. 4–5.
44. Mars, *Derniers souvenirs*, pp. 3, 26; Mars, *Auffay*, pp. 155–6, 228–9.
45. LeParquier, *Cahiers*, p. 52 (article 3).
46. Ibid., p. 53 (article 6).
47. Ibid., pp. 53, 55 (articles 7 and 14).
48. ADSM 6MP5114, L277, L5118.
49. ADSM Parish Registers.
50. Ibid.
51. Ibid.
52. Daoust, *Auffay*, p. 6; Mars, *Auffay*, pp. 164–70; Mars, *Derniers souvenirs*, p. 64.
53. Mars, *Derniers souvenirs*, pp. 50–1.
54. Ibid., pp. 56–9.
55. Ibid., p. 4.
56. Unfortunately, Mars, who is the only source of information about La Mort d'Auffay, tells us nothing about the origins of the skeleton or about whether the display of artificial skeletons was common in the Caux in the eighteenth century. Its origins may have lain in the seventeenth century, when, according to Philippe Ariès, skeletons or bones were found on almost every tomb and even appeared in houses as decorations. See Philippe Ariès, *Western Attitudes toward Death: From the Middle Ages to the Present*, translated by Patricia M. Ranum (Baltimore: The Johns Hopkins University Press, 1974), p. 40.
57. Mars, *Auffay*, pp. 172–4.
58. Mars, *Derniers souvenirs*, p. 34.

59. Ibid., pp. 34–5; William E. Monter, *Witchcraft in France and Switzerland: The Borderlands during the Reformation* (Ithaca; N.Y.: Cornell University Press, 1976).
60. Mars, *Auffay*, pp. 107–116.
61. LeParquier, *Cahiers*, p. 54, n. 1 (article 9).
62. ADSM 6MP5113.
63. Eugene Marchand, *Etude statistique, économique et chimique sur l'agriculture du pays de Caux* (Paris: Bouchard-Huzard, 1869), pp. 126–7.
64. Bloch, *French Rural History*, pp. 30–2; Sion, *Paysans*, p. 228; Jerome Blum, *The End of the Old Order in Rural Europe* (Princeton: Princeton University Press, 1978), p. 126.
65. ADSM Parish Registers, Auffay, 1751–90.
66. ADSM L1772.
67. Bloch, *French Rural History*, pp. 21–2.
68. Steven L. Kaplan, *Bread, Politics and Political Economy in the Reign of Louis XV*, vol. I (The Hague, Netherlands: Martinus Nijhoff, 1976), p. xvi.
69. Charles Desmarest, *Le commerce des grains dans la généralité de Rouen à la fin de l'ancien régime* (Paris: Jouve & Cie., 1926), pp. 95, 216–19.
70. ADSM C107, 108; Desmarest, *Commerce des grains, pp. 120–237 passim*.
71. Kaplan, *Bread, Politics and Political Economy*, pp. 67–8; Desmarest, *Commerce des grains*, pp. 38–9.
72. The grain shortage and market riots in 1775 followed a poor harvest in 1774 and Turgot's freeing of the grain trade between French provinces in September of that year. The severity of the riots, especially in the provinces around Paris, earned them the name *"le guerre des farines."* They have sometimes been regarded as having been provoked by Turgot's opponents. It seems more likely, however, that the peasants were simply responding to high prices and short grain supplies and not to outside agitators. For more information, see Desmarest, *Commerce des grains*, pp. 197–9; Gérard Walter, *Histoire des paysans de France* (Paris: Flammarion, 1963), pp. 309–20; Alfred Cobban, *A History of Modern France*, Vol. I: *Old Regime and Revolution, 1715–1799* (Middlesex, England: Penguin, 1963), pp. 104–6.
73. ADSM C107, C108.
74. Sion estimated the population density of the Caux in 1806 to be 99 inhabitants per square kilometer. In the neighboring pays de Bray and Vexin normand, it was 52.2 and 53.9, respectively. The estimates are based on an examination of the population figures for one canton in each *pays*. See, Sion, *Paysans*, p. 435.
75. Desmarest, *Commerce des grains*, pp. 225, 231–7.
76. Ibid., pp. 199–201; ADSM C107.
77. ADSM 6MP5111; Mars, *Derniers souvenirs*, p. 32; Sion, *Paysans*, p. 474.
78. ADSM C1730, 219BP364; LeParquier, *Cahiers*, p. 51.
79. Sion, *Paysans*, p. 468.
80. Ibid., p. 469.
81. Mars, *Derniers souvenirs*, p. 32; Sion, *Paysans*, p. 472; ADSM Notarial Registers, Auffay, 1751–1800 (marriage contracts and inventories of possessions); E. P. Thompson, "Time, Work-Discipline and Industrial Capitalism," *Past and Present*, no. 38 (1967): 56–97; David Landes, *Revolution in Time: Clocks and the Making of the Modern World* (Cambridge: Harvard University Press, 1982), pp. 81–2.
82. Sion, *Paysans*, p. 472; Mars, *Derniers souvenirs*, p. 32.
83. Sion, *Paysans*, pp. 472–3.
84. ADSM 6MP5111.
85. M. M. Bouloiseau, "Aspects socieaux de la crise cotonnière dans les campagnes Rouennaises en 1788–1789," in *Actes de 81e Congrès National des Sociétés Savantes*,

Rouen-Caen, 1956 (Paris: Presses Universitaires de France, 1956), p. 407; Dardel, *Bolbec,* pp. 23.

86. LeParquier, *Cahiers,* lii–liii.

Proto-industrial theory and the pays de Caux

1. Charles Tilly and Richard Tilly, "Agenda for European Economic History in the 1970's," *Journal of Economic History,* XXXI (1971): 186.

2. Franklin F. Mendels, "Industrialization and Population Pressure in Eighteenth-Century Flanders," Ph.D dissertation, University of Wisconsin, 1969. Subsequently published by Arno Press, 1981.

3. E. J. T. Collins, "Labour Supply and Demand in European Agriculture, 1800–1880," in E. L. Jones and S. J. Woolf, eds., *Agrarian Change and Economic Development* (London: Methuen, 1969), p. 64; E. L. Jones and S. J. Woolf, "Introduction: The Historical Role of Agrarian Change in Economic Development," in Jones and Woolf, eds., *Agrarian Change,* pp. 10–11.

4. Franklin F. Mendels, Proto-Industrialization: The First Phase of the Industrialization Process," *Journal of Economic History,* XXXII (1972): 241–6.

5. Pierre Deyon, "Un modele à l'épreuve; Le développement industriel de Roubaix de 1762 à la fin du XIXeme siècle," *Revue du Nord,* LXIII (1981): 59–66; Pat Hudson, "Proto-industrialisation: The Case of the West Riding Wool Textile Industry in the Eighteenth and Early Nineteenth Centuries," *History Workshop,* no. 12 (1981): 34–61. James R. Lehning, *The Peasants of Marlhes: Economic Development and Family Organization in Nineteenth-Century France* (Chapel Hill: University of North Carolina Press, 1980); David Levine, *Family Formation in an Age of Nascent Capitalism* (New York: Academic Press, 1977); David Levine, "The Demographic Implications of Rural Industrialization: A Family Reconstitution Study of Shepshed, Leicestershire, 1600–1851," *Social History,* no. 2 (1976): 177–96; Hans Medick, "The Proto-Industrial Family Economy: The Structural Function of Household and Family during the Transition from Peasant Society to Industrial Capitalism," *Social History,* no. 3 (1976): 296–7; Peter Kriedte, Hans Medick, and Jurgen Schlumbohm, *Industrialization Before Industrialization: Rural Industry in the Genesis of Capitalism,* translated by Beate Schempp (Cambridge: Cambridge University Press, 1981). See also Charles Tilly, "The Historical Study of Vital Processes" in Charles Tilly, ed., *Historical Studies of Changing Fertility* (Princeton: Princeton University Press, 1978), pp. 3–56; the collected papers for the Eighth International Congress of Economic History (Budapest (1982), Section A2: Protoindustrialization: Theory and Reality; Serge Chassagne, "La diffusion rurale de l'industrie cotonnière en France (1750–1850)," *Revue du Nord,* LXI (1979): 97–114; and, Wolfram Fischer, "Rural Industrialization and Population Change," *Comparative Studies in Society and History,* 15 (1973): 158–70.

For critiques of proto-industrial theory, see Maxine Berg, Pat Hudson, and Michael Sonescher, eds., *Manufacture in Town and Country before the Factory* (Cambridge: Cambridge University Press, 1983) (see especially, Berg, Hudson, and Sonenscher, "Manufacture in Town and Country before the Factory," pp. 1–32; J. K. J. Thomson, "Variations in Industrial Structure in Pre-Industrial Languedoc," pp. 61–91; and, Pat Hudson, "From Manor to Mill: The West Riding in Transition," pp. 124–44. D. C. Coleman, "Proto-Industrialization: A Concept too Many," *Economic History Review,* Second Series, XXXVI (August 1983): 435–48; Myron P. Gutmann and René Leboutte, "Rethinking Proto-industrialization and the Family," *Journal of Interdisciplinary History,* XIV, no. 3 (Winter 1984): 587–608; Rab Houston and K. D. M. Snell, "Proto-Industrialization? Cottage Industry, Social Change, and Industrial Revolution,"

The Historical Journal, 27 (1984): 473–92; Pierre Jeannin, "La proto-industrialization: développement ou impasse?", *Annales: Economies, Sociétés, Civilisations,* 35a (1980): 52–65; James Lehning, "Nuptiality and Rural Industry: Families and Labor in the French Countryside," *Journal of Family History,* (Winter 1983): 333–45; Eckart Schremmer, "Proto-Industrialisation: A Step towards Industrialization?," *Journal of European Economic History,* 10 (Winter 1981): 653–70; Paul G. Spagnoli, "Industrialization, Proletarianization, and Marriage: A Reconsideration," *Journal of Family History,* 8 (Fall 1983): 230–47; Charles Vandenbroeke, "Mutations économiques et sociales en Flandre au cours de la phase proto-industrielle, 1650–1850," *Revue du Nord,* LXIII, no. 248 (Janvier-Mars 1981): 73–94; Gay L. Gullickson, "Proto-Industrialization, Demographic Behavior and the Sexual Division of Labor in Auffay, France, 1750–1850," *Peasant Studies,* 9 (Winter 1982): 106–118; and, Gay L. Gullickson, "Agriculture and Cottage Industry: Redefining the Causes of Proto-Industrialization," *Journal of Economic History,* XLIII (December 1983): 831–50. With the exception of the last article on agriculture and cottage industry, these critiques have focused on one of two issues: the demographic consequences of proto-industrialization and the relationship between proto-industrialization and industrialization.

6. E. Tarlé, *L'industrie dans les campagnes en France à la fin de l'ancien régime* (Paris: Edouard Cornely et Cie., 1910); Henri Sée, "Remarques sur le caractère de l'industrie rurale en France et les causes de son extension au XVIIIe siècle," *Revue historique,* CXLII (1923): 47–53.

7. Joan Thirsk, "Industries in the Countryside," in F. J. Fisher, ed., *Essays in the Economic and Social History of Tudor and Stuart England* (Cambridge: The University Press, 1961); Rudolf Braun, *Industrialisierung und Volksleben* (Erlenbach-Zurich und Stuttgard: Rentsch, 1960); Rudolf Braun, "The Impact of Cottage Industry on an Agricultural Population," in David Landes, ed., *The Rise of Capitalism* (New York: Macmillan, 1966), pp. 53–64; Rudolf Braun, "Early Industrialization and Demographic Change in the Canton of Zurich," in Charles Tilly, ed., *Historical Studies of Changing Fertility* (Princeton: Princeton University Press, 1978), pp. 289–334; E. L. Jones, "Agricultural Origins of Industry," *Past and Present,* no. 40 (1968): 58–71, reprinted in E. L. Jones, *Agriculture and the Industrial Revolution* (Oxford: Blackwell, 1974), pp. 128–42 (all subsequent references are to this edition); Jan de Vries, "The Role of the Rural Sector in the Expansion of the Dutch Economy, 1500–1700" (unpublished Ph.D. dissertation, Yale University, 1970); Jan de Vries, *The Dutch Rural Economy in the Golden Age, 1500–1700* (New Haven: Yale University Press, 1974); Herbert Kisch, "The Textile Industries in Silesia and the Rhineland: A Comparative Study in Industrialization," in Kriedte, Medick, and Schlumbohm, *Industrialization Before Industrialization,* pp. 178–200.

8. Franklin F. Mendels, "Seasons and Regions in Agriculture and Industry During the Process of Industrialization," in Sidney Pollard, ed., *Region und Industrialisierung* (Göttingen: Vanderhoeck & Ruprecht, 1980), pp. 177–95. See also, Pierre Deyon and Franklin Mendels, "Programme de la section A2 du huitième Congrès international d'histore économique: La Proto-Industrialisation: Théorie et Réalité (Budapest 1982)," *Revue du Nord,* LXIII (1981): 11–19.

9. Franklin F. Mendels, "Agriculture and Peasant Industry in Eighteenth-Century Flanders," in William N. Parker and Eric L. Jones, eds., *European Peasants and Their Markets* (Princeton: Princeton University Press, 1975), pp. 200–1; Collins, "Labour Supply and Demand," pp. 61–94 passim; Mendels, "Seasons and Regions," pp. 179–80; Tarlé, *L'industrie dans les campagnes,* pp. 79–80.

10. Jones, "Agricultural Origins," pp. 129–38.

11. Mendels, "Agriculture and Peasant Industry," pp. 200, 202.

12. Mendels, "Proto-Industrialization," p. 247; Mendels, "Seasons and Regions," p. 181.

13. Mendels, "Proto-Industrialization," pp. 247–8.
14. Mendels, "Seasons and Regions," pp. 178–83.
15. Ibid., p. 183.
16. Jones, "Agricultural Origins," p. 133.
17. Mendels, "Agriculture and Peasant Industry," p. 189.
18. Tarlé, *L'industrie dans les campagnes,* p. 79.
19. Braun, "Impact of Cottage Industry," p. 55; Braun, "Early Industrialization," p. 296.
20. Levine, *Family Formation,* p. 19. Levine is quoting G. E. Fussell, "Four Centuries of Leicestershire Farming," in *Studies in Leicestershire Agrarian History,* edited by W. G. Hoskins (Leicester: The Leicestershire Archaeological Society), p. 158.
21. Pat Hudson, "From Manor to Mill: The West Riding in Transition," in Berg, Hudson, and Sonenscher, eds., *Manufacture in Town and Country,* p. 127.
22. Lehning, *Peasants of Marlhes,* pp. 3–34. In an interesting variation on Jones's argument, Lehning has found that it was the growth of urban demand for dairy products combined with improvements in the mountain roads, not the failure to compete successfully for urban cereal markets (because the region had never produced cereals for sale), that led the Stephanois region to concentrate on dairy herding in the nineteenth century. See Lehning, pp. 43–4.
23. Braun, "Impact of Cottage Industry," p. 53; Braun, "Early Industrialization," p. 299.
24. Levine, *Family Formation,* pp. 6–9.
25. Lutz K. Berkner, "Family, Social Structure and Rural Industry: A Comparative Study of the Waldviertel and the Pays de Caux in the Eighteenth Century," (Ph.D. dissertation, Harvard University, 1973), pp. 121–63, 290–1.
26. Kisch, "Textile Industries," pp. 179–80.
27. Thirsk, "Industries in the Countryside," p. 77.
28. Medick, "The Proto-Industrial Family Economy, pp. 296–7. This is not a totally new argument. Henry Sée, examining cottage industry in eighteenth-century Picardy and Normandy, argued in 1923 that it was the abundance of landless workers that "best explains the extension of rural industry" in those regions. See Sée, "Remarques," p. 50.
29. Hudson, "From Manor to Mill", pp. 125–31.
30. Mendels, "Agriculture and Peasant Industry," pp. 198–203.
31. Braun, "Impact of Cottage Industry," p. 64; Braun, "Early Industrialization," pp. 300, 322.
32. Levine, *Family Formation,* pp. 19, 61–5.
33. Braun, "Impact of Cottage Industry," p. 55.
34. Jones, "Agricultural Conditions," p. 131; Tarlé, *L'industrie dans les campagnes,* p. 59.
35. Mendels, "Seasons and Regions," p. 183.
36. Maxine Berg, Pat Hudson, and Michael Sonenscher have also recently called for further analysis of the relationships between towns and countryside in proto-industrial studies. See their "Manufacture in Town and Country," pp. 25–8.
37. Arthur Young, *Travels in France during the Years 1787, 1788, 1789,* edited by Jeffry Kaplow (Garden City, New York: Anchor Books, 1969), p. 433.
38. Jules Sion, *Les paysans de la Normandie Orientale: Pays de Caux, Bray, Vexin Normand, Vallée de la Seine. Etude géographique* (Paris: Armand Colin, 1909), p. 6.
39. Marc Bloch, *French Rural History: An essay on its Basic Characteristics,* translated by J. Sondheimer (Berkeley: University of California Press, 1966), p. 207.
40. E. LeParquier, *Cahiers de doléances du Bailliage d'Arques (secondaire de Caudebec) pour les états généraux de 1789* (Lille: Camille Robbe, 1922), p. xix.
41. Tarlé, *L'industrie dans les campagnes,* pp. 16–17.
42. Ibid.

43. Sion, *Paysans*, pp. 29–32, 67–76.
44. Ch. de Beaurepaire, *Renseignements statistiques sur l'état de l'agriculture vers 1789* (Rouen: Cagniard, 1889), p. 55.
45. LeParquier, *Cahiers*, p. xxii.
46. Beaurepaire, *Renseignements statistiques*, p. 55.
47. Michel Morineau, *Les faux-semblants d'un démarrage économique: agriculture et démographie en France au XVIIIe siècle* (Paris: Armand Colin, 1971), pp. 25, 35–6.
48. Steven L. Kaplan, *Bread, Politics and Political Economy in the Reign of Louis XV*, Vol. 1 (The Hague, Netherlands: Martinus Nijhoff, 1976), p. 21; Jean Vidalenc, "L'agriculture dans les départements normands à la fin du premier empire," *Annales de Normandie*, VII (1957): 185.
49. Young, *Travels in France*, p. 433.
50. Ibid., p. 437.
51. LeParquier, *Cahiers*, p. xxii; Jeffry Kaplow, *Elbeuf during the Revolutionary Period* (Baltimore: The Johns Hopkins University Press, 1964), p. 109.
52. For a similar argument, see Henri Baudrillart, *Les populations agricoles de la France*, vol. I: *Normandie et Bretagne* (Paris: Hachette, 1885), pp. 206–7.
53. Jerome Blum, *The End of the Old Order in Rural Europe*, (Princeton: Princeton University Press, 1978), p. 140.
54. Ibid., pp. 257–63.
55. André J. Bourde, *The Influence of England on the French Agronomes, 1750–1789* (Cambridge: The University Press, 1953), p. 114.
56. Bloch, *French Rural History*, pp. 214–15; Sion, *Paysans*, pp. 225–6.
57. LeParquier, *Cahiers*, pp. xxii–xxiii; Sion, *Paysans*, p. 226.
58. LeParquier, *Cahiers*, p. 313 (article 6).
59. Bourde, *Influence of England*, pp. 34–5.
60. Blum, *End of the Old Order*, p. 263.
61. Ibid., pp. 262–3.
62. LeParquier, *Cahiers*, p. 285 (article 6).
63. Bloch, *French Rural History*, p. 49.
64. Ibid., pp. 206–8.
65. Blum, *End of the Old Order*, p. 269.
66. Sion, *Paysans*, p. 229.
67. ADSM 6MP5113; 6MP5110; 6MP5107; Beaurepaire, *Renseignements statistiques*, pp. 13–14.
68. Collins, "Labour Supply," pp. 64, 74.
69. The Caux may have needed a large indigenous labor force more than other commercial agricultural areas because it was surrounded on three sides by water. Many migrant harvest workers who came from outside the *pays* would have had to cross the Seine River. This barrier would have made it more difficult and more expensive to rely on migrant harvest workers than was the case for many cereal regions.
70. ADSM L367; Parish and Civil Registers, Auffay.
71. ADSM L367.
72. ADSM 6MP5113.
73. Based on Charles Ernest Labrousse, *Esquisse du mouvement des prix et des revenus en France au XVIIIe siècle* (Paris: Librairie Dalloz, 1933), pp. 583–90. Labrousse estimated that a family of five (father, mother, and three children aged six to nine) would consume seven pounds of bread a day, with the male head himself consuming three pounds. Extrapolating from this estimate it seems reasonable to assume that, on the average, adults consumed at least two pounds of bread daily.
74. ADSM 6MP5113; Sion, *Paysans*, p. 156.
75. ADSM 3PP27[4]. The acre was the principal unit of land in Normandy before the French

Revolution. It may have been carried to the region by Norman knights returning from the conquest of England in 1066. The normand acre was approximately the same as an American and English acre – 4,047 square meters. During the French Revolution, it was replaced by the metric arpent, which equalled 1.46 acres.

> *Equivalencies*
> 1 acre = 160 square perches
> 1 arpent metric = 1 acre 73 square perches

See Ronald Edward Zupko, *French Weights and Measures Before the Revolution: A Dictionary of Provincial and Local Units* (Bloomington: Indiana University Press, 1978), pp. 1–3.

76. ADSM 3PP27[1].
77. Sion, *Paysans*, p. 265. This sale of noble land indicates the weakness of manorial control in the Caux. Since communal control was equally weak, building was not controlled and population was allowed to grow. As Lutz Berkner has noted, this weak manorial and communal control helped make the Caux attractive to the Rouen merchants. See Berkner, "Family, Social Structure and Rural Industry," pp. 232–93.
78. LeParquier, *Cahiers*, p. 89 (article 1).
79. Ibid., p. 523.
80. Sion, *Paysans*, p. 272.
81. LeParquier, *Cahiers*, p. 89; ADSM C1730.
82. ADSM C1730.
83. ADSM C537.
84. ADSM C1730; 3PP27[1].
85. ADSM C537.
86. Sion, *Paysans*, p. 273.
87. Ibid., p. 274.
88. LeParquier, *Cahiers*, pp. 54–5; David Houard, *Dictionnaire analytique, historique, étymologique, critique et interprétatif de la coutume de Normandie* (Rouen, 1780–82).
89. LeParquier, *Cahiers*, passim; Sion, *Paysans*, pp. 290–1.
90. LeParquier, *Cahiers*, p. 27 (article 3); p. 116 (article 3).
91. Pierre Dardel, *Histoire de Bolbec des origines à la Révolution: Le commerce et l'industrie à Bolbec avant 1789* (Rouen: Lestringant, 1939), pp. 81–3.
92. Sion, *Paysans*, p. 290.
93. ADSM 6MP5118–5124.
94. Messance, *Recherches sur la population des généralités d'Auvergne, de Lyon, de Rouen et de quelques provinces et villes du royaume* (Paris, 1766), p. 76; Guy Lemarchand, "Structure sociale d'après les rôles fiscaux et conjoncture économique dans le Pays de Caux: 1690–1789," *Bulletin de la Société d'histoire moderne*, LXVIII (1969): 7; Sion, *Paysans*, 290–1. Messance's study of 541 parishes revealed 123,037 births and 111,738 deaths, or a population growth of 11,299 between 1752 and 1761 simply as a result of natural increase. Areas near the Caux in which there was no cottage industry also watched their populations steadily depart for the plain, however, and the overall growth of the region came partly from immigration. Both sources of population growth lie behind the 45 percent increase in the number of households in 226 *cauchois* villages studied by Lemarchand for the years 1700 and 1789.
95. Sion, *Paysans*, pp. 432–5.
96. Cited in Sion, *Paysans*, p. 177.
97. Cited in Sion, *Paysans*, p. 178.
98. ADSM L367.
99. Sion, *Paysans*, p. 184; William M. Reddy, "The Textile Trade and the Language of the Crowd at Rouen, 1752–1871," *Past and Present*, no. 74 (1977): 68.

100. There are no carders, per se, in Auffay records between 1751 and 1800, which probably means that carding was one of the tasks of spinners rather than a separate occupation. ADSM Parish and Civil Registers, Auffay, 1751–1800; C1730; 219BP364.
101. ADSM L367; 6M83.
102. Sion, *Paysans*, p. 315.
103. Marc Bouloiseau, "Aspects socieaux de la crise cotonnière dans les campagnes rouennaises en 1788–1789," in *Actes de 81e Cóngrés National des Sociétés Savantes, Rouen-Caen, 1956* (Paris: Presses Universitaires de France, 1956), p. 406; G. Olphe-Galliard, "Les industries rurales à domicile dans la Normandie Orientale," *La Science Sociale* (1913): 22–3; Sion, *Paysans*, p. 444; ADSM 6MP5113.
104. Sion, *Paysans*, pp. 446–7.
105. Ibid., pp. 445–6.
106. ADSM L367; 6M83.
107. ADSM 6MP5154; Eugene Marchand, *Etude statistique, économique et chimique sur l'agriculture du Pays de Caux* (Paris: Mme. Veuve Bouchard-Huzard, 1869), p. 128.
108. Paul Hohenberg, "Change in Rural France in the Period of Industrialization, 1830–1914," *Journal of Economic History*, XXXII (1972): 229. See also Sion, *Paysans*, pp. 439–47.
109. J. Levainville, *Rouen: Etude d'une agglomeration urbaine* (Paris: Armand Colin, 1913), pp. 188, 190–3; Dardel, *Histoire de Bolbec*, p. 56; Sion, *Paysans*, pp. 172–3.
110. Dardel, *Histoire de Bolbec*, pp. 74–5.
111. AN F^{12}560, M. Latapie, "Réflexions préliminaires sur un mémoire intitulé Voyage de Rouen ou observations sur l'état actuel des arts et manufactures de Rouen, Elbeuf, Louviers, Evreux et Andely faites dans le mois de mai, juin et juillet 1773"; Dardel, *Histoire de Bolbec*, pp. 77–80. There is some controversy over the date of Delarue's creation of *siamoises*. Sion places the event in 1701; Dardel, in 1694. Dardel's case is the stronger of the two.
112. Morel, Inspecteur des Manufactures, 1750, cited in Dardel, *Histoire de Bolbec*, p. 87.
113. Dardel, *Histoire de Bolbec*, pp. 91–3. Dardel believes the figures for the period after 1779 are highly unreliable.
114. Ibid., pp. 89, 91; Louis Reybaud, *Rapport sur la condition morale, intellectuelle et materielle des ouvriers qui vivent de l'industrie du coton* (Paris, 1862), p. 267.
115. ADSM 6MP5122; Levainville, *Rouen*, pp. 196–9; Reybaud, *La condition morale*, pp. 164–7; E. LeParquier, *Cahiers*, pp. xx–xxi; Sion, *Paysans*, p. 309; Claude Fohlen, *L'industrie textile au temps du Second Empire* (Paris, 1956), pp. 198–9.
116. Michel Mollat, ed., *Histoire de Rouen* (Toulouse: Edouard Privat, 1979), pp. 218–23; AN F^{12}650 (Report of Goy, Inspecteur des manufactures à Rouen, 1782).
117. AN F^{12}650 (Report of Goy, 1782).
118. Levainville, *Rouen*, 202; Sion, *Paysans*, pp. 179–80.
119. Tarlé, *L'industrie dans les campagnes*, p. 4.
120. Dardel, *Histoire de Bolbec*, p. 91.
121. ADSM 6MP5122.
122. LeParquier, *Cahiers*, pp. xx–xxi; Sion, *Paysans*, p. 309; Fohlen, *L'industrie textile*, pp. 198–9.
123. Olphe-Galliard, "Les industries rurales" 35; Sion, *Paysans*, p. 35.
124. J. K. J. Thomson has found that the province of Languedoc was also a region of both commercial agriculture and a proto-industrial textile industry in the eighteenth century. See his "Variations in Industrial Structure in Pre-Industrial Languedoc," in Berg, Hudson, and Sonenscher, eds., *Manufacture in Town and Country*, pp. 61–91.
125. Ivy Pinchbeck, *Women Workers in the Industrial Revolution, 1750–1850* (1930; reprinted London: Frank Cass, 1977), pp. 59–62, 73; Collins, "Labour Supply," pp. 64–74.

126. Pinchbeck, *Women Workers*, pp. 59–62.
127. Ibid., p. 59.

The golden age of spinning

1. Remonstrances du Parlement de Rouen, 22 Avril 1722. Cited in Jules Sion, *Les paysans de la Normandie Orientale: Pays de Caux, Bray, Vexin Normand, Vallée de la Seine. Etude géographique* (Paris: Armand Colin, 1909), p. 177.
2. Pierre Dardel, *Histoire de Bolbec des origines à la Révolution: Le commerce et l'industrie à Bolbec avant 1789* (Rouen: Lestringant, 1939), pp. 51–4.
3. Louis Reybaud, *Rapport sur la condition morale, intellectuelle et materielle des ouvriers qui vivent de l'industrie du coton* (Paris, 1862), pp. 268–9; AN F^{12}560 (Report of Goy, Inspecteur des Manufactures à Rouen, 1782).
4. Sion, *Paysans*, pp. 174–5; Claude Fohlen, *L'industrie textile au temps du Second Empire* (Paris, 1956), p. 193.
5. Dardel, *Histoire de Bolbec*, p. 84.
6. AN F^{12}560.
7. ADSM L367.
8. Arthur Young, *Travels in France during the Years 1787, 1788, 1789*, edited by Jeffry Kaplow (Garden City, New York: Anchor Books, 1969), p. 83.
9. ADSM Notarial Records, Auffay.
10. There were 19,865 looms in 1782. See AN F^{12}560. Levainville's estimate of spinners to weavers were higher than Goy's. He believed that twelve spinners were needed for every *siamoise* weaver, not including children and the elderly who carded cotton. See Levainville, *Rouen*, p. 205.
11. ADSM L367.
12. ADSM Notarial Records, Auffay, 10 November 1778.
13. Remonstrances du Parlement de Rouen, 22 Avril 1722. Cited in Sion, *Paysans*, p. 177.
14. ADSM Parish Registers, Auffay and other villages.
15. Sion, *Paysans*, p. 469; Ivy Pinchbeck, *Women Workers and the Industrial Revolution, 1750–1850* (1930; reprinted London: Frank Cass, 1969), pp. 113–14.
16. An F^{12}560, M. Latapie, "Réflexions préliminaires sur un mémoire intitulé Voyage de Rouen ou observations sur l'état actuel des arts et manufactures de Rouen, Elbeuf, Louviers, Evreux et Andely faites dans le mois de mai, juin et juillet, 1773," p. 79.
17. Ibid., pp. 79–80.
18. Isidore Mars, *Derniers souvenirs du bon vieux temps d'Auffay depuis 1793 jusqu'à 1840 environ* (Dieppe: Paul Leprêtre & Cie., 1876), pp. 34, 38; Pinchbeck, *Women Workers*, pp. 129–30.
19. AN F^{12}560: Latapie, "Voyage de Rouen," pp. 80–82.
20. E. Tarlé, *L'industrie dans les campagnes en France à la fin de l'ancien régime* (Paris: Edouard Cornely et Cie., 1910), pp. 31–3; Young, *Travels in France*, pp. 436, 503 (1792 ed.); AN F^{12}560 (Goy's Report).
21. ADSM 6MP5113.
22. Mars, *Derniers souvenirs*, p. 34.
23. Dardel, *Histoire de Bolbec*, p. 96.
24. Mars, *Derniers souvenirs*, pp. 38–9.
25. Dardel, *Histoire de Bolbec*, pp. 96–7.
26. ADSM Notarial Records, Auffay, 10 November 1778.
27. Latapie, "Voyage de Rouen," pp. 101–8.
28. Ibid., p. 100.
29. Pinchbeck, *Women Workers*, pp. 115–16.

30. Charles Ballot, *L'introduction du machinisme dans l'industrie française* (Paris: F. Rieder & Cie, 1922), pp. 247–52.

31. Latapie, "Voyage de Rouen," pp. 109–10.

32. Charles Noiret, *Mémoires d'un ouvrier rouennais* (Rouen: François, 1836), p. 25.

33. Ibid., pp. 17, 23–5, 30–1.

34. ADSM 6MP5122.

35. M. M. Bouloiseau, "Aspects sociaux de la crise cotonnière dans les campagnes rouennaises en 1788–1789," *Actes de 81e Congrès National des Sociétés Savantes, Rouen-Caen, 1956* (Paris: Presses Universitaires de France, 1956), p. 406, n. 3.

36. An $F^{12}560$ (Goy's Report). For other contrasts in urban and rural wages see E. Levasseur, *Histoire des classes ouvrières et de l'industrie en France de 1789 à 1870*, II, 2d ed. (New York: AMS Press, 1969), p. 253; Reybaud, *La condition morale*, p. 276.

37. Descriptions of the living conditions of Rouen textile workers come from the early nineteenth century. Conditions in the eighteenth century could not have been much better. See Levainville, *Rouen*, p. 227; Noiret, *Mémoires*, pp. 29, 42; Reybaud, *La condition morale*, p. 276.

38. AN $F^{12}560$ (Goy's Report) *(fileuses 10–15 sous, tisserands 25)*; Bouloiseau, "Aspects sociaux," pp. 405–406 *(fileuses 8–15 sous, fileurs 25, tisserands 30–40)*; Sion, *Paysans*, pp. 184–185 *(fileuses 8–12 sous, tisserands 20)*; Evrard, "Les ouvriers du textile dans la région rouennaise (1789–1802)," *Annales historiques de la Révolution française*, no. 108 (1947): 349–50 *(fileuses 12–14 sous, toiliers and siamoisiers 15–18)*. Figures in parentheses are estimated daily earnings.

39. Noiret, *Mémoires*, p. 22.

40. Bouloiseau, "Aspects sociaux," p. 406; Sion, *Paysans*, p. 184.

41. Latapie, "Voyage de Rouen" pp. 77–8; Evrard, "Les ouvriers du textile," p. 345; Levainville, *Rouen*, p. 213.

42. Evrard, "Les ouvriers du textile," p. 349; Bouloiseau, "Aspects sociaux," p. 406.

43. François Furet and Jacques Ozouf, "Literacy and Industrialization: The Case of the Département du Nord in France," *Journal of European Economic History*, V (Spring 1976): 27, 42–3.

44. ADSM Parish and Civil Registers, Auffay.

45. Auffay Family Reconstitution Study.

46. LeParquier, *Cahiers*, passim. The cahier from Auffay complained that "the cafés, buvettes and billards, established in the bourgs, ought to be suppressed and prohibited: in ruining those who frequent them, they also corrupt their morals and drive them often into crime." (LeParquier, *Cahiers*, p. 53.)

47. ADSM 219BP364, C1730. This conclusion is supported by the 1796 census. In that year, forty-one of the sixty-one women who headed their own households were employed as spinners. See ADSM L367.

48. Olwen H. Hufton, *The Poor of Eighteenth-Century France, 1750–1789* (Oxford: The Clarendon Press, 1974), p. 33.

49. Auffay Family Reconstitution Study.

50. ADSM 219BP364, C1730; Parish Registers, Auffay.

51. ADSM C1730.

52. These and the following figures for male occupations are taken from eighteenth-century tax roles and parish registers. See ADSM 219BP364, C1730, and Parish Registers, Auffay.

53. Auffay Family Reconstitution Study.

54. Dardel, *Histoire de Bolbec*, p. 96.

55. Hans Medick, "The Proto-Industrial Family Economy: The Structural Function of Household and Family during the Transition from Peasant Society to Industrial Capitalism," *Social History*, no. 3 (1976): 296–7; Hans Medick, "The Proto-Industrial

Family Economy," in Peter Kriedte, Hans Medick, and Jurgen Schlumbohm, *Industrialization Before Industrialization*, translated by Beate Schempp, (New York: Cambridge University Press, 1981), pp. 61–3.

56. Louise A. Tilly and Joan W. Scott, *Women, Work and Family* (New York: Holt, Rinehart and Winston, 1978), pp. 176–213; Lynn Lees, *Exiles of Erin* (Ithaca, New York: Cornell University Press, 1979), pp. 155–63; Pinchbeck, *Women Workers*, p. 312.

57. Mars, *Derniers souvenirs*, pp. 34, 37–8.

58. LeParquier, *Cahiers*, passim.

59. Georges Dubosc, "Le jeu de dominos en Normandie," *Par Ci, Par La: Etudes normandes de moeurs et d'histoire* (Rouen, 1927), p. 48. Unfortunately, Dubosc does not tell us how long these names had been attached to the dominoes.

Crisis and change in the Caux

1. Eden consulted with English manufacturers before the negotiations to determine what kind of treaty they wanted. He offered advantages to the French only on products that the English did not produce. Vergennes, controller general of foreign affairs and the French negotiator, believed that the French had to make trade concessions to the English to prevent them from retaliating for France's role in the American Revolution, and he was predisposed toward the laissez-faire views of the Physiocrats. The only advantages he won for the French were in the tariffs England would charge on agricultural products. Shepard Bancroft Clough, *France: A History of National Economics, 1789–1939* (New York: Charles Scribner's Sons, 1939), pp. 26–7, 386–7, note 85.

2. That the slump in the textile industry began before the treaty became effective in July 1787 has given rise to debate over the treaty's role in the French economic crisis of 1786–1787. See Clough, *France*, pp. 27–8, 387–9, note 89; F. Dumas, *Etude sur le traité de commerce de 1786 entre la France et l'Angleterre* (Toulouse: Privat, 1904). There was considerable confusion about the effective date of the treaty. This, I would argue, coupled with the anticipation of disaster, made the treaty a major factor in the crisis despite its delayed beginning date.

3. Louis Reybaud, *Rapport sur la condition morale, intellectuelle et materielle des ouvriers qui vivent de l'industrie du coton* (Paris: Institut Imperial de France, 1862). See also ADSM 6MP5106 (Rapport sur le commerce de Rouen); Pierre Dardel, *Histoire de Bolbec des origines à la Révolution: Le commerce et l'industrie à Bolbec avant 1789* (Rouen: Lestringant, 1939), pp. 26–27; M. M. Bouloiseau, "Aspects sociaux de la crise cotonnière dans les campagnes rouennaises en 1788–1789," *Actes de 81e Congrès National des Sociétés Savantes, Rouen-Caen, 1956* (Paris: Presses Universitaires de France, 1956), p. 410.

4. Jules Sion, *Les paysans de la Normandie Orientale: Pays de Caux, Bray, Vexin Normand, Vallée de la Seine. Etude géographique* (Paris: Armand Colin, 1909), p. 296. Bouloiseau cites an even steeper decline from 15 to 3 *sous* for women spinners (*fileuses*) and from 25 to 12–14 *sous* for male spinners (*fileurs*). His initial figures are probably high for the Caux, however. Bouloiseau, "Aspects sociaux," p. 414.

5. E. LeParquier, *Cahiers de doléances du Bailliage d'Arques (secondaire de Caudebec) pour les états généraux de 1789* (Lille: Camille Robbe, 1922), p. 59.

6. Ibid., p. 275. See also, Dumas, *Le traité de commerce*, p. 182.

7. LeParquier, *Cahiers*, p. xxii.

8. Ibid., pp. xliii–xlix.

9. Ibid., pp. 527–8.

10. Ibid., p. 52.

11. Ibid., pp. 421–2.

12. Ibid., p. 162.

13. LeParquier, *Cahiers*. See especially the *cahiers* from La Heuze, article 2; Saint-Martin-de-Veules, article 1; La Chapelle-sur-Dun, article 13; Bois-Robert, article 5; and, Saint-Denis d'Acquelon, article 7.

14. Ibid., p. xiv.

15. Ibid., p. 120.

16. Ibid., p. 404.

17. Ibid., p. 90.

18. Ibid., pp. xliii–xlv; E. Gosselin, *Journal des principaux épisodes de l'époque révolutionnaire à Rouen et dans les environs, de 1789 à 1795* (Rouen: E. Cagniard, 1867), pp. 6–7; ADSM 202BP14bis.

19. Gosselin, *Principaux épisodes*, pp. 7–8.

20. Ibid., pp. 18–19.

21. LeParquier, *Cahiers*, pp. 147–8.

22. Ibid., p. 148.

23. LeParquier, *Cahiers*.

24. *Journal de Rouen*, 25 Juillet, 1791, p. 1008.

25. Ibid., 24 Juillet 1791, p. 1004.

26. Gosselin, *Principaux épisodes*, pp. 1–15. Gosselin's account is based on the minutes of the Bailliage Criminel in Rouen.

27. For a discussion of women's participation in crowds, see George Rudé, *The Crowd in the French Revolution* (London: Oxford University Press, 1959), pp. 67–74; Natalie Zemon Davis, "Women on Top," in her *Society and Culture in Early Modern France* (Stanford: Stanford University Press, 1965), pp. 124–51; E. P. Thompson, *The Making of the English Working Class* (New York: Vintage, 1966), pp. 63–5; Louise Tilly, "The Food Riot as a Form of Political Conflict in France," *Journal of Interdisciplinary History*, II (1971): 23–58.

28. Charles Tilly, *The Vendée* (Cambridge Mass.: Harvard University Press, 1964).

29. T. J. A. LeGoff and D. M. G. Sutherland, "The Social Origins of Counter-Revolution in Western France," *Past and Present*, no. 99 (May 1983), pp. 65–87.

30. ADSM L319.

31. Ibid.

32. Ibid. (Emphasis is mine.)

33. Ibid.

34. ADSM L277 and L277bis.

35. ADSM L277.

36. Ibid.

37. Ibid. The list is undated.

38. Isidore Mars, *Auffay, ou le vieil Isnelville* (Rouen: Lecointe Frères, 1857), pp. 196–201.

39. ADSM L5116–5123.

40. The following description of the advances in spinning in England comes from Ivy Pinchbeck, *Women Workers and the Industrial Revolution, 1750–1850* (reprinted New York: Augustus M. Kelley, 1969), pp. 115–17, 148–53; David Landes, *The Unbound Prometheus: Technological Change and Industrial Development in Western Europe from 1750 to the Present* (Cambridge: Cambridge University Press, 1972), pp. 84–6; and, L. S. Wood and A. Wilmore, *The Romance of the Cotton Industry in England* (London: Oxford University Press, 1927), pp. 72–94. Productivity was linked directly to the number of spindles in operation and increased as the size of the machines increased. The early jennies contained sixteen spindles. Later models contained as many as eighty. For the merchant, the cost of the machines was quickly absorbed by the

increases in productivity, and merchants who did not provide machines for their workers or force them to buy jennies could not long compete on the open market with
merchants who had introduced the new machines.

41. Wood and Wilmore, *The Cotton Industry in England*, p. 82.
42. Claude Fohlen, "The Industrial Revolution in France, 1700–1914," in *The Fontana
    Economic History of Europe*, Vol. 4, edited by Carlo M. Cipolla (Glascow: Fon-
    tana/Collins, 1973), pp. 64–5; Landes, *Unbound Prometheus*, p. 139; Sion, *Paysans*,
    p. 295; Edmund Perrée, *Les origines de la filature mecanique de coton en Normandie*
    (Rouen: Cagniard, 1923), p. 20.
43. ADSM 6MP5106; Perrée, *Filature mecanique de coton*, p. 4.
44. AN F^{1c}V, S–Inf, I, cited in Sion, *Paysans*, p. 297.
45. Clough, *France*, pp. 45, 65.
46. Landes, *Unbound Prometheus*, p. 162.
47. ADSM L367. This partial census of the population (only persons aged twelve and over
    are listed) has been preserved only for the canton of Auffay.
48. ADSM 6MP5105, 5119, 5120, 5123. The first reference to this mill is in *an* IX (1800–
    1801).
49. ADSM 6MP5106.
50. Most historians accept the government reports. André Dubuc, however, notes that the
    price of a jenny was equal to five months salary for a spinner. See André Dubuc,
    "L'industrie textile en Haute Normandie au cours de la Révolution et de l'Empire,"
    Le Textile en Normandie: Etudes Diverses (Rouen: Société d'emulation de la Seine-
    Maritime, 1975), p. 134.
51. J. Levainville, *Rouen: Etude d'une agglomeration urbaine* (Paris: Armand Colin, 1913),
    pp. 225–6.
52. ADSM 6MP5123.
53. Fernand Evrard, "Les ouvriers du textile dans la région rouennaise (1789–1802),"
    Annales historiques de la Révolution française, no. 108, (1947): pp. 345–6, 351.
54. ADSM 6MP5118.
55. ADSM L367.
56. ADSM 6MP5118.
57. ADSM 6MP5123–5124.
58. ADSM 6MP5124.
59. Ibid.; Landes, *Unbound Prometheus*, p. 162; Clough, *France*, p. 88.
60. ADSM 6MP5129, 6MP5118.
61. ADSM 6MP5124.
62. ADSM 6MP5124, 6MP5113. Between 1789 and 1805, the annual earnings of most
    farm employees doubled. Shepherds went from 150 to 300 francs per year; ploughmen
    from 120–130 to 250; general workers from 100 to 200; and harvest workers from
    25–30 to 45.
63. Auffay Family Reconstitution Study.
64. Ibid.
65. The entry of women into weaving also cannot be accounted for by technological changes
    in weaving. No substantive changes in hand looms occurred in the Caux before 1818.
    Moreover, the looms used in the Caux were generally small and could have been used
    by women from the beginning. See Landes, *Unbound Prometheus*, p. 86.
66. ADSM L367.
67. Valerie Kincade Oppenheimer, *The Female Labor Force in the United States* (Berkeley:
    Institute of International Studies, University of California, 1970), p. 102. For a general
    discussion of the factors that influence sexual divisions of labor also see Cynthia B.
    Lloyd, ed., *Sex, Discrimination, and the Division of Labor* (New York: Columbia
    University Press, 1975); Judith K. Brown, "A Note on the Division of Labor by Sex,"

American Anthropologist 72 (1970): 1073–8; Martha Blaxell and Barbara Reagan, eds., *Woman and the Workplace: The Implications of Occupational Segregation* (Chicago: The University of Chicago Press, 1976).

68. ADSM 6M1100; AN F^{12}4476C. By the mid-nineteenth century, the spinning mills in the arrondissements of Rouen, Dieppe, and Le Havre employed 6224 men, 5628 women, and 5596 children. At least two-thirds of these workers were in the Rouen area.

The golden age of cottage weaving

1. Jules Sion, *Les paysans de la Normandie Orientale: Pays de Caux, Bray, Vexin Normand, Vallée de la Seine. Etude géographique* (Paris: Armand Colin, 1909), pp. 300–1, 308.
2. ADSM Civil Registers, Auffay. The marriage records list an occupation for only thirty-four of the 167 women who married during these years. An additional twenty-one women, for whom there is no bridal occupation, appear in subsequent records with an occupation, but this still accounts for only one-third of the brides. The occupations that are recorded are revealing, however. Only nine women are ever listed as spinners (four at their weddings, five later). In contrast, twenty-five were weavers either at the time of their marriages (eleven) or later (fourteen). The absence of female occupations from the marriage registers during theses years is probably the result of two factors: (1) recording failures (many, if not all, of the brides with no listed occupation who appear in later records with an occupation probably were working in the same job when they married) and (2) unemployment. An employer as large as cottage spinning had been was not easily replaced.
3. Ibid.
4. AN F^{12}560. The 1780s figure is based on the assumption of a 10 to 1 ratio of spinners to weavers and a total number of textile workers of 188,000. G. Olphe-Galliard, "Les industries rurales à domicile dans la Normandie Orientale," *La Science Sociale* (1913): 30.
5. ADSM 6M83.
6. ADSM 6MP5154.
7. Sion, *Paysans*, p. 314.
8. Isidore Mars, *Derniers souvenirs du bon vieux temps d'Auffay depuis 1793 jusqu'à 1840 environ* (Dieppe: Paul Leprêtre, 1876), p. 33.
9. Sion, *Paysans*, p. 314; Charles Noiret, *Mémoires d'un ouvrier rouennais* (Rouen: François, 1836), pp. 18–19.
10. Noiret, *Mémoires*, pp. 18–19. (Emphasis is mine.)
11. Sion, *Paysans*, p. 304.
12. ADSM 6MP5154.
13. Sion, *Paysans*, p. 308. The premiere job in the textile industry was not urban weaving but factory spinning. Spinners earned 2.00 francs a day at midcentury.
14. ADSM 6MP5154.
15. Municipal Council Minutes, Auffay, 1849.
16. Sion, *Paysans*, pp. 312–14; Claude Fohlen, *L'industrie textile au temps du Second Empire* (Paris: Plon, 1956), p. 193.
17. Fohlen, *L'industrie textile*, pp. 148–53.
18. Ibid., p. 199; Sion, *Paysans*, p. 303; Fernand Evrard, "Les ouvriers du textile dans la région rouennaise (1789–1802)," *Annales historiques de la Révolution française*, no. 108 (1947): 338.
19. Noiret, *Mémoires*, p. 46.
20. Sion, *Paysans*, p. 310.

21. ADSM 6MP5154. It is not clear whether these wages are averaged on an annual basis or are what was paid during the work season. The question arises because of indications that day laborers were much poorer than the weavers in Auffay. See Tables 6.1 and 6.2.
22. Municipal Council Records, Auffay, 1849.
23. Ibid., 1833–51. Tuition was assessed as follows: morality and religion, 0.75 francs; writing, 1.00; French 1.25; weights and measures and geometry, 1.50.
24. ADSM L367.
25. ADSM 6M83.
26. ADSM 6MP3004.
27. ADSM L367, 6M83.
28. Ibid. The communes are Bracquetuit, Fresnay Lelong, Montreuil, St. Denis sur Scie, St. Maclou de Folleville, St. Victor L'Abbaye, and Vassonville.
29. ADSM L367, 6M23, 6M83.
30. ADSM 6MP5154, L367.
31. ADSM 6M83.
32. Sion, *Paysans*, p. 317. The first mechanical looms appeared in the Caux in 1825.
33. E. Levasseur, *Histoire des classes ouvrières de l'industrie en France de 1789 à 1870*, tome II, 2d ed. (New York: AMS Press, 1969), p. 274.
34. ADSM 6M83.
35. Noiret, *Mémoires*, pp. 23–5.
36. Ibid., pp. 30–1.
37. ADSM L367.
38. Municipal Council Records, Auffay, 1849.
39. ADSM 6M83.
40. Municipal Council Records, Auffay, 1849.
41. ADSM 6M23, 6M64, 6M83.
42. Municipal Council Records, Auffay, 1832–50; Isidore Mars, *Auffay, ou le vieil Isnelville* (Rouen: Lecointe Frères, 1857), pp. 228–9, 260–1; Mars, *Derniers souvenirs*, pp. 79–81.
43. ADSM Civil Registers, Auffay. The first reference to this mill is in 1838.
44. No factory owner appears in the 1841, 1846, and 1851 Auffay censuses. See ADSM 6M23, 6M64, 6M83.
45. ADSM Civil Registers, Auffay, 1838–50.
46. ADSM Parish and Civil Registers, Auffay, 1751–1850.
47. Ibid.; ADSM 1J35 [1], 1J35 [2].
48. Mars, *Derniers souvenirs*, p. 11.
49. ADSM Parish and Civil Registers, Auffay, 1751–1850.
50. Mars, *Auffay*, pp. 155–6; Mars, *Derniers souvenirs*, pp. 108–9.
51. ADSM Parish and Civil Registers, Auffay, 1751–1850.
52. André Cauchois, *Démographie de la Seine-Inférieure* (Rouen: Laine, 1929), p. 15; Sion, *Paysans*, p. 317.
53. ADSM L367, 6M83; Civil Registers, Auffay, 1801–50.
54. AN F[1c] III, S–Inf., 9. Cited in Sion, *Paysans*, p. 318.
55. Auffay Family Reconstitution Study.
56. Olphe-Galliard, "Les industries rurales," p. 30; Sion, *Paysans*, p. 441; J. Levainville, "Les ouvriers du coton dans la région de Rouen," *Annales de Géographie*, XX: 58–9.
57. Sion, *Paysans*, pp. 320–1, 432–58; Paul Hohenberg, "Change in Rural France in the Period of Industrialization, 1830–1914," *Journal of Economic History*, 32 (March 1972), 229.

Marriage and family in proto-industrial Auffay

1. ADSM Parish Registers, Auffay, 1783.
2. Isidore Mars, *Derniers souvenirs du bon vieux temps d'Auffay depuis 1793 jusqu'à 1840 environ* (Dieppe: Paul Leprêtre, 1876), pp. 61–4. Unfortunately, Mars does not tell us whether this ritual was always performed in the same way, if both women and men participated at all stages, who cooked the meal, who paid for the food, who was invited to the wedding, and so forth. For further descriptions of wedding ceremonies and charivaris, see Natalie Zemon Davis, "The Reasons of Misrule," in *Society and Culture in Early Modern France* (Stanford: Stanford University Press, 1965), pp. 97–123; and Martine Segalen, *Mari et femme dans la société paysanne* (Paris: Flammarion, 1980).
3. This and subsequent information about Varin and Frichet is drawn from the Auffay Family Reconstitution Study.
4. Olwen Hufton, "Women and the Family Economy in Eighteenth-Century France," *French Historical Studies*, IX, (Spring 1975): 7–8; Louise A. Tilly and Joan W. Scott, *Women, Work and Family* (New York: Holt, Rinehart and Winston, 1978), pp. 24–5.
5. Charles Noiret, *Mémoires d'un ouvrier rouennais* (Rouen: François, 1836), pp. 17, 30–1.
6. Tilly and Scott, *Women, Work and Family*, pp. 24, 43; J. Hajnal, "European Marriage Patterns in Perspective," in D. V. Glass and D. E. C. Eversley, eds., *Population in History* (London: E. Arnold, 1965), p. 133; André Armengaud, *La Famille et l'enfant en France et en Angleterre du XVIe au XVIIIe siècle. Aspects démographiques.* (Paris: Société d'Édition d'Enseignement Supérieur, 1975), p. 145.
7. Tilly and Scott, *Women, Work and Family*, p. 26; Etienne Gautier and Louis Henry, *La population de Crulai, paroisse normande: Etude historique* (Paris: Presses Universitaires de France, 1958), p. 236; Martine Segalen, *Nuptialité et alliance* (Paris: G.-P. Maisonneuve et Larose, 1972), p. 41.
8. Franklin F. Mendels, "Proto-Industrialization: The First Phase of the Industrialization Process," *Journal of Economic History*, 32 (March 1972): 250–2.
9. David Levine, *Family Formation in an Age of Nascent Capitalism* (New York: Academic Press, 1977), pp. 61–4.
10. Rudolf Braun, "The Impact of Cottage Industry on an Agricultural Population," in *The Rise of Capitalism* edited by David Landes (New York: Macmillan, 1966), p. 57.
11. Ibid., p. 59.
12. Hans Medick, "The Proto-Industrial Family Economy," in Peter Kriedte, Hans Medick, and Jurgen Schlumbohm, *Industrialization Before Industrialization*, translated by Beate Schempp (New York: Cambridge University Press, 1981), p. 56.
13. E. A. Wrigley, "Family Limitation in Pre-Industrial England," *Economic History Review*, 2d Series, vol. 19 (1966): 123; Levine, *Family Formation*, pp. 61–4. Levine's study shows that lowering the age of marriage increased population growth in two ways: Women bore more children (those who married before the age of twenty had an average completed family size of 7.2 whereas those who married between the ages of thirty and thirty-five had an average completed family size of only 3.4), and the intervals between generations became shorter so "more children were born in each unit of time."
14. Wolfram Fischer, "Rural Industrialization and Population Change," *Comparative Studies in Society and History*, vol. 15 (March 1973): 162; Levine, *Family Formation*, pp. 27–8, 80–1. Braun, "Impact of Cottage Industry," p. 62. If the work of children and adolescents was not segregated by sex, then both sexes were equally desirable. But if

more work was available for one sex than for another, they were not. In the Zurich highlands, cottage workers desired daughters more than sons and delayed or prevented their marrying whenever possible. In Shepshed, sons were probably more desired than daughters because they learned to knit earlier than girls and could earn almost as much money as adults. Women as well as men operated the knitting frames, but, according to contemporaries, were unable to earn as much because of their lesser physical strength and stamina.

15. Levine, *Family Formation*, p. 79.
16. Pierre Deyon, "L'enjeu des discussions autour du concept de 'proto-industrialization'," *Revue de Nord*, 61 (1979): 12.
17. Medick, "The Proto-Industrial Family Economy," in Kriedte, Medick, and Schlumbohm, *Industrialization Before Industrialization*, p. 56.
18. Myron P. Gutmann and René Leboutte, "Rethinking Protoindustrialization and the Family," *Journal of Interdisciplinary History*, XIV (Winter 1984): 595.
19. James Lehning, "Nuptiality and Rural Industry: Families and Labor in the French Countryside," *Journal of Family History* (Winter 1983): 333–45.
20. Rab Houston and K. D. M. Snell, "Proto-Industrialization? Cottage Industry, Social Change, and Industrial Revolution," *The Historical Journal*, 27 (1984): 482.
21. Based on analysis of ADSM Parish Registers, Auffay, 1751–86.
22. Ibid.
23. Gautier and Henry, *Population de Crulai*, p. 75.
24. Hajnal, "European Marriage Patterns," p. 102.
25. Based on an analysis of ADSM Parish and Civil Registers, Auffay, 1787–1817.
26. ADSM 6M83.
27. ADSM Civil Registers, Auffay, 1841–50.
28. ADSM 6M83.
29. J. Levainville, *Rouen: Etude d'une agglomeration urbaine* (Paris: Armand Colin, 1913), pp. 230–1; J. Levainville, "Les ouvriers du coton dans la région de Rouen," *Annales de Géographie*, XX (1911); 63–4; Claude Fohlen, *L'industrie textile au temps du Second Empire* (Paris: Plon, 1956), p. 199; Jules Sion, *Les paysans de la Normandie Orientale: Pays de Caux, Bray, Vexin Normand, Vallée de la Seine. Etude Géographique* (Paris: Armand Colin, 1909), p. 317.
30. ADSM L367.
31. Auffay Family Reconstitution Study. This conclusion is based on the assumption that young men and women who were living in the same village as their parents were also living in the same household with them. There is no way to determine whether this was true in all cases, but the 1796 census of the village lends support to the assumption. In that year, only four households were headed by single women whereas an additional sixteen were headed by women of indeterminate marital status. Even if all of these women had never married, it remains the case that the vast majority of unmarried women whose parents lived in Auffay were living at home. See ADSM L367.
32. Ibid.
33. ADSM 6M83.
34. Auffay Family Reconstitution Study.
35. Ibid.
36. ADSM L367.
37. Hufton, "Women and the Family Economy," pp. 8–10; Louise A. Tilly, Joan W. Scott, and Miriam Cohen, "Women's Work and European Fertility Patterns," *Journal of Interdisciplinary History*, VI (Winter, 1976): 463–7; Jacques Depauw, "Illicit Sexual Activity and Society in Eighteenth-Century Nantes," translated by Elborg Forster and Patricia M. Ranum, in *Family and Society*, edited by Robert Forster and Orest Ranum (Baltimore: The Johns Hopkins University Press, 1976), pp. 162–5, 188–91.

38. Noiret, *Mémoires,* p. 19.
39. This was true far beyond the Caux. In the United States, the reluctance of New England farm families to let their daughters move unprotected to the city prompted the owners of the textile mills in Lowell, Massachusetts, to construct boarding houses for their female employees, where strict moral codes were imposed and enforced. See Thomas Dublin, *Women at Work: The Transformation of Work and Community in Lowell, Massachusetts, 1826–1860.* (New York: Columbia University Press, 1979), pp. 75–85.
40. Albert Soboul, *The French Revolution, 1787–1799,* translated by Alan Forrest and Colin Jones (New York: Vintage Books, 1975), p. 329.
41. ADSM L367.
42. These and all subsequent figures on marriage ages and occupations are from the 590 marriages in the Auffay Family Reconstitution Study in which both spouses were marrying for the first time.
43. Segalen, *Nuptialité et alliance,* p. 59.
44. Gautier and Henry, *Population de Crulai,* p. 233.
45. Ibid.; Segalen, *Nuptialité et alliance,* p. 59.
46. Hajnal, "European Marriage Patterns," pp. 108–11. Hajnal estimates that the mean marriage age for single women in Western Europe was between twenty-four and twenty-six; for single men, between twenty-six and twenty-eight.
47. Auffay Family Reconstitution Study.
48. ADSM Parish and Civil Registers, Auffay, 1751–1850.
49. Levine, *Family Formation,* pp. 62–3.
50. ADSM 6MP5154.
51. All the examples and data on occupations and endogamy in this section are taken from the Auffay Family Reconstitution Study.
52. ADSM 219BP364; E. LeParquier, *Cahiers de doléances du bailliage d'Arques (secondaire de Caudebec) pour les états généraux de 1789* (Lille: Camille Robbe, 1922). In a *grand gabelle* region like the Caux, households were required to purchase a certain amount of salt from the government based on the size of the household and the number of animals.
53. Municipal Council Records, Auffay, 1832–50; Isidore Mars, *Auffay, ou le vieil Isnelville* (Rouen: Lecointe Frères, 1857), pp. 228–9, 260–1; Mars, *Derniers souvenirs,* pp. 79–81.
54. ADSM 219BP364; Municipal Council Records, Auffay, 1832–50.
55. Mars, *Derniers souvenirs,* pp. 33–4.
56. Auffay Family Reconstitution Study.
57. Mars, *Derniers souvenirs,* pp. 34, 37–8.
58. For a discussion of the concept of innate skills and the sexual divison of labor, see Valerie Kincade Oppenheimer, *The Female Labor Force in the United States* (Berkeley: Institute of International Studies, University of California, 1970), p. 102.
59. Medick, "The Proto-Industrial Family Economy," in Kriedte, Medick, and Schlumbohm, *Industrialization Before Industrialization,* pp. 61–3.
60. Braun, "Impact of Cottage Industry," pp. 58–60.
61. Medick, "The Proto-Industrial Family Economy," in Kriedte, Medick, and Schlumbohm, *Industrialization Before Industrialization,* pp. 61–3.
62. Ibid.
63. These and all subsequent figures in this chapter are from the Auffay Family Reconstitution Study. Only first marriages for both spouses have been used in the calculations.
   The conception figures are remarkably stable for the entire period. The percentage of brides who bore their first child within a year of marriage ranges from 61.1 to 62.3 to 62.2 for the three marriage cohorts. The percentage who bore their first child within

the first two years of marriage ranges from 88.9 to 86.1 to 85.8. The percentage of pregnant brides varies more, ranging from 19.4 to 30.3 to 22.2. These changes are linked to other changes in the illegitimacy rates for the village and are analyzed in Chapter 9.

64. Auffay Family Reconstitution Study.

65. Jane Mencken, James Trussel, and Susan Watkins, "The Nutrition Fertility Link: An Evaluation of the Evidence," *The Journal of Interdisciplinary History* II (1981); 432.

66. The following demographic and occupational information on completed families is drawn from the larger Auffay Family Reconstitution Study.

67. Hufton, "Women and the Family Economy," pp. 11–13; Robert J. Bezucha, *The Lyon Uprising of 1834: Social and Political Conflict in the Early July Monarchy* (Cambridge, Mass.: Harvard University Press, 1974), p. 42.

68. ADSM Parish Registers, Auffay. This is close to the average infant mortality rate of 168 for France in the mid-nineteenth century. See E. A. Wrigley, *Population and History* (New York: World University Library, 1969), p. 171.

69. For an analysis of the significance of increasing birth intervals see E. A. Wrigley, "Family Limitation in Pre-Industrial England," *Economic History Review*, 2d Series, Vol. 19 (1966): 82–109.

70. In 1978, Rose Frisch gathered a variety of scientific and historical evidence to support the hypothesis that "undernutrition and 'hard living' " explain the lower than expected fertility of various European groups in the mid-nineteenth century. She argued that undernourished women and men are less fecund than well-nourished people, that women "low in fecundity" bred at greater intervals at all ages, beginning with the first birth, and that the interval between all births lengthens for undernourished women because they have a higher probability of miscarriage and stillbirth than do well-nourished women. See Rose E. Frisch, "Population, Food Intake, and Fertility," *Science,* 199 (1978): 22–4.

   In 1981, Jane Mencken, James Trussel, and Susan Watkins argued, in contradistinction to Frisch, that changes in nutrition levels for populations that are chronically undernourished do not significantly affect the ability of women to conceive and bear live children. Reductions in fertility levels that are associated with reductions in nutrition are more likely to be the result of reductions in the frequency of intercourse (as a result of the separation of the spouses, due to the temporary or permanent migration of men to seek jobs, or stress that either "reduces sexual desire or performance, or [leads] couples deliberately [to] decide to abstain until conditions seem more propitious for having a child") than of reduced fecundity. See Mencken, Trussel, and Watkins, "The Nutrition Fertility Link," p. 441.

71. ADSM Parish and Civil Registers, Auffay, 1751–1850. See Appendix.

72. The infant mortality rate was calculated from the formula $I.M.R = k(D_0/B)$, where D_0 = number of deaths to children under 1 year of age in year X, B = number of live births in year x, and $k = 1,000$. Cf. James A. Palmore, *Measuring Mortality: A Self-Teaching Guide to Elementary Measures* (Papers of the East–West Population Institute, revised June 1973).

73. Wrigley, "Family Limitation," pp. 82–109.

74. The following examples are taken from the Auffay Family Reconstitution Study.

75. Levine, *Family Formation,* pp. 66–7, 108.

Widowhood, remarriage, and the sexual division of labor

1. Auffay Family Reconstitution Study.

2. Jean-Louis Flandrin, *Familles: parenté, maison, sexualité dans l'ancienne société* (Paris: Librarie Hachette, 1976), pp. 114–15.

3. Micheline Baulant, "The Scattered Family: Another Aspect of Seventeenth-Century Demography," in *Family and Society*, edited by Robert Forster and Orest Ranum, translated by Elborg Forster and Patricia M. Ranum (Baltimore: The Johns Hopkins University Press, 1967), p. 106.

4. Ibid.

5. Edward Shorter, *The Making of the Modern Family* (New York: Basic Books, 1975), pp. 57–8.

6. Ibid., p. 57.

7. Ibid., pp. 55, 57.

8. Ibid., p. 59.

9. François Lebrun, *La vie conjugale sous l'ancien régime* (Paris: Librarie Hachette, 1976), p. 83. (Emphasis is mine.)

10. Louise A. Tilly and Joan W. Scott, *Women, Work and Family* (New York: Holt, Rinehart and Winston, 1978), p. 53.

11. Ibid., p. 52.

12. Martine Segalen, *Mari et femme dans la société paysanne* (Paris: Flammarion, 1980); Françoise Zonabend, *La mémoire longue* (Paris: Presses Universitaires de France, 1980).

13. Zonabend, *La mémoire longue*, p. 196.

14. Ibid.

15. Ibid., p. 193.

16. Segalen, *Mari et femme*, Chapter 3.

17. Ibid., p. 121.

18. Auffay Family Reconstitution Study.

19. Ibid.

20. ADSM Parish and Civil Registers, Auffay.

21. Auffay Family Reconstitution Study.

22. ADSM 6M83.

23. Auffay Family Reconstitution Study. Percentages are based on men and women who were married and widowed in Auffay and who continued to live in the village until they either remarried or died.

24. Ibid.

25. Ibid. Four women died within the first week after giving birth; five, within the second week; two, within the third week; four, in six to seven weeks; and two, between two and five months after giving birth. Ten of these women were in their twenties, six were in their thirties, and one was forty.

26. Auffay Family Reconstitution Study.

27. Ibid.

28. ADSM Parish and Civil Registers, Auffay.

29. Auffay Family Reconstitution Study.

30. ADSM Parish and Civil Registers, Auffay.

31. *A Present for a Servant Maid* (1743) cited in Ivy Pinchbeck, *Women Workers and the Industrial Revolution, 1750–1850* (1930; reprinted New York: Augustus M. Kelley, 1969), pp. 1–2.

32. Godefroy Berault, *Commentaires sur la Coutume de Normandie*, nouvelle édition, (Rouen, 1776), pp. 5–6; Emmanuel Le Roy Ladurie, "A System of Customary Law: Family Structures and Inheritance Customs in Sixteenth-Century France," in *Family and Society*, edited by Forster and Ranum, p. 89.

33. The following information is taken from the Auffay Family Reconstitution Study.

34. David Levine, *Family Formation in an Age of Nascent Capitalism* (New York: Academic Press, 1977), p. 56.

35. ADSM 219BP364.

36. ADSM L367. The number of female-headed households may have been higher than

usual in Auffay in 1796 because many men were serving in the army and were absent from the village. Army pay was not calculated to allow men to support dependents, however, and even the married women who were heads of households probably were surviving solely on their own and their children's earnings.

37. The marital status of sixteen female heads of households is unclear in the records and cannot be determined from the Family Reconstitution Study. Some of these women were probably widows. Because they headed their own households, determining their marital status would simply increase the percentage of widows who were able to support themselves.

38. ADSM 6M83.

39. Tilly and Scott, *Women, Work and Family*, p. 52.

40. ADSM Notarial Registers, 11 Ventose, AN VIII.

Unwed mothers and their children

1. Auffay Family Reconstitution Study.

2. Ibid.; ADSM Parish Registers, Auffay.

3. Ibid.; ADSM Civil Registers, Auffay.

4. Auffay Family Reconstitution Study; ADSM Civil Registers, Auffay. More brides may, of course, have been unwed mothers than is apparent from the records because any woman who bore an illegitimate child outside of the village and whose child either was not fathered by the groom or was no longer living at the time of the marriage escapes the detection of the historian. This problem exists throughout the entire 1751–1850 period. Thus, although the absolute number of unwed mothers who married in Auffay may be inaccurate, the increase revealed by the available data is not.

5. Auffay Family Reconstitution Study; ADSM Parish and Civil Registers, Auffay.
   In addition to the illegitimate births included in the figures and tables for Auffay, sixty-two unmarried women who were not Auffay residents bore children in the village at the home of the midwife, Marie Prudence Bavent, between 1838 and 1850. Although the Auffay records give no explanation for the presence of so many unmarried women in Auffay at the time of their confinement, Bavent was probably the *sage-femme* who was designated by the Bureau de Bienfaisance to deliver illegitimate children in this part of the Caux. As the Bureau's official midwife, she would have charged the unwed mothers-to-be according to their ability to pay and have received the rest of her fee from the government, a strong inducement to poor pregnant women to travel to Auffay for their *accouchements*. For information on how this system worked, see Paul Strauss, *Paris Ignoré* (Paris, 1892). I am indebted to Rachel Fuchs for this reference.
   The presence of so many nonresident unmarried women in Auffay at the time of their *accouchements* poses a serious problem for the demographic historian. Clearly, the civil birth records for other villages in the Auffay region underrecord the number of illegitimate births and hence the illegitimacy ratio. Similarly, counting the births to non-Auffay residents in the Auffay statistics would seriously exaggerate the incidence of illgitimacy in that community. I have thus eliminated these births from the illegitimacy figures and from the total birth figures for the village.

6. Auffay Family Reconstitution Study; ADSM Parish and Civil Registers, Auffay.

7. Ibid.

8. Edward Shorter, *The Making of the Modern Family* (New York: Basic Books, 1975).

9. Ibid., p. 159.

10. Ibid., p. 166.

11. Ibid., pp. 258–9.

12. Ibid.
13. Louise A. Tilly, Joan W. Scott, and Miriam Cohen, "Women's Work and European Fertility Patterns," *Journal of Interdisciplinary History* 6 (1976), pp. 463–7.
14. Ibid., p. 470.
15. David Levine and Keith Wrightson, "The Social Context of Illegitimacy in Early Modern England," unpublished paper, 1975.
16. Ibid., pp. 29–30, 37.
17. Cissie Fairchilds, "Female Sexual Attitudes and the Rise of Illegitimacy: A Case Study," *Journal of Interdisciplinary History* VIII (1978), pp. 459–76, reprinted in Rotberg and Rabb, eds., *Marriage and Fertility*, p. 190.
18. ADSM LP8255. Pregnancy Declarations for Auffay can be found in two sets of records – the Notarial Registers and the Justice of the Peace Records (ADSM LP 8245–8259). For more information about illegitimacy records, see Marie-Claude Phan, "Les déclarations de grossesse en France (XVIe–XVIIIe siècles): Essai institutionnel," *Revue d'Histoire Moderne et Contemporaine*, XVII (1975), pp. 61–88.
19. ADSM Notarial Records, Auffay, and LP8247–8259.
20. ADSM LP8250; Auffay Family Reconstitution Study.
21. Not all of the unwed mothers who married in Auffay had borne their children in the village.
22. ADSM LP8251–2.
23. ADSM Notarial Records, Auffay, 1775, 1790; LP8247; Jean-Marie Gouesse, "Parenté, famille et mariage en Normandie aux XVIIe et XVIIIe siècles: Presentation d'une source et d'une enquête," *Annales: Economies, Sociétés, Civilisations*, 27e Année (1972), pp. 1139–54.
24. ADSM LP8253.
25. ADSM LP8247.
26. ADSM LP8249.
27. ADSM LP8252.
28. ADSM Notorial Records, Auffay, 1775, 1776, 1777.
29. ADSM Notarial Records; LP8245–8259.
30. Fairchilds, "Female Sexual Attitudes," in Rotberg and Rabb, eds., *Marriage and Fertility*, pp. 173–6; Olwen Hufton, "Women and the Family Economy in Eighteenth-Century France," *French Historical Studies*, 9 (Spring 1975), p. 8.
31. ADSM C1730; 219BP364.
32. ADSM Parish Registers, Auffay.
33. ADSM C1730.
34. ADSM Civil Registers, Auffay.
35. ADSM Parish and Civil Registers, Auffay. The age of unmarried women when they gave birth to children is not recorded before the 1780s. In the 1790s, however, the average marriage age for single women was 25.8 years whereas the average age at which single (i.e., not widowed) women became unwed mothers for the first time was 25.25. There is no reason to believe that the age of unwed mothers was substantially different earlier in the century, especially since it changed little throughout the proto-industrial period. Between 1818 and 1850, the ages of the two groups were 25.3 and 24.4, respectively.
36. David Levine, *Family Formation in an Age of Nascent Capitalism* (New York: Academic Press, 1977), p. 141.
37. ADSM L367.
38. See Chapter 7.
39. ADSM L5119.
40. ADSM L277.
41. ADSM 1J35[1]; 1J35[2].

42. Joan W. Scott and Louise A. Tilly, "Women's Work and the Family in Nineteenth-Century Europe," *Comparative Studies in Society and History*, vol. 17 (1975), p. 56. Scott and Tilly argue that the migration of young women to cities was an important factor in increasing illegitimacy rates because it removed them from "their own parents and the community which could have enforced compliance with an agreement to marriage which preceded sexual relations."
43. ADSM Civil Registers, Auffay; 1J35[1], 1J35[2].
44. ADSM L367, 6M23, 6M64, 6M83.
45. Ibid.
46. Peter Laslett, *Family Life and Illicit Love in Earlier Generations* (Cambridge: Cambridge University Press, 1977), pp. 108, 147.
47. Auffay Family Reconstitution Study and ADSM Parish and Civil Registers, Auffay.
48. Jacques Depauw, "Illicit Sexual Activity and Society in Eighteenth-Century Nantes," in *Family and Society,* edited by Robert Forster and Orest Ranum (Baltimore: The Johns Hopkins University Press, 1976), p. 177.
49. All of the above examples come from the Auffay Family Reconstitution Study.
50. Auffay Family Reconstitution Study. Although the identity of the father was often well known in the community, it is only known to the historian when he married the mother of his living child. If the child died before the marriage or if no marriage occurred, the man's identity is, unfortunately, permanently hidden from history. Most of the traceable links to illegitimacy are thus female links, and the number of couples in each cohort, but especially in the third cohort, would be higher if we knew which men had fathered illegitimate children.
51. Ibid.
52. Ibid.

Bibliography

~~~~~~

I. Archival sources

A. *Archives Départementales de la Seine-Maritime*

Série B: Courts and Jurisdictions

202BP14 bis	Procés verbal de la révolte (1789) Bacqueville
219BP364	Salt Tax Roles, Auffay, 1694–1789

Série C: Provincial Administration before 1790

C 106	Grain Pillaging, 1784
C 107	Grain Pillaging, 1768 and 1775
C 95–99	Courses in Midwifery, 1779
C 259	Number of Households, *Sergenterie* of Auffay, 1751
C 537	*Vingtième* Roles, Auffay, 1770, 1790
C 809	Men Eligible and Ineligible for the Army, 1775
C 882	*Atelier de charité*, Auffay, 1777–80
C 1002	Fear of Brigands, 1776
C 1730	*Taille* Roles, Auffay
C 2156	Cotton Spinning, 1787, 1789
C 2161	Courses in Midwifery, 1788
C 2173	Spinning
C 2210–2212	State of the Poor in 1788
C 2391	*Taille* Roles, Auffay, 1755
2C9	Collateral and Direct Successions, Auffay

Série E: Manors, Communes, and Families

	Notarial Registers (*Tabellionages*), Auffay, 1751–1850
	Parish Registers, Auffay, 1751–93
	Civil Registers, Auffay, 1793–1850
5E 1–4	Auffay Tanners' Records, 1753, 1758–66

Série J: Religious Records

1J35[1]	Parish Registers, Auffay, 1803–45
1J35[2]	Parish Registers, Auffay, 1846–50
16J31	Parlement Records – Dieppe
1JP1	Pastoral Visit of Bishop to Auffay, 1825

Série L: Administration of Department, Districts, and Cantons, 1790–1800 (Revolution Period)

L 277 and 277bis	Counter-revolutionary Activity
L 309	Food Prices
L 319	Religious Dissension, Auffay, 1792
L 320	Pillage of Grain Shipments, 1795
L 347	Rural Militia
L 367	Enumerated Census, Auffay, *an* IV (1796); Population Totals, Auffay Canton, *an* VIII (1800)
L 368–369	Population of Department, *an* VIII (1800)
L 1280	Salaries of Priests, Auffay, 1790–91

L 1723–1724   Harvest Statistics, 1791, 1795
L 1772   Fairs and Markets, Auffay, *an* II (1794)
L 1408   Requests for Iron and Charcoal, *an* II (1794)
L 5116–5123   Reports of Auffay Municipal Council, *an* II (1794)
L 5597   Minutes of the *Société populaire,* Auffay, 1792
LP 7324   Pregnancy Declarations, 1787–*an* II (1794)
LP 8245–8259   Justice of the Peace Records, Canton of Auffay, 1790–*an* IX
                     (1801)
LP 8726–8733   Laws and Decrees Received in Auffay, 1790–*an* II (1794)

Série M: Nineteenth-Century Administration
6M1   1831 Census, Arrondissement of Dieppe
6M21   1841 Census, Canton of Longueville
6M23   1841 Census, Canton of Totes
6M56bis   Summary of 1846 Census for the Department
6M62   1846 Census, Canton of Longueville
6M64   1846 Census, Canton of Totes
6M82bis   Summary of 1851 Census for Department
6M83   1851 Census, Canton of Totes
6MP2509–2510   Cholera Epidemic, 1832
6MP5101   Price of Grain, Population, Mendicity, *ans* VIII–IX (1799–1801)
6MP5103   Price of Grain and Food, *ans* XI–XIII (1802–05)
6MP5105   Agriculture and Industry, *ans* VIII–IX (1799–1801)
6MP5106   Population, *an* IX (1800–1801); Report on Commerce
6MP5107   Agricultural Inquiry, *an* IX (1800–1801)
6MP5108   Population, *an* XIII (1805)
6MP5110   Description of the Department, *an* IX (1800–1801)
6MP5111   Agricultural Reports, Auffay, *ans* IX–X, XIII–XIV (1800–1802,
                     1804–1805)
6MP5113   Agricultural Report, *an* IX (1800), 1807
6MP5114   Principal Families, Arrondissement of Dieppe, 1809
6MP5115   Industrial Report
6MP5118–5121   Industrial Reports, 1807, 1811, 1812, 1815
6MP5122   Cotton Industry, *an* X (1801–1802), 1809
6MP5123   Cotton Industry, 1810–18
6MP5124   Cotton Industry, Number of Workers, Wages
6MP5129   Linen Industry, 1810–18
6MP5142   Tanning Industry, 1820–5
6MP5154   Departmental Reports on Manufacturing, 1855
6MP5158   Departmental Reports on Manufacturing, 1861

Série P: Finances
3PP27^1 Auffay Cadastre, 1822
3PP27^4 Auffay Cadastre, First Empire (undated)

                        B. Archives Nationales

Série F^{12}560   *Reports on textile industry, including* M. Latapie's "Réflexions
                     préliminaires sur un mémoire intitulé Voyage de Rouen ou ob-
                     servations sur l'état actuel des arts et manufactures de Rouen,
                     Elbeuf, Louviers, Evreux et Andely faites dans le mois de mai,
                     juin et juillet 1773."

F¹²650   Goy's Report on Rouen textile industry (1782)
F¹²658   Goy's Report on Rouen textile industry (1779)
F²⁰382   Active Citizens in Canton of Auffay, 1790

C. Bibliotheque Nationale

N.A.F. 3338–3343 Poésies populaires de la France (1877)

D. La Mairie d'Auffay

Municipal Council Records, Auffay, 1833–51

E. Service du Cadastre, Dieppe

Maps of Auffay, First Empire

II. Printed primary sources

Berault, Godefroy. *Commentaires sur la Coutume de Normandie.* Nouvelle édition. Rouen, 1776.
Dictionnaire universel de commerce. Paris: 1741.
Flaust, Baptiste. *Explication de la coutume et de jurisprudence de Normandie.* 2 vols. Rouen, 1781.
Gouhier, Pierre; Vallez, Anne; and Vallez, Jean Marie. *Atlas historique de Normandie.* Tome I: *Cartes des communautés d'habitants généralités de Rouen, Caen et Alençon, 1636–1789.* Caen, 1967.
Houard, David. *Dictionaire analytique, historique, étymologique, critique et interprétatif de la coutume de Normandie.* 4 vols. Rouen, 1780–82.
Journal de Rouen et du Département de la Seine-Inférieure. 1791.
LeParquier, E. *Cahiers de doléances du bailliage d'Arques (secondaire de Caudebec) pour les états généraux de 1789.* 2 vols. Lille: Camille Robbe, 1922.
Mars, Isidore. *Auffay, ou le vieil Isnelville.* Rouen: Lecointe Frères, 1857.
Derniers souvenirs du bon vieux temps d'Auffay depuis 1793 jusqu'à 1840 environ. Dieppe: Paul Leprêtre & Cie., 1876.
Noiret, Charles. *Mémoires d'un ouvrier rouennais.* Rouen: François, 1836.
Young, Arthur. *Travels in France during the Years 1787, 1788, and 1789.* Edited by Jeffry Kaplow. New York: Anchor Books, 1969.

III. Secondary sources

Adelmann, Gerhard. "Structural Change in the Rhenish Linen and Cotton Trades at the Outset of Industrialization." In *Essays in European Economic History, 1789–1914,* edited by F. Crouzet, W. H. Chaloner, and W. M. Stern. New York: St. Martin's Press, 1969.
Agulhon, Maurice. *La Republique au village (Les populations du Var de la Révolution à la Seconde Republique).* Paris: Plon, 1970.
La vie sociale en Provence Intérieure au lendemain de la Révolution. Paris: Société des Etudes Robespierristes, 1970.
Allard, Paul. *Paysans cauchois à la fin de l'ancien régime.* Rouen: Cagniard, 1895.

Anderson, Michael. *Family Structure in Nineteenth-Century Lancashire.* Cambridge: Cambridge University Press, 1971.

Ardouin-Dumazet. *Les petites industries rurales.* Paris: Victor Lecoffre, 1912.

Aries, Philippe. *Western Attitudes toward Death: From the Middle Ages to the Present.* Translated by Patricia M. Ranum. Baltimore: The Johns Hopkins University Press, 1974.

Armengaud, A. *La famille et l'enfant en France et en Angleterre du XVIe au XVIIIe siècle. Aspects démographiques.* Paris: Société d'Edition d'Enseignement Supérieur, 1975.

"Population in Europe, 1700–1914." In *The Industrial Revolution,* vol. 3 of *The Fontana Economic History of Europe,* edited by Carlo M. Cipolla. London: Collins/ Fontana Books, 1973.

Audiganne, Armand. *Les populations ouvrières et les industries de la France dans le mouvement social du XIX siècle.* Paris: Capelle, 1854.

Babeau, Albert. *Les artisans et les domestiques d'autrefois.* Paris: Firmin-Didot et Cie., 1886.

Ballot, Charles. *L'introduction du machinisme dans l'industrie française.* Paris: F. Rieder & Cie., 1922.

Baudrillart, Henri. *La Normandie (Passé et Présent): Enquête.* Paris: Hachette, 1880.

Les populations agricoles de la France. Vol. I: Normandie et Bretagne. Paris: Hachette, 1885.

Baulant, Micheline. "The Scattered Family: Another Aspect of Seventeenth-Century Demography." In *Family and Society. Selections from the Annales: Economies, Sociétés, Civilisations,* edited by Robert Forster and Orest Ranum. Translated by Elborg Forster and Patricia M. Ranum. Baltimore: The Johns Hopkins University Press, 1976.

Beaurepaire, Charles de Robillard de. "Recherches sur la population de la généralité et du diocese de Rouen avant 1789." *Mémoires de la Société des Antiquaires de Normandie* 3e série, 8e tome (1870): 361–433.

Renseignements statistiques sur l'état de l'agriculture vers 1789. Rouen: Cagniard, 1889.

Benoit, F. *Histoire de l'outillage rural et artisanal.* Paris, 1947.

Berg, Maxine. "Political Economy and the Principles of Manufacture 1700–1800." In *Manufacture in Town and Country before the Factory,* edited by Maxine Berg, Pat Hudson, and Michael Sonenscher. Cambridge: Cambridge University Press, 1983.

Berg, Maxine; Hudson, Pat; and Sonenscher, Michael, eds. *Manufacture in Town and Country before the Factory.* Cambridge: Cambridge University Press, 1983.

Bergues, Helene; Ariès, Philippe; Helin, Etienne; Henry, Louis; Piquet, R. P. Michel; Suavy, Alfred; and Sutter, Jean. *La prévention des naissances dans la famille. Ses origines dans les temps modernes.* I.N.E.D. Travaux et Documents, Cahier no. 35. Paris: Presses Universitaires de France, 1960.

Berkner, Lutz K. "Family, Social Structure and Rural Industry: A Comparative Study of the Waldviertel and the Pays de Caux in the Eighteenth Century." Ph.D. dissertation, Harvard University, 1973.

"Recent Research on the History of the Family in Western Europe." *Journal of Marriage and the Family,* 35 (August 1973): 395–405.

"Rural Family Organization in Europe: A Problem in Comparative History." *Peasant Studies Newsletter,* 1 (October 1972): 145–56.

"The Stem Family and the Developmental Cycle of the Peasant Household: An Eighteenth-Century Austrian Example." *American Historical Review,* 77 (April 1972): 398–418.

"The Use and Misuse of Census Data for the Historical Analysis of Family Structure." *Journal of Interdisciplinary History* 4 (Spring 1975): 721–38.

Berkner, Lutz K., and Mendels, Franklin F. "Inheritance Systems, Family Structure, and Demographic Patterns in Western Europe, 1700–1900." In *Historical Studies of*

Changing Fertility, edited by Charles Tilly. Princeton: Princeton University Press, 1978.

Besnier, Robert. *La Coutume de Normandie: Histoire externe.* Paris: Librairie du Recueil Sirey, 1935.

Bloch, Marc. *French Rural History: An Essay on its Basic Characteristics.* Translated by Janet Sondheimer. Berkeley: University of California Press, 1966.

Blum, Jerome. *The End of the Old Order in Rural Europe.* Princeton: Princeton University Press, 1978.

Bois, Paul. *Paysans de l'Ouest. Des structures économiques et sociales aux options politiques depuis l'époque révolutionnaire dans la Sarthe.* Paris: Flammarion, 1971.

Boserup, Ester. "Preface," *Signs* 3 (Autumn 1977): xi–xiv.

Woman's Role in Economic Development. London: George Allen and Unwin, Ltd., 1970.

Bouard, Michel de. *Histoire de la Normandie.* Toulouse: Edouard Privat, 1970.

Bouloiseau, M. M. "Aspects socieaux de la crise cotonnière dans les campagnes Rouennaises en 1788–1789." In *Actes de 81e Congrès National des Sociétés Savantes, Rouen-Caen, 1956.* Paris: Presses Universitaires de France, 1956.

"La fiscalité du sel dans la France du XVIIIe siècle: son intérêt pour l'histoire économique et sociale." In *Le rôle du sel dans l'histoire*, edited by Michel Mollat. Paris: Presses Universitaires de France, 1968.

Bourde, Andre J. *The Influence of England on the French Agronomes, 1750–1789.* Cambridge: The University Press, 1953.

Bourgeois-Pichat, J. "The General Development of the Population of France since the Eighteenth Century." In *Population in History*, edited by D. V. Glass and D. E. C. Eversley. London: E. Arnold, 1965.

Braudel, Fernand, and Labrousse, Ernest. *Histoire économique et sociale de la France.* Tome II: *Des derniers temps de l'age seigneurial aux préludes de l'age industriel (1660–1789)* and Tome III: *L'avènement de l'ère industrielle (1789–années 1880).* Paris: Presses Universitaires de France, 1976.

Braun, Rudolf. "Early Industrialization and Demographic Change in the Canton of Zurich." In *Historical Studies of Changing Fertility*, edited by Charles Tilly. Princeton: Princeton University Press, 1978.

"The Impact of Cottage Industry on an Agricultural Population." In *The Rise of Capitalism*, edited by David Landes. New York: Macmillan, 1966.

Industrialisierung und Volksleben. Erlenbach-Zurich und Stuttgart: Rentsch, 1960.

Brown, Judith K. "A Note on the Division of Labor by Sex." *American Anthropologist* 172 (1970): 1073–8.

Bruneau, Marguerite. "Le costume normand." *Connaître Rouen* III (1976).

Bunel, M. l'Abbe J., and Tougard, l'Abbé. *Géographie du département de la Seine-Inférieure.* Tome V: *Arrondissement de Dieppe.* Rouen: E. Cagniard, 1877.

Cauchois, Dr. André. *Démographie de la Seine-Inférieure.* Rouen: Laine, 1929.

Chambers, J. D. "Enclosure and Labour Supply in the Industrial Revolution." In *Agriculture and Economic Growth in England, 1650–1815*, edited by E. L. Jones. London: Methuen, 1967.

Chassagne, Serge. "Industrialisation et désindustrialisation dans les campagnes français: Quelques refléxions à partir du textile." *Revue du Nord* LXIII, no. 248 (Janvier-Mars 1981): 35–57.

"La diffusion rurale de l'industrie cotonnière en France (1750–1850)." *Revue du Nord* LXI, no. 240 (Janvier-Mars 1979): 97–114.

Chatelain, Abel. "Migrations et domesticité féminine urbaine en France, XVIIIe siècle–XXe siècle." *Revue d'histoire économique et sociale* 47 (1969): 506–28.

Chaunu, Pierre. "Réflexions sur la démographie normande." In *Hommage à Marcel Reinhard.* Paris: Société de Démographie Historique, 1973.

Chauvet, Stephan. *La Normandie ancestrale: Ethnologie, vie, coutumes, meubles, usten-siles, costumes, patois.* Paris, 1921.

Circuits commerciaux, foires et marchés en Normandie. Vologenes: IXe Congrès des So-ciétés historiques, archéologiques et ethnolgiques de Normandie, Octobre 1974.

Clough, Shepard Bancroft. *France: A History of National Economics, 1789–1939.* New York: Charles Scribner's Sons, 1939.

Clout, Hugh. *Agriculture in France on the Eve of the Railway Age.* Totowa, New Jersey: Barnes & Noble, 1980.

Themes in the Historical Geography of France. New York: Academic Press, 1977.

Cobb, Richard. "Disette et mortalité: La crise de l'an III et de l'an IV à Rouen." *Annales de Normandie* (1956): 267–91.

Coleman, D. C. "Proto-Industrialization: A Concept Too Many." *Economic History Re-view,* Second Series, 36 (August 1983): 435–48.

"Textile Growth," In *Textile History and Economic History,* edited by N. B. Harte and K. G. Ponting. Manchester: Manchester University Press, 1973.

Collier, Frances. *The Family Economy of the Working Classes in the Cotton Industry, 1784–1833.* 1964. Reprint. New York: Augustus M. Kelley, 1968.

Collins, E. J. T. "Labour Supply and Demand in European Agriculture, 1800–1880." In *Agrarian Change and Economic Development: The Historical Problems,* edited by E. L. Jones and S. J. Woolf. London: Methuen, 1969.

Cordier, M. Alphonse. *La crise cotonnière dans la Seine-Inférieure: Ses causes et ses effets.* Rouen: Lapierre, 1864.

Corneille, M. A. *La Seine-Inférieure: Industrielle et Commerciale.* Rouen: Herpin, 1873.

Crouzet, F. "England and France in the Eighteenth Century: A Comparative Analysis of Two Economic Growths." In *The Causes of the Industrial Revolution in England,* edited by R. M. Hartwell. London: Methuen, 1967.

Dardel, Pierre. *Commerce, industrie et navigation à Rouen et au Havre au XVIIIeme siècle.* Rouen, 1966.

Crises et faillités à Rouen et dans la Haute-Normandie de 1740 à l'an V. Paris: Marcel Rivière, 1948.

Histoire de Bolbec des origines à la Révolution: Le commerce et l'industrie à Bolbec avant 1789. Rouen: Lestringant, 1939.

Navires et marchandises dans les ports de Rouen et du Havre au XVIIIe siècle. Paris: Ecole pratique des hautes études – VIe section, 1963.

Davies, Alan. "The New Agriculture in Lower Normandy, 1750–1789." *Transactions of the Royal Historical Society* (1957): 129–46.

Davis, Natalie Zemon. "Ghosts, Kin, and Progeny: Some Features of Family Life in Early Modern France." In *The Family,* edited by Alice S. Rossi, Jerome Kagan, and Tamara Hareven. New York: Norton, 1978.

"Women on Top." In her *Society and Culture.* Stanford: Stanford University Press, 1965.

Davranches, L. Chanoine. *La vie sociale pendant la première partie de la Révolution, 1789–1798: Rouen et environs.* Rouen: Lecerf Fils, 1916.

Depauw, Jacques. "Illicit Sexual Activity and Society in Eighteenth-Century Nantes." In *Family and Society: Selections from the Annales: Economies, Sociétés, Civilisations,* edited by Robert Forster and Orest Ranum. Translated by Elborg Forster and Patricia M. Ranum. Baltimore: The Johns Hopkins University Press, 1976.

Deprez, Paul, ed. *Population and Economics: Proceedings of Section V of the Fourth Con-gress of the International Economic History Association, 1968.* Winnipeg, Canada: University of Manitoba Press, 1970.

Desmarest, Charles. *Le commerce des grains dans la généralité de Rouen à la fin de l'ancien régime.* Paris: Jouve & Cie., 1926.

de Vries, Jan. *The Dutch Rural Economy in the Golden Age, 1500–1700.* New Haven: Yale University Press, 1974.

Deyon, Pierre. "Un modele à l'épreuve: Le développement industriel de Roubaix de 1762 à la fin du XIXeme siècle." *Revue du Nord,* LXI (1979): 97–114.

Deyon, Pierre, and Mendels, Franklin. "Programme de la section A2 du huitième Congrès international d'histoire économique: La Proto-Industrialization: Théorie et Réalité (Budapest 1982)." *Revue du Nord* LXIII, no. 248 (January-March 1981): 11–19.

Drake, Michael. *Population and Society in Norway, 1735–1865.* Cambridge: The University Press, 1969.

Dubois, Georges. *La Normandie économique à la fin du XVIIe siècle, d'après les mémoires des intendants.* Paris: Rivière, 1934.

――― *Les subsistances dans la Seine-Inférieure de 1793 à 1795. Application des lois sur le maximum, requisitions des blés et pillages de grains.* Rouen: Laine, 1936.

Dubosc, Georges. "La moisson les 'aouteux'." *Par Ci, Par La: Etudes normandes de moeurs et d'histoire,* 6e série (1929): 31–48.

――― "Le bonnet de cotton en Normandie." *Par Ci, Par La: Etudes normandes de moeurs et d'histoire,* 5e série (1927): 93–105.

――― "Le jeu de dominos en Normandie." *Par Ci, Par La: Etudes normandes de moeurs et d'histoire,* 5e série (1927): 47–58.

――― "Le tissage à la main en Normandie." *Par Ci, Par La: Etudes normandes de moeurs et d'histoire,* 4e série (1927): 99–111.

――― "Les coiffes normandes." *Par Ci, Par La: Etudes normandes de moeurs et d'histoire,* 5e série (1927): 107–19.

Dubuc, M. André. "La culture du lin et du chanvre dans la Seine-Inférieure (1810–1818)." In *Le textile en Normandie: Etudes diverses.* Rouen: Société libre d'Emulation de la Seine-Maritime, 1975.

――― "L'industrie textile en Haute Normandie au cours de la Révolution et de l'Empire." In *Le textile en Normandie: Etudes diverses.* Rouen: Société libre d'Emulation de la Seine-Maritime, 1975.

――― "Un ancien marché au coton à Pont-Saint-Pierre." In *Le textile en Normandie: Etudes diverses.* Rouen: Société libre d'Emulation de la Seine-Maritime, 1975.

Dumas, François. *Etude sur le Traité de Commerce de 1786 entre la France et l'Angleterre.* Toulouse: Edouard Privat, 1904.

Dunham, Arthur Louis. *The Industrial Revolution in France, 1815–1848.* New York: Exposition Press, 1955.

Dupaquier, Jacques. "Les caractères originaux de l'histoire démographique française au XVIIIe siècle." *Revue d'histoire moderne et contemporaine* 23 (April-June 1976): 182–202.

Esmonin, Edmond. *La Taille en Normandie au temps de Colbert (1661–1683).* Paris: Hachette, 1913.

Estaintot, V. R. d'. *Recherches sur l'introduction de la filature mécanique du coton dans la Haute-Normandie.* Rouen: Henry Boissel, 1865.

Evrard, Fernand. "Les ouvriers du textile dans la région rouennaise (1789–1802)." *Annales historiques de la Révolution française,* no. 108 (1947): 333–52.

Fairchilds, Cissie. "Female Sexual Attitudes and the Rise of Illegitimacy: A Case Study." *Journal of Interdisciplinary History,* VIII (1978): 459–476.

Faucher, Daniel. *Le paysan et la machine.* Paris: Les éditions de minuit, 1954.

Fischer, Wolfram. "Rural Industrialization and Population Change." *Comparative Studies in Society and History,* 15 (March 1973): 158–70.

Flandrin, Jean-Louis. "Contraception, mariage et relations amoureuses dans l'Occident chrétien." *Annales: Economies, Sociétés, Civilisations,* no. 26 (1969): 1370–90.

242   *Bibliography*

Flandrin, Jean-Louis. *Familles: parenté, maison, sexualité dans l'ancienne société.* Paris: Hachette, 1976.

Flaubert, Gustave. *Madame Bovary: Moeurs de province.* Paris: M. Levy Frères, 1857.

Fleury, Michel, and Henry, Louis. *Nouveau manuel de dépouillement et d'exploitation de l'état civil ancien.* I.N.E.D. Paris: Presses Universitaires de France, 1965.

Fohlen, Claude. *L'industrie textile au temps du Second Empire.* Paris: Plon, 1956.

"The Industrial Revolution in France 1700–1914." In *The Emergence of Industrial Societies,* vol. 4 of *The Fontana Economic History of Europe,* edited by Carlo M. Cipolla. London: Collins/Fontana, 1973.

Fougeyrollas, Pierre. "Prédominance du mari ou de la femme dans le ménage. Une enquête sur la vie familiale." *Population* 6 (1951): 83–102.

Fouquet, Henri. *Histoire civile, politique et commerciale de Rouen,* II. Rouen, 1876.

Frémont, André. "L'agriculture dans la partie occidentale du pays de Caux (Région du Havre)." *Etudes normandes,* no. 80 (1957): 157–84.

Frémont, Armand. *L'élevage en Normandie: Etude géographique,* vols. I and II. Caen: Association des Publications de la Faculté des Lettres et Sciences Humaines de l'Université de Caen, 1967.

Frisch, Rose E. "Population, Food Intake, and Fertility." *Science,* 199 (6 January 1978): 22–30.

Furet, François, and Ozouf, Jacques. "Literacy and Industrialization: The Case of the Département du Nord in France." *Journal of European Economic History,* V (1976): 5–44.

Ganiage, Jean. *Trois villages d'Ille-de-France au XVIIIe siècle. Etude démographique.* I.N.E.D. Travaux et Documents, Cahier no. 40. Paris: Presses Universitaires de France, 1958.

Gautier, Etienne, and Henry, Louis. *La population de Crulai, paroisse Normande: Etude historique.* I.N.E.D. Travaux et Documents, Cahier no. 33. Paris: Presses Universitaires de France, 1958.

Gillispie, Charles Coulston, ed. *A Diderot Pictorial Encyclopedia of Trades and Industry: Manufacturing and the Technical Arts in Plates Selected from "L'Encyclopédie, ou Dictionnaire Raisonné des Sciences, des Arts et des Metiers" of Denis Diderot.* New York: Dover Publications Inc., 1959.

Glass, D. V., and Grebenik, E. "World Population, 1800–1950." In *The Industrial Revolutions and After,* vol. VI of *The Cambridge Economic History of Europe,* edited by H. J. Habakkuk, and M. Postan. Cambridge: Cambridge University Press, 1977.

Goode, William J. *World Revolution and Family Patterns.* New York: The Free Press, 1970.

Goody, Jack, ed. *The Character of Kinship.* Cambridge: The University Press, 1973.

Goody, Jack. "The Evolution of the Family." In *Household and Family in Past Time,* edited by Peter Laslett and Richard Wall. Cambridge: Cambridge University Press, 1972.

"Inheritance, Property and Women: Some Comparative Considerations." In *Family and Inheritance: Rural Society in Western Europe, 1200–1800,* edited by Jack Goody, Joan Thirsk, and E. P. Thompson. Cambridge: Cambridge University Press, 1976.

"Strategies of Heirship." *Comparative Studies in Society and History,* 15 (January 1973): 3–20.

Gosselin, E. *Journal des principaux episodes de l'époque révolutionnaire à Rouen et dans les environs, de 1789 à 1795. L'extrait de la Revue de la Normandie,* années 1865, 1866, 1867. Rouen: E. Cagniard, 1867.

Goubert, Pierre. *Beauvais et les Beauvaisis de 1600 à 1730. Contribution a l'histoire sociale de la France du XVIIe siècle.* Paris: S.E.V.P.E.N., 1960.

"Historical Demography and the Reinterpretation of Early Modern French History: A Research Review." In *The Family in History: Interdisciplinary Essays,* edited by Theodore K. Rabb and Robert I. Rotberg. New York: Harper & Row, 1971.

"Legitimate Fecundity and Infant Mortality in France during the Eighteenth Century: A Comparison." *Daedalus.* Historical Population Studies (Spring 1968): 593–603.

"Recent Theories and Research in French Population between 1500 and 1700." In *Population in History,* edited by D. V. Glass and D. E. C. Eversley. London: E. Arnold, 1965.

Gouesse, Jean-Marie. "Parenté, famille et mariage en Normandie aux XVIIe et XVIIIe siècles: Presentation d'une source et d'une enquête." *Annales: Economies, Sociétés, Civilisations,* 27 année (1972): 1139–54.

Gricourt, M.-C. "Etude d'histoire démographique, sociale et religieuse de cinq paroisses de l'archidiaconé du Petit Caux: Doudeville, Cauville, Bacqueville, Brachy et Luneray du milieu du XVIIe siècle à la fin de l'Ancien Régime." *Annales de Normandie,* cahier no. 3, 1963.

Gross, Edward. "Plus ça change . . . ? The Sexual Structure of Occupations over Time." *Social Problems,* 16: 198–208.

Gullickson, Gay L. "Agriculture and Cottage Industry: Redefining the Causes of Proto-Industrialization." *Journal of Economic History,* 43 (December 1983): 831–50.

"Proto-Industrialization, Demographic Behavior and the Sexual Division of Labor in Auffay, France, 1750–1850." *Peasant Studies,* 9 (Winter 1982): 106–18.

"The Sexual Division of Labor in Cottage Industry and Agriculture in the Pays de Caux: Auffay, 1750–1850." *French Historical Studies,* 12 (Fall 1981): 177–99.

Gutmann, Myron P., and Leboutte, René. "Rethinking Proto-industrialization and the Family," *Journal of Interdisciplinary History,* 14 no. 3 (Winter 1984): 587–608.

Habakkuk, H. J. "Family Structure and Economic Change in Nineteenth-Century Europe." *Journal of Economic History,* 15 (1955): 1–12.

Population Growth and Economic Development Since 1750. Leicester: Leicester University Press, 1971.

Hajnal, J. "European Marriage Patterns in Perspective." In *Population in History,* edited by D. V. Glass and D. E. C. Eversley. London: E. Arnold, 1965.

"Two Kinds of Pre-Industrial Household Formation Systems." In *Family Forms in Historic Europe,* edited by Richard Wall, in collaboration with Jean Robin, and Peter Laslett. Cambridge: Cambridge University Press, 1983.

Harte, N. B., and Ponting, K. G., eds. *Textile History and Economic History.* Manchester: Manchester University Press, 1973.

Hartmann, Heidi. "Capitalism, Patriarchy, and Job Segregation by Sex." *Signs,* I (1976): 137–69.

Havinden, M. A. "Agricultural Progress in Open-Field Oxfordshire." In *Agriculture and Economic Growth in England 1650–1815,* edited by E. L. Jones. London: Methuen, 1967.

Hebert, P., Abbé. "La Révolution à Rouen et dans le pays de Caux (1791–1793)." *Revue Catholique de Normandie,* 12 (1902): 185–301.

Henderson, W. O. *The Industrial Revolution on the Continent: Germany, France, Russia, 1800–1914.* 2d ed. London: Frank Cass & Co., Ltd., 1967.

Henry, Louis. "The Population of France in the Eighteenth Century." In *Population in History,* edited by D. V. Glass and D. E. C. Eversley. London: E. Arnold, 1965.

Herr, Richard. *The Eighteenth-Century Revolution in Spain.* Princeton: Princeton University Press, 1958.

Himes, Norman. *A Medical History of Contraception.* Baltimore: Williams and Wilkins, 1936.

Hohenberg, Paul. "Change in Rural France in the Period of Industrialization, 1830–1914." *Journal of Economic History,* 32 (March 1972): 219–40.

Houston, Rab, and Snell, K. D. M. "Proto-Industrialization? Cottage Industry, Social Change, and Industrial Revolution." *The Historical Journal,* 27 (1984): 473–92.

Hudson, Pat. "Proto-industrialisation: The Case of the West Riding Wool Textile Industry in the Eighteenth and Early Nineteenth Centuries," *History Workshop,* no. 12 (Autumn 1981): 34–61.

"From Manor to Mill: The West Riding in Transition." In *Manufacture in Town and Country before the Factory,* edited by Maxine Berg, Pat Hudson, and Michael Sonenscher. Cambridge: Cambridge University Press, 1983.

Hufton, Olwen H. *The Poor of Eighteenth-Century France, 1750–1789.* Oxford: The Clarendon Press, 1974.

"Women and the Family Economy in Eighteenth-Century France." *French Historical Studies,* IX (Spring 1975): 1–22.

"Women, Work and Marriage in Eighteenth-Century France." In *Marriage and Society: Studies in the Social History of Marriage,* edited by R. B. Outhwaite. London: St. Martin's Press, 1981.

Jeannin, Pierre. "La proto-industrialisation: développement ou impasse?" *Annales: Economies, Sociétés, Civilisations,* 35 (1980): 52–65.

Jones, Eric L. "Afterword." In *European Peasants and Their Markets: Essays in Agrarian Economic History,* edited by William N. Parker and Eric L. Jones. Princeton: Princeton University Press, 1975.

"Agricultural Origins of Industry." *Past and Present,* no. 40 (1968): 58–71.

"The Environment and the Economy," In *The New Cambridge Modern History,* Vol. XIII, edited by Peter Burke. Cambridge: Cambridge University Press, 1979.

Jones, Erik L., and Woolf, S. J., eds. *Agrarian Change and Economic Development.* London: Methuen, 1969.

Káplan, Steven L. *Bread, Politics and Political Economy in the Reign of Louis XV,* 2 vols. The Hague, Netherlands: Martinus Nijhoff, 1976.

Kaplow, Jeffry. *Elbeuf during the Revolutionary Period: History and Social Structure.* Baltimore: The Johns Hopkins University Press, 1964.

Klima, Arnost. "The Role of Rural Domestic Industry in Bohemia in the Eighteenth Century." *Economic History Review,* 2d ser., 27 (1974): 48–56.

Kriedte, Peter; Medick, Hans; and Schlumbohm, Jurgen. *Industrialization before Industrialization.* Translated by Beate Schempp. New York: Cambridge University Press, 1981.

Labrousse, Charles Ernest. *Esquisse du mouvement des prix et des revenus en France au XVIIIe siècle.* Paris: Librairie Dalloz, 1933.

Lacotte, Daniel. *Traditions et legendes en Normandie.* Coutances: OCEP, 1981.

Landes, David S. *The Unbound Prometheus: Technological Change and Industrial Development in Western Europe from 1750 to the Present.* Cambridge: Cambridge University Press, 1972.

Laslett, Peter. *Family Life and Illicit Love in Earlier Generations: Essays in Historical Sociology.* Cambridge: Cambridge University Press, 1977.

"Introduction: The History of the Family." In *Household and Family in Past Time,* edited by Peter Laslett and Richard Wall. Cambridge: Cambridge University Press, 1972.

"Mean Household Size in England since the Sixteenth Century." In *Household and Family in Past Time,* edited by Peter Laslett and Richard Wall. Cambridge: Cambridge University Press, 1972.

The World We Have Lost: England Before the Industrial Age. 2d ed. New York: Charles Scribner's Sons, 1971.

Laslett, Peter, and Wall, Richard, eds. *Household and Family in Past Time.* Cambridge: Cambridge University Press, 1972.

Lebrun, François. *La vie conjugale sous l'ancien régime.* Paris: Armand Colin, 1975.

Lecarpentier, G. *Le pays de Caux (Etude géographique).* Rouen, 1906.

Lefebvre, Georges. *The French Revolution from its Origins to 1793.* Vol. 1. Translated by Elizabeth Moss Evanson. New York: Columbia University Press, 1962.

La grande peur de 1789. Paris: Armand Colin, 1970.

Les paysans du Nord pendant la Révolution Française. Paris: F. Rieder, 1924.

LeGoff, T. J. A., and Sutherland, D. M. G. "The Revolution and the Rural Community in Eighteenth-Century Brittany." *Past and Present,* no. 62 (February 1974): 96–119.

"The Social Origins of Counter-Revolution in Western France." *Past and Present,* no. 99 (May 1983): 65–87.

Lehning, James. "Nuptiality and Rural Industry: Families and Labor in the French Countryside." *Journal of Family History* (Winter 1983): 333–45.

The Peasants of Marlhes: Economic Development and Family Organization in Nineteenth-Century France. Chapel Hill: The University of North Carolina Press, 1980.

Lemarchand, Guy. "Les troubles de subsistances dans la généralité de Rouen." *Annales historiques de la Révolution Française,* no. 4 (1963): 401–27.

"Structure sociale d'après les rôles fiscaux et conjoncture économique dans le Pays de Caux: 1690–1789." *Bulletin de la Société d'histoire moderne,* LXVIII (1969): 7–11.

LeParquier, E. "La démographie de la Normandie Orientale, d'après Louis Leroux. Etude sur le mouvement de la population dans un certain nombre de cantons de la Seine-Inférieure et de l'Eure." *Société des Etudes Locales: Groupe de la Seine-Inférieure Bulletin,* (Mai 1932–Mai 1933): 145–52.

Une enquête sur le pauperisme et la crise industrielle dans la région rouennaise en 1788. Rouen: Albert Laine, 1936.

LePlay, Frederic. *Les ouvriers européens. Etudes sur les travaux, la vie domestique et la condition morale des populations ouvrières de l'Europe.* Paris: Imprimerie Imperiale, 1855.

Leroy, Charles. *Paysans normands au XVIIIe siècle: La vie rurale, la communauté, la paroisse.* 2d ed. Rouen: Schneider, 1912.

Le Roy Ladurie, Emmanuel. "A System of Customary Law: Family Structure and Inheritance Customs in Sixteenth-Century France." In *Family and Society: Selections from the Annales: Economies, Sociétés, Civilisations,* edited by Robert Forster and Orest Ranum. Translated by Elborg Forster and Patricia M. Ranum. Baltimore: The Johns Hopkins University Press, 1976.

Levainville, J. "Les ouvriers du coton dans la région de Rouen." *Annales de Géographie,* XX (1911): 52–64.

Rouen: Etude d'une agglomeration urbaine. Paris: Armand Colin, 1913.

Levasseur, E. *Histoire des classes ouvières et de l'industrie en France de 1789 à 1870,* tome II, 2d ed. New York: AMS Press, 1969.

Levine, David. "The Demographic Implications of Rural Industrialization: A Family Reconstitution Study of Shepshed, Leicestershire, 1600–1851." *Social History,* no. 2 (May 1976): 177–96.

Family Formation in an Age of Nascent Capitalism. New York: Academic Press, 1977.

Levine, David, and Wrightson, Keith. "The Social Context of Illegitmacy in Early Modern England." Unpublished paper. 1975.

Levy, Marion J., Jr. "Aspects of the Analysis of Family Structure." In *Aspects of the Analysis of Family Structure,* edited by Ansley J. Coale et al. Princeton: Princeton University Press, 1965.

Lloyd, Cynthia B., ed. *Sex, Discrimination, and the Division of Labor.* New York: Columbia University Press, 1975.

Mandrou, Robert. *De la culture populaire aux 17e et 18e siècles: La bibliotheque bleue de Troyes.* Paris: Stock, 1964.

Mantoux, Paul. *The Industrial Revolution in the Eighteenth Century: An Outline of the Beginnings of the Modern Factory System in England.* Rev. ed. New York: Harper & Row, 1961.

Marchand, Eugene. *Etude statistique, économique et chimique sur l'agriculture du pays de Caux.* Paris: Mme Veuve Bouchard-Huzard, 1869.

Medick, Hans. "The Proto-Industrial Family Economy: The Structural Function of Household and Family during the Transition from Peasant Society to Industrial Capitalism." *Social History*, no. 3 (October 1976): 291–315.

Mencken, Jane; Trussell, James; and Watkins, Susan. "The Nutrition Fertility Link: An Evaluation of the Evidence." *The Journal of Interdisciplinary History*, 11, no. 3 (Winter 1981): 425–41.

Mendels, Franklin F. "Proto-Industrialization: The First Phase of the Industrialization Process." *Journal of Economic History* XXXII (March 1972): 241–61.

"Agriculture and Peasant Industry in Eighteenth-Century Flanders." In *European Peasants and Their Markets: Essays in Agrarian Economic History*, edited by William N. Parker and Eric L. Jones. Princeton: Princeton University Press, 1975.

"Seasons and Regions in Agriculture and Industry During the Process of Industrialization." In *Region und Industrialisierung*, edited by Sidney Pollard. Göttingen: Vandenhoeck & Ruprecht, 1980.

Industrialization and Population Pressure in Eighteenth-Century Flanders. New York: Arno Press, 1981.

"General Report, Eighth International Economic History Congress, Section A.2: Proto-industrialization: Theory and Reality." Budapest, August 16–22, 1982.

"Social Mobility and Phases of Industrialization." MSSB Conference on International Comparisons of Social Mobility in Past Societies. Princeton, Institute for Advanced Studies, June 15–17, 1972.

Messance. *Recherches sur la population des généralités d'Auvergne, de Lyon, de Rouen et de quelques provinces et villes du royaume*. Paris, 1766. Rpr. 1973.

Meuvret, J. "Demographic Crisis in France from the Sixteenth to the Eighteenth Century." In *Population in History*, edited by D. V. Glass and D. E. C. Eversley. London: E. Arnold, 1965.

Mitchell, Harvey. "Resistance to the Revolution in Western France," *Past and Present*, no. 63 (1974): 94–131.

Mollat, Michel, ed. *Histoire de Rouen*. Toulouse: Edouard Privat, 1979.

Morineau, Michel. *Les faux-semblants d'un démarrage économique: agriculture et démographie en France au XVIIIe siècle*. Paris: Armand Colin, 1971.

"Y a-t-il eu une révolution agricole en France au XVIIIe siècle?" *Revue historique*, XCII (1968): 299–326.

Musset, René. "A propos de la maison normande: du pays de Caux au Bocage normand. Problèmes et recherches à faire." *Annales de Normandie*, V (1955): 271–87.

La Normandie. Paris: Colin, 1960.

Noel, Eugene. *Rouen, Rouennais, Rouenneries*. Rouen: Schneider Frères, 1948.

Noel, J. B. "Résumé de l'enquête de l'an IX." In *Le textile en Normandie: Etudes diverses*. Rouen: Société Libre d'Emulation de la Seine-Maritime, 1975.

Olphe-Galliard, G. "Les industries rurales à domicile dans la Normandie Orientale." *La Science Sociale*, (Dec. 1913): 1–75.

Oppenheimer, Valerie Kincade. *The Female Labor Force in the United States*. Berkeley: Institute of International Studies, University of California, 1970.

Ourliac, Paul, and Malafosse, J. de. *Histoire du droit privé*. Tome III: *Le droit familial*. Paris: Presses Universitaires de France, 1968.

Parish, William L., Jr., and Schwartz, Moshe. "Household Complexity in Nineteenth-Century France." *American Sociological Review*, 37 (1972): 154–73.

Perrée, Edmond. *Les origines de la filature mécanique de coton en Normandie*. Rouen: Cagniard, 1923.

Perrot, J. C. "Note sur les contrats de mariage normands." In *Structures et relations sociales à Paris au milieu du XVIII siècle*, by A. Daumard and F. Furet. Paris: Cahiers des Annales, 1961.

Phan, Marie-Claude. "Les Declarations de grossesse en France (XVI–XVIIIe siècle): Essai institutionnel." *Revue d'histoire moderne et contemporaire,* XVIII (Janvier-Mars 1975): 61–88.

Phillips, Roderick. "Women and Family Breakdown in Eighteenth-Century France: Rouen 1780–1800." *Social History,* no. 2 (May 1976): 197–218.

Pinchbeck, Ivy. *Women Workers and the Industrial Revolution, 1750–1850.* 1930. Reprint. New York: Augustus M. Kelley, 1969.

Pleck, Elizabeth. "Two Worlds in One: Work and Family." *Journal of Social History,* X: 178–95.

Pollard, Sidney, ed. *Region und Industrialisierung. Studien zur Rolle der Region in der Wirthschaftsgeschichte der letzen zwei Jahrhunderte.* Göttingen: Vandenhoeck & Ruprecht, 1980.

La Protoindustrialisation: Théorie et Realité. Rapports. Tome I and II. VIIIe Congrès International d'Histoire Economique, (section A2), Budapest, August 16–22, 1982. Compiled by Université des Arts, Lettres et Sciences Humaines de Lille.

Ragache, Jean-Robert; Lepelley, René; Henry, Jacques; Lerond, Michel; Desert, Gabriel; Bertaux, Jean-Jacques. *Normandie: Ecologie, Economie, Art, Litterature, Langue, Histoire, Traditions populaires.* Christine Bonneton, 1978.

Reddy, William M. *The Rise of Market Culture: The Textile Trade and French Society, 1750–1900.* Cambridge: Cambridge University Press, 1984.

"The Textile Trade and the Language of the Crowd at Rouen 1752–1871." *Past and Present,* no. 74 (1977): 62–89.

Reinhard, Marcel; Armengaud, André; and Dupaquier, Jacques. *Histoire générale de la population mondiale.* 3d ed. Paris: Editions Montchrestien, 1968.

Renoult, Robert. "Metiers et gens de metier de nos villages." *Société des Etudes Locales: Groupe de la Seine-Inférieure Bulletin,* (Mai 1933–Mai 1934): 98–103.

"Note sur le logement rural dans le pays de Caux: Les 'couverts' et les 'fours' ". *Société des Etudes Locales: Groupe de la Seine-Inférieure Bulletin,* (Mai 1932–Mai 1933): 142–44.

"Notes sur le logement, l'ameublement et le costume dans le pays de Caux." *Société des Etudes Locales: Groupe de la Seine-Inférieure Bulletin,* (Mai 1935–Mai 1936): 86–92.

Reybaud, Louis. *Rapport sur la condition morale, intellectuelle et materielle des ouvriers qui vivent de l'industrie du coton.* Paris: Institut Imperial de France, 1862.

Roussel, M. "Mémoire de M. Roussel sur l'industrie des tissus en lin, chanvre et coton du pays de Caux, depuis plusieurs siècles jusqu'à nos jours." *Annuaire de la Normandie,* (1878): 388–425.

Rudé, George. *The Crowd in the French Revolution.* London: Oxford University Press, 1959.

Sabean, David. "Aspects of kinship behaviour and property in Rural Western Europe before 1800." In *Family and Inheritance: Rural Society in Western Europe, 1200–1800,* edited by Jack Goody, Joan Thirsk, and E. P. Thompson. Cambridge: Cambridge University Press, 1976.

Schlumbohm, Jürgen. "Seasonal Fluctuations and Social Division of Labour: Rural Linen Production in the Osnabrück and Bielefeld Regions and the Urban Woolen Industry in the Niederlausitz, c. 1770–c. 1850." In *Manufacture in Town and Country before the Factory,* edited by Maxine Berg, Pat Hudson, and Michael Sonenscher. Cambridge: Cambridge University Press, 1983.

Schofield, Roger. "Age Specific Mobility in an Eighteenth-Century English Parish." *Annales de démographie historique,* (1970): 261–74.

Schremmer, Eckart. "Proto-Industrialisation: A Step towards Industrialisation?" *Journal of European Economic History,* 10 (Winter 1981): 653–70.

Scott, Joan W., and Tilly, Louise A. "Women's Work and the Family in Nineteenth-Century Europe." *Comparative Studies in Society and History,* 17 (January 1975): 36–64.

Seccombe, Wally. "Marxism and Demography." *New Left Review,* 137 (January-February 1983): 22–47.

Sée, Henri. "Remarques sur le caractère de l'industrie rurale en France et les causes de son extension au XVIIIe siècle." *Revue historique,* CXLII (1923): 47–53.

Segalen, Martine. *Amours et mariages de l'ancienne France.* Paris: Berger-Levrault, 1981.
Mari et femme dans la société paysanne. Paris: Flammarion, 1980.
Nuptialité et alliance: Le choix du conjoint dans une commune de l'Eure. Paris: B.-P. Maisonneuve et Larose, 1972.

Sheridan, George J., Jr. "Household and Craft in an Industrializing Economy: The Case of the Silk Weavers of Lyons." In *Consciousness and Class Experience in Nineteenth-Century Europe,* edited by John M. Merriman. New York: Holmes & Meier, 1979.

Shorter, Edward. "Female Emancipation, Birth Control, and Fertility in European History." *American Historical Review,* 78 (1973): 605–640.
"Illegitimacy, Sexual Revolution, and Social Change in Modern Europe." In *The Family in History: Interdisciplinary Essays,* edited by Theodore K. Rabb and Robert I. Rotberg. New York: Harper Torchbooks, 1971.
The Making of the Modern Family. New York: Basic Books, 1975.

Sion, Jules. *Les paysans de la Normandie Orientale: Pays de Caux, Bray, Vexin Normand, Vallée de la Seine. Etude géographique.* Paris: Armand Colin, 1909.

Slicher van Bath, B. H. *The Agrarian History of Western Europe, A.D. 500–1800.* London: Edward Arnold, 1963.

Smelser, Neil J. *Social Change in the Industrial Revolution.* Chicago: University of Chicago Press, 1959.
"Sociological History: The Industrial Revolution and the British Working-Class Family." *Journal of Social History,* I (1967): 17–35.

Soboul, Albert. *The French Revolution 1787–1799: From the Storming of the Bastille to Napoleon.* Translated by Alan Forrest and Colin Jones. New York: Vintage Books, 1975.

Sonenscher, Michael. "Work and Wages in Paris in the Eighteenth Century." In *Manufacture in Town and Country before the Factory,* edited by Maxine Berg, Pat Hudson, and Michael Sonenscher. Cambridge: Cambridge University Press, 1983.

Spagnoli, Paul G. "Industrialization, Proletarianization, and Marriage: A Reconsideration." *Journal of Family History.* 8 (Fall 1983): 230–47.

Sullerot, Evelyne. *Histoire de sociologie du travail feminin.* Paris: Editions Gonthier, 1968.

Tarlé, E. *L'industrie dans les campagnes en France à la fin de l'ancien régime.* Paris: 1910.
Le textile en Normandie: Etudes diverses. Rouen: Société libre d'Emulation de la Seine-Maritime, 1975.

Thirsk, Joan. "Industries in the Countryside." In *Essays in the Economic and Social History of Tudor and Stuart England,* edited by F. J. Fisher. Cambridge: The University Press, 1961.

Thompson, E. P. "The Moral Economy of the English Crowd in the Eighteenth Century." *Past and Present,* no. 50 (1971): 76–136.
"Time, Work-Discipline, and Industrial Capitalism." *Past and Present,* no. 38 (1967): 56–97.

Thomson, J. K. J. "Variations in Industrial Structure in Pre-Industrial Languedoc." In *Manufacture in Town and Country before the Factory,* edited by Maxine Berg, Pat Hudson, and Michael Sonenscher. Cambridge: Cambridge University Press, 1983.

Tilly, Charles. "The Historical Study of Vital Processes." In *Historical Studies of Changing Fertility,* edited by Charles Tilly. Princeton: Princeton University Press, 1978.

"Population and Pedagogy in France." *History of Education Quarterly,* 13 (Summer 1973): 113–28.

"Sociology, History, and the Origins of the European Proletariat." American Historical Association Annual Meeting, December 1976.

The Vendée. Cambridge, Mass.: Harvard University Press, 1968.

Tilly, Charles, and Tilly, Richard. "Agenda for European Economic History in the 1970's." *Journal of Economic History,* 31 (1971): 184–98.

Tilly, Louise. "The Food Riot as a Form of Political Conflict in France." *Journal of Interdisciplinary History,* II (1971): 23–58.

Tilly, Louise, and Scott, Joan W. *Women, Work, and Family.* New York: Holt, Rinehart and Winston, 1978.

Tilly, Louise; Scott, Joan; and Cohen, Miriam. "Women's Work and European Fertility Patterns." *Journal of Interdisciplinary History,* 6 (Winter 1976): 447–76.

Toutain, J. C. *La population de la France de 1700 à 1959.* Paris: I.S.E.A., 1963.

Le produit de l'agriculture française de 1700 à 1958. Paris: I.S.E.A., 1961.

Treble, J. H. "The Seasonal Demand for Adult Labour in Glasgow, 1890–1914." *Social History,* vol. 3, no. 1 (January 1978): 43–60.

L'univers du paysan cauchois aux XVIIIe et XIXe siècles (1750–1900). Archives de la région de Haute-Normandie et du Département de la Seine-Maritime, Catalogue de l'Exposition, 1977.

Usher, Abbott Payson. *The History of the Grain Trade in France, 1400–1710.* Cambridge: Harvard University Press, 1913.

Vandenbroeke, Charles. "Mutations économiques et sociales en Flandre au cours de la phase proto-industrielle, 1650–1850." *Revue du Nord,* LXIII, no. 248 (Janvier-Mars 1981): 73–94.

Van de Walle, Etienne. "Alone in Europe: The French Fertility Decline until 1850." In *Historical Studies of Changing Fertility,* edited by Charles Tilly. Princeton: Princeton University Press, 1978.

The Female Population of France in the Nineteenth Century. Princeton: Princeton University Press, 1974.

Vidalenc, Jean. "L'agriculture dans le départements normands à la fin du premier empire." *Annales de Normandie,* VII (1957): 179–201.

Aspects de la Seine-Inférieure sous la Restauration, 1814–1830. Rouen: Centre Regional de Documentation Pedagogique, 1976.

"L'industrie dans les départements normands à la fin du premier empire." *Annales de Normandie,* VII (1957): 281–307.

La Société française de 1815 à 1848. Tome I: *Le peuple des campagnes.* Paris: Marcel Rivière, 1970.

Textes sur l'histoire de la Seine-Inférieure à l'époque napoleonienne (1800–1814). Rouen: Centre Regional de Documentation Pedagogique, 1976.

Vigarie, A. "Recherche d'une explication de la maison cauchoise." *Norois,* XVI, no. 63 (1969): 491–501.

Villermé, Louis-René. *Tableau de l'état physique et moral des ouvriers employés dans les manufactures de coton, de laine, et de soie.* Tome II. Paris: 1840.

Wall, Richard. "Woman Alone in English Society." *Annales de Démographie Historique* (1981): 303–17.

Watkins, Susan Cotts, and Van de Walle, Etienne. "Nutrition, Mortality, and Population Size: Malthus' Court of Last Resort." *Journal of Interdisciplinary History,* 14, no. 2 (Autumn 1983): 205–26.

Wrigley, E. A. "Family Limitation in Pre-Industrial England." *Economic History Review.* 2d Series, XIX (1966): 82–109.

"Mortality in Pre-Industrial England: The Example of Colyton, Devon, over Three Centuries." *Daedalus*, (1968): 546–80.

Population and History. New York: McGraw-Hill, World University Library, 1969.

Yver, Jean. *Les caractères originaux de la coutume de Normandie*. Caen: Ch. Le Tendre, 1952.

Les caractères originaux du groupe coutumes de l'Ouest de la France. Paris: Librairie du Recueil Sirey, 1952.

Zimmerman, Carle C., and Frampton, Merle E. *Family and Society: A Study of the Sociology of Reconstruction*. London: Williams and Norgate, 1935.

Zonabend, Françoise. *La mémoire longue: Temps et histoires au village*. Paris: Presses Universitaires de France, 1980.

Zupko, Ronald E. *French Weights and Measures before the Revolution: A Dictionary of Provincial and Local Units*. Bloomington: Indiana University Press, 1978.

Index

~~~~~~

agricultural revolution (pays de Caux), 49–52, 114–16

agriculture: compatibility with cottage industry, 40, 47–52, 59–61, 65–7; labor shortage, 60–1, 126; seasonal labor demand, 39–40, 52–3, 61, 65, 67; triennial crop and field rotation (pays de Caux), 10, 30–1, 49–50; see also agricultural revolution; Caux, pays de; cereal agriculture; commercial agriculture; day laborers; domestic servants/farm domestics; enclosure; fallow farming; harvest; land fragmentation; open-field agriculture; proto-industrialization; seasonal division of labor; sexual division of labor, agriculture; subsistence agriculture; threshing; wages

Anglo–French Treaty of 1786, see Eden Treaty

artificial meadows, 50, 52, 59, 114

Auffay, 3, 5; administrative functions, 21; *cahier de doléances*, 25, 87, 221 n46; Committee of Public Safety, 95; confraternities in, 27–9; canton of, 52; description of, 20–1, 118–19; education in, 23–4, 113, 121–2, 226 n23; fairs and festivals, 21–2, 24, 31–2; *hameaux*, 16–17; history, 17–20; itinerant peddlers and merchants, 21–3; living conditions in, 20–1, 23–4, 35–7, 55, 73, 118–19; location, 15, 20–2; Municipal Council, 113, 119; population, 15–17; *Soeurs-Grises*, 23–4, 121; tanneries, 21; village life, 20–3, 118–22, 194; see also birth intervals; bridal pregnancy; celibacy rates; childbearing; child mortality; civil marriages; completed families; Dufossé family; endogamy; family limitation; family reconstitution, examples of; female occupations; fertility; heads of households; illegitimacy; infant mortality; La Mort d'Auffay; literacy; male occupations; marriage age; marriage customs; marriage frequency; marriage, seasonality of; maternal mortality; mendicants; migration; names; religion; remarriage; seamstresses; spin-

ning mills; Thomas de Bosmelet; unwed mothers; widowhood; widows

Bacqueville, 33–4, 73, 88–9, 91

Baulant, Micheline, 163–5

Belleville-en-Caux, 54, 88

Berkner, Lutz, 43

birth intervals (Auffay), 155, 157–9, 229 n63

Bloch, Marc, 47

boys' names, see names

Braun, Rudolf, 2, 4, 38, 42, 45, 131–3, 150–1

Bray, pays de, 8, 47–8, 65

bread consumption, 217 n73

bridal pregnancy (Auffay), 152–3, 178–84, 229 n63

cafés (pays de Caux), 37, 84–5, 152, 221 n46

cahiers de doléances (pays de Caux), 25, 47, 50, 84, 86–8, 90, 221 n46

Caletes, 7–8

calico, 109–10, 125, 135, 150, 200

carding, 60, 69–71, 73, 96, 219 n100; machine, 97

Cartier, Sub-prefect, 58, 101

Caux, pays de, 3–4; agricultural practices, 46–52; boundaries, 8, 14; climate, 8–10, 14, 47, 73; crops, 10; general characteristics, 8–15; grain production, 32, 48–50; location, 7, 62; quality of land, 8, 47–8; roads, 64–5; topography, 8, 47; see also agricultural revolution; agriculture; cafés; children's work; conscription; cottage industry; cotton; counter-revolution; courtship; *coutume de Caux; curés;* day-laborers; domestic servants/farm domestics; dominoes; emigration; fallow farming; female weavers; French Revolution; grain shipments; harvest; immigration; inheritance; land distribution; land fragmentation; linen industry; male spinners; male weavers; market riots; *masures;* mechanical

251